R.E.M.
ALBUM BY ALBUM

R.E.M.

ALBUM BY ALBUM

R.E.M.
ALBUM BY ALBUM

MAX PILLEY

WHITE OWL

AN IMPRINT OF PEN & SWORD BOOKS LTD.
YORKSHIRE – PHILADELPHIA

First published in Great Britain in 2023 by
PEN AND SWORD WHITE OWL
An imprint of
Pen & Sword Books Ltd
Yorkshire - Philadelphia

ISBN 978 1 39901 762 6

Typeset in Times New Roman 11.5/14 by
SJmagic DESIGN SERVICES, India.
Printed and bound in the UK by CPI Group (UK) Ltd.

Pen & Sword Books Ltd incorporates the Imprints of Pen & Sword Books
Archaeology, Atlas, Aviation, Battleground, Discovery, Family History, History,
Maritime, Military, Naval, Politics, Railways, Select, Transport, True Crime,
Fiction, Frontline Books, Leo Cooper, Praetorian Press, Seaforth Publishing,
Wharncliffe and White Owl.

For a complete list of Pen & Sword titles please contact
PEN & SWORD BOOKS LIMITED
47 Church Street, Barnsley, South Yorkshire, S70 2AS, England
E-mail: enquiries@pen-and-sword.co.uk
Website: www.pen-and-sword.co.uk

Or

PEN AND SWORD BOOKS
1950 Lawrence Rd, Havertown, PA 19083, USA
E-mail: Uspen-and-sword@casematepublishers.com
Website: www.penandswordbooks.com

Contents

Prologue

"The ocean is the river's goal
A need to leave the water knows"

I got in just before midnight on 6 July 2007, giddy. I had recently turned 19 and was readying to leave home to study a hundred miles away, a new career in a new town. It felt like my world was finally starting to open up. I had spent the evening with a girl I liked watching the band Bright Eyes at the Birmingham Academy, having only recently returned home from the first music festival of my life. None of my usual cocktail of anxieties could mask the fact that at this particular moment, I was happy.

My dad was still up when I came through the door. He was watching *Later...with Jools Holland*; in fact, he was cackling at it. He liked to put on the subtitles so that he could catch the performers' lyrics and as Jack White limbered up for the last verse of 'Icky Thump', he hadn't expected to hear something as pithy as, "White Americans, what, nothing better to do? Why don't you kick yourself out, you're an immigrant too". Our good moods rarely coincided, so when he asked if I fancied a drink, it was an easy yes.

What he produced was not a drink, but multiple boxes of red wine, decanted over several hours into pint glasses, and enough marijuana to calm a feral lion. We played a never-ending series of backgammon games – I won, which he denied the next day – and listened to music, the one thing that truly bonded us.

Music was his passion, the bass guitar in particular. He was, in some ways, the quintessential boomer, bred on that first blazing rush of 60s rock guitar and the revolutionary zeal of the counter-culture. Taste-wise, he was of the John Peel school, and although he could be prone to falling into the trap of believing that everything that happened after New Year's

Eve 1969 was inherently lesser-than, he still wanted to know it all, and feel it all. He had an insatiable desire to stay alert to the comings and goings of on-trend music, far beyond the traditional decade-long window during which most people are interested, understanding the capacity of great popular music to access a truth that was otherwise too well hidden by real life's chaotic order.

That night, he leaned into some of his favourites: Pink Floyd's *Ummagumma* and *Atom Heart Mother*, Weather Report's *Heavy Weather* and Cream's *Disraeli Gears*. When it was my turn to choose, I reached for my CD copy of *Automatic for the People*, which although not strictly from my generation, was easily strong enough, I felt, to pass his austere credibility test. It did, but only because he already knew the damn thing inside out.

My dad was predisposed to thinking deeply about the world. Politics was never off our screens in my childhood, nor out of our daily conversations, and he encouraged me to try to understand the bigger picture on all occasions. When *Automatic for the People* reached its final track 'Find the River', though, I learned quite how far I still had to go. It was a song that I already loved, but I had never been able to coax much meaning out of its opaquely written lyrics. My dad, on the other hand, had given it some considerable thought.

The song was about death, my dad told me, or at least about the inevitability of dying. Michael Stipe sings about the river winding inexorably towards its destination, on a mission beyond its control to join the ocean to rest, losing its own identity on arrival but becoming part of a greater, universal energy instead. What impressed my dad about the song was not the metaphor in particular, but the maturity of the narrator in being able to express their own finite existence in such a way that did not come across as mawkish or self-pitying, nor couched in airy-fairy, quasi-religious allusions, but with clear vision. It is only our consciousness that resists not being alive anymore; our bodies, our vessels, they understand that there is a need to leave. You can't be born unless you are also going to die.

My dad was dying. He had been gravely ill for well over a year, outliving his doctors' expectations, and his situation had certainly afforded him special insight into the song's meaning. Stipe sings as though the dying man is desperate to pass along the wisdom that comes from facing down your own life's end, and my dad spoke to me that night the same way. He was frustrated that it had taken him until he knew that his river's journey was nearly complete to realise that there is peace to be found in the understanding that dying is part of something far bigger than our own self-awareness. Just as Stipe's narrator implores a younger person to slow down and try to take in this message, my dad tried to get me to do the same. Perhaps it was my youthful naïveté, or perhaps it was all the wine and the pot, but as astonished as I was by my dad's ability to turn my choice of music into an impossibly profound life lesson, the full effect of his words took several years to start making an impact.

Thanks to the diet of morphine that he was on at the time, my dad was up and ready to go the next morning, while I couldn't move off the sofa I'd fallen asleep on for two days. Nine days later, he died.

If it took too long for his 'Find the River'-inspired wisdom to get through to me, then it took me even longer to realise that growing up surrounded by his passion for music and art and his idea of its place in the world had made me want to become a writer, and in particular to write about music. So, this one's for you, dad; I'm finally ready to pick up here and chase the ride.

Arriving in Athens

5 January 1978
Great Southeast Music Hall, Atlanta, GA

To the Sex Pistols, it was just another crowd. They had spent two years sneering out at them by now and nothing that any new city did could impress them. Groups of young punks would show up, blinking in disbelief that there were hundreds of other like-minded souls from their own hometown; it was a nightly revolution. The tectonic shift in youth culture had taken effect so quickly that a Pistols gig was often the first chance for the local gaggle of misfits to congregate together under the same roof. As the cliché goes, half of them would go on to form the great bands of the future.

They couldn't have known it, but the six hundred in attendance in Atlanta that night were particularly fortunate. It was the Pistols' first ever show in the United States, the opening night of a tour of the Deep South that would prove to be the last shows they would ever play, assuming that we agree to overlook their toe-curling 1990s revival. Sid Vicious was in grave condition, his heroin problem requiring that his off-stage hours were spent alternating between bar fights, bust deals and hospital visits. Nine days later, John Lydon would utter his famous withering words on stage in San Francisco: "Ever get the feeling you've been cheated?". The band's breakup was formally announced within the fortnight.

That the London *enfants terribles* should find themselves in the Southern states at all for their first American shows was a deliberately obtuse move, straight from the playbook of their manager Malcolm McLaren, who had sought to exploit the media paranoia that had blown up around punk at the time. New York and Los Angeles were craving the Sex Pistols, but McLaren, in his wisdom, chose to deny them.

1

Atlanta had simply not been a player in the new wave of music culture in the same way that the coastal hubs had. Sure, they had The Fans, a Brian Eno-inspired art rock band that had a mild local following, but word travelled slowly and those Georgia youngsters bitten by the punk bug were made to feel isolated. Turning up that night would have been a culture shock for anyone.

But, alas, this fairy tale origin story ends before it begins. Instrumental though it may have been in the lives of many, the concert played next to no direct role in the formation of R.E.M. Only one quarter of the band was even living in Atlanta at the time, and although Peter Buck did have a ticket, he saw very little of the show.

Being their US debut, the gig was an insider music industry event as much as anything else and as McLaren had no doubt hoped, an influx of journalists and record label executives from New York made up a significant proportion of the crowd. Through just the sort of cobbled mismanagement that you would expect from a Sex Pistols tour, the two tickets that Buck had pre-ordered with his mother's credit card had both found their way into the hands of travelling critics instead and through no fault of his own, one of Atlanta's few genuine punk connoisseurs was faced with a challenge.

Fortunately, Buck's gig partner on this occasion was a friend of a friend, and while he may not have been a Sex Pistols obsessive, he certainly knew how to throw his weight around. When the doorman attempted to explain the snafu with the tickets, Buck's accomplice cared little for the finer details of the matter and, as Buck explained to *Rolling Stone* in 1990, "he kicked the door in and we got in". Buck managed to evade the capture of the bouncers for the opening couple of songs before he was heavy-handedly ejected and given short shrift on his way to the curb outside. He would later reflect on the episode, accurately, as "pretty much the quintessential Sex Pistols experience".

It's probably a safe bet that quite a few of the locals in attendance would not have been there if not for Buck as for most of 1977, he had been working in Wuxtry Records in Atlanta, during the era that record store staff were looked to as arbiters of what was and was not to be listened to. It was the ideal chance at last for Buck to parade the refined taste that he had long been cultivating. Any intrepid customer could expect a *High Fidelity*-worthy lecture from the imposing beanpole figure behind the counter on the merits of their chosen records.

Born in Berkeley, California on 6 December 1956, Peter Lawrence Buck had been passionate about music from the moment that his memories came online. A childhood love of The Beatles, The Monkees and Motown was just the beginning; he moved into teenagerhood at just the moment that the music magazines he pored over started to feature new bands with a more devious, subversive take on pop and rock music. In came The Velvet Underground, New York Dolls, Roxy Music and The Stooges and out went the young Buck's musical naiveté.

The Buck family moved around California throughout the 1960s before relocating to Roswell, Georgia and then finally Atlanta when Buck was fifteen. Peter's younger brother Ken, no doubt inspired by the record collection he had inherited from his sibling, took it upon himself to learn to play guitar, later going on to complete a classical guitar degree at the University of Georgia. He taught Peter the basics, but it was the mythology of musical history and the joy of indulging in niche subcultures that animated Peter and so, for now, any serious thought of developing a playing career took a back seat.

After graduating with honours from Crestwood High School, Buck, like so many others, found himself directionless and drifting; he enrolled in a course at Emory University in Atlanta but dropped out within a year. Exactly what made the Wuxtry store owner Mark Methe approach him with a job offer one day in early 1977 is somewhat unclear – perhaps Buck didn't need to be working there to be overheard espousing the virtues of the month's best new underground releases – but nevertheless, it was an easy yes when he did.

From his new vantage point at the centre of the Atlanta music world, the glacial pace of progress in the city became painfully clear. He was able to strike up relationships with many of the regulars, including Kathleen O'Brien, an Atlanta native whose interests mapped neatly onto Buck's own, and Danny Beard, who owned a rival music store named Wax 'n' Facts. Through his time living in the nearby college town of Athens, Beard had developed a relationship with a local band there who went by the name of The B-52's.

Beard had made The B's a series of promises during a hedonistic trip they made together to New York City in late 1977, the most pressing of which upon their return home was that he would be able to provide the circumstances for their first ever show in Atlanta. Having sobered up and with a sense of guilt-ridden duty, Beard turned to Buck for help. It

3

speaks to Buck's fast rise to the level of chief Atlanta scenester that he was considered the man for the job. He answered Beard's request and duly hired a room on the college campus for $25.

The B-52's may only have played their first gig ten months earlier but they had already figured out the formula that would propel them to international cult status by the decade's end. Siblings Ricky and Cindy Wilson and their friend Keith Strickland had all grown up in Athens, while vocalists Kate Pierson and Fred Schneider had arrived separately from New Jersey, but together they struck upon an otherworldly style that could only have come from a place without its own musical signature.

The trip to New York City with Danny Beard came about thanks to an invitation from their friends in The Fans, but the show they played at the iconic Max's Kansas City – a booking that the band themselves struggled to believe could be real – spotlighted how out of step they were with the prevailing wind. Where the Ramones were surly, The B-52's were bubbly; where Television were po-faced, The B-52's allowed themselves to be daft. They dressed brightly and performed with abandon and were in many respects the 1977 precursors to the 21st century poptimists. Lux Interior, frontman of The Cramps, was one of the few punters at the Max's show and called them his "new favourite band". They were the niche of the niche in New York, but back home in Athens, they were already superstars.

Until The B-52's, the only reason to know about Athens, Georgia was because it was the site of the University of Georgia, or UGA. An old cotton mill town, it had been termed the 'Manchester of the South' during the industrial revolution, but by the late 20th century, UGA had taken centre stage. During term time, the population of the city would swell from 50,000 to 75,000.

Up until this point, local live music in Georgia had generally meant southern boogie in the vein of home-state heroes the Allman Brothers Band and Marshall Tucker, or traditional blues rock, with at best a hangover of late 60s flower power as the one discernible trace of the counter-culture. But with Athens' student base, there was at least the fuel for a new revolution and thanks to UGA's much sought-after art department, there was a very particular craving for something innovative to call their own. It just needed someone to light the touch paper and The B-52's filled that role with glee.

The B-52's brought dozens of their most enthusiastic Athens fans to the gig that Buck organised for them in Atlanta in Christmas week 1977 and Buck was instantly entranced. The band's aesthetic style was informed by their friends on the drag scene and their music seemed to be a reaction against the angry-young-man mould of punk. You didn't often find Debbie Harry shrieking with joy like Kate Pierson, nor Joe Strummer banging maniacally on a cowbell like Fred Schneider. They brought a ray of sunshine into a decidedly self-serious movement, without sacrificing a shred of the artfulness. Their set that night included 'Planet Claire' and, most pointedly, 'Rock Lobster', which Danny Beard loved so much that he decided to release it on his own newly-formed label DB Records in April 1978. The B-52's' first release, the single quickly gained traction in New York's clubs and was an underground sensation, leading the band to sign with Warner Bros in short order and rack up chart hits at home and abroad the following year.

Buck was so taken by the band's performance that night and the rabid audience they had established that when Methe offered him a job at Wuxtry's Athens branch later in the week, he snapped it up. If Atlanta had started to seem stale, Athens seemed gripped by the shock of the new. By the time the Sex Pistols arrived in Atlanta in the first week of the new year, Buck made the journey there from his new Athens apartment. Superficially, little connected the performances of The B-52's and the Sex Pistols, but the two crowds shared the same electricity, borne from an identical outburst of new energy, that full-throated yell of opposition to the status quo (and, indeed, the Status Quo). For the first time in these people's lives, they were reclaiming live music spaces from the grips of an older generation.

Several key players in the burgeoning Athens scene managed to watch the entirety of the Pistols' show, including Paul Butchart, future drummer for The Side Effects, and Johnny Hibbert, the soon-to-be founder of Hib-Tone Records and frontman of that night's opening band Cruis-o-Matic. Of more imminent impact on the pre-nascent R.E.M., however, was the presence of one Ian Copeland.

Copeland was out of place in Georgia. The son of a CIA officer, he had grown up in the Middle East and had served with distinction in Vietnam, before settling in London in the early 1970s and immersing himself into the music business. His younger brother Stewart would find global fame and success as the drummer in The Police, while Ian's older brother Miles would amass a fortune as The Police's manager, which he would later funnel into forming his own record label, I.R.S. Records. Ian, meanwhile, was not riding the same gravy train and instead found himself working for the Paragon booking agency in Macon, Georgia, an affiliate of the towering Capricorn Records label, the spiritual home of Southern rock.

The problem was, Southern rock was dwindling and being quickly swamped by the new sound, and Paragon knew it. Bringing in Ian Copeland was a reaction to this, knowing his connections to the contemporary London scene. Copeland, understanding that his brief was to revamp the company's image, brought as many of the Paragon staff as he could with him to see the Sex Pistols

His bosses told him beforehand that they didn't understand punk, but after the gig they actively hated it. Copeland, an enthusiastic, borderline obnoxious promoter whose approach to pushing a band would make Sisyphus green with envy, was mostly met with hostility. There was, however, one kid working in the company's mail room, a 19-year-old named Bill Berry, who not only got it, but was immediately swooning over Copeland's arrival.

Copeland emitted the kind of cool that Berry craved for himself. After the Pistols debacle – a show Berry had to miss in order to cover for everybody else's absence from the Paragon office – Copeland's bosses were starting to lose their patience, so the Pistols' sudden demise shortly afterwards was no bad news. Bruised by the stubborn brick wall of resistance that his hard punk suggestions had met, Copeland turned to the softer, more New Wave bands that were starting to come out of England and found that Squeeze, Dire Straits and The Police were much more readily received.

When Squeeze arrived in Macon a few months later, Copeland took charge of the booking and, realising the paucity of resources available to him, he set about developing a novel, thrifty model for promoting the show. He had disused billboards spray-painted with propaganda, put the band up in the cheapest available accommodation and talked various local small club owners into promoting each other's live shows. He was, in effect, establishing the independent touring blueprint that would become the norm for small bands for the next four decades, relying as much on word of mouth and verbal agreements as on sound financial backing. The same tactics were used when The Police toured the

Southern states later in the year, and all the while Copeland ensured that Berry was at his right hand, learning these guerrilla tactics for possible future use.

William Thomas Berry was born on 31 July 1958 in Duluth, Minnesota, the same town that gave us Bob Dylan. A fairly nomadic childhood beckoned, with the Berry family calling Wauwatosa, Milwaukee and Sandusky home before settling in Macon, Georgia when Bill was fourteen. Like Buck, he was devoted to music from an early stage, including a heavy dose of The Beatles, and by the time he was attending Mount de Sales Academy in Macon, he was handy with a keyboard, guitar or ukulele, although it was already the drums that appealed to him the most.

Unlike Buck, Berry was eager to join a band, so when he was invited to a jam session by a couple of school acquaintances, he jumped at the opportunity. Not unusually for a teenage boy, Berry could be judgmental in his attitude to his peers, so when a bespectacled, undersized kid that Berry faintly recognised from school walked into the rehearsal room strapped with his bass, Berry's shackles went up. Berry and Mike Mills were separated by nature, by high school tribe and by lifestyle, but out of politeness they nonetheless went through the motions of the fledgling band practice. Within minutes, something had clicked. The desire to play together quickly outlasted the impulses of peer pressure and by the afternoon's end, an indelible connection had been established.

Michael Edward Mills, born 17 December 1958 in Orange County, California, was the son of an opera singing father, a formative detail that may go some way towards explaining his attraction to an infectious melody line. Like Buck and Berry, Mills was a teenager when he arrived with his family to live in Georgia and he immediately signed up for the school band, playing tuba and sousaphone. In truth, he could turn his hand to most instruments that he came into contact with, his bookish instincts and quest for knowledge teeing him up with a technical musical expertise.

The band that Mills and Berry created that fateful afternoon would go on to be called Shadowfax, named for Gandalf's horse, and later the Back Door Band. A straight-ahead stomp through classic rock, with dashes of blues and Southern boogie, they found themselves playing just the sort of music that they would soon be forming bands in order to stamp out. A small measure of regional success was achieved, but the rhythm section of Mills and Berry, now close friends, decided to quit the band in 1976, after sensing that the group had reached their natural ceiling. The two moved into an apartment together in Macon, whereupon Berry managed to land himself the job at Paragon.

Mills did not land on his feet quite so quickly after leaving school, bouncing between jobs in department stores, before finally enrolling on a course at UGA. His flatmate Berry decided to do the same, eyeing up a future role on the business side of the music industry, having been enthused by Copeland's methods. The two upped sticks and hitched their wagon to Athens, signing up for classes on 4 January 1979. They didn't know it at the time, but further down the same registration paper hid a scrawled name that would change the course of their lives.

The First Gig

Craig Franklin just needed a singer and by this point anyone would do. The Collinsville High School summer talent show was around the corner and his fledgling band lacked a frontperson. Under pressure but determined not to let the opportunity pass, Franklin mustered up the courage one afternoon for what he probably considered a long shot and approached a shy, bushy haired acquaintance of his in the junior year with a proposal.

The two knew each other a little, well enough to understand that they had a mutual interest in music and art, but not so well that such a significant favour was easy to broach, and Franklin's initial pitch was met with nothing but resistance. How could this guy not want to be a singer, Franklin wondered, when his hair seems deliberately coiffed to look like that of Roger Daltrey or Robert Plant?

"I don't sing," was 16-year-old Michael Stipe's reply.

But Franklin had overcome the first hurdle just by asking and he wasn't prepared to give up so easily now. He persisted forcefully enough to coerce Stipe into agreeing to at least come round to his house one night so that they could talk it over and figure out a middle ground. When Stipe arrived with sheet music for The Who and The Rolling Stones under his arm, it was clear that the allure of the proposition was growing on him. Franklin explained that they would need to perform two songs for the show and while they quickly agreed that Stipe's idea of 'Gimme Shelter' would be good for one, Franklin's own suggestions were a harder sell.

Franklin was very much a mainstream rock guy. He loved Boston and Kansas, whereas Stipe's mind had already been convulsed by Patti Smith and his tastes were shifting quickly. 'Working Man' by Rush was about as far from his consciousness as you could have got in summer 1976 but it was the song that the rest of the band knew best so Stipe relented and set about learning the lyrics.

All that was needed, now that the running order had been hammered out, was a band name. They flirted with several – Nasty Habits and The Jotz were two Stipe suggestions – but come the big night nothing had been agreed upon, so in a hurried moment Franklin decided that The Band would suffice, safe in his assumption that Robbie Robertson's 1960s Americana heroes would probably let it slide. By all accounts they gave a decent showing, but they were ultimately pipped to victory by a piano/singer duo who performed a cover of Bette Midler's 'The Rose'.

That was more or less it for The Band, although Stipe and Franklin remained friends for life and Franklin would eventually release two albums of his own material in the 2000s at Stipe's encouragement. But the impact of losing his stage performance virginity, however modestly, cannot be underestimated when understanding the emergence of one of the most enigmatic and compelling rock stars of his generation.

John Michael Stipe was born on 4 January 1960 in Decatur, Georgia, the eldest child of Marianne and John, the latter of whom served for most of his adult life in the US Army, meaning the Stipe family would move with regularity, making homes in West Germany, Texas and Alabama. The similarities between the four band members' childhoods are impossible to ignore, all nomadic to various degrees, although only Stipe can lay claim to having genuine roots in the band's home state, with at least three previous generations of Stipes calling Georgia their home.

The longest spell of stability for the young Michael began in 1973 when they settled in Collinsville, Illinois, fifteen miles east of St. Louis. Discussion of his childhood has been fairly effectively fenced off by Stipe over the years, thanks both to his tendency toward personal mystique and his generally wary attitude with journalists, although descriptions by both friends and biographers have often leaned into the phrase "painfully shy". In a rare moment of clarity, however, Stipe himself once proclaimed, "I had an unbelievably happy childhood" and in truth there is no evidence to the contrary.

High school, though, may have proved more difficult. The challenge of managing wildly erratic hormonal impulses alongside the chaos and cruelty of the hierarchical social rules of teenage life is a struggle for many and Stipe has described the fear that attending Collinsville High instilled in him. However, if he was aching for an outlet for his anxieties, then it arrived with a bang in the form of a long player that he purchased in December 1975.

Patti Smith's *Horses* is the record that has launched a thousand careers. Stipe, having taken out a subscription to *Village Voice* magazine earlier in the year, had read something that spiked his interest in this performance-poet-cum-rockstar from an impossibly subversive alternate reality and once he was finally able to lay his hands on the album itself, it was a race against the clock to meet his destiny.

Stipe sat up listening to *Horses* all night long, hanging so intently onto Smith's every iconoclastic, blasphemy-ridden word that he didn't notice that the cherries he was gorging on were beginning to congeal into one gelatinous mass in his stomach. His rush to the bathroom to throw them back up may have been the only thing that night to break his listening trance.

Smith's lyrics were impressionistic, drawing clearly enough from real world familiarities that they drew you in, but always stopping short of making lucid narrative sense. The effect was to paint the first half of a mental image and then leave the listener with the tools necessary to complete it. If Stipe had never considered writing before, the thought of it may have begun to percolate here. What's more, Smith's voice dripped with sweat and her band, led by the vastly underrated Lenny Kaye, tore from the speaker with revolutionary zeal, scything down the pomposity of 1970s indulgence and re-framing rock music as immediate and impatient. It was the auditory embodiment of the New York underground and it filled teenage listeners stuck in quiet towns everywhere with dreams of making it there one day.

And even beyond that, *Horses* struck a yet more intimate note with Stipe. From the iconic Robert Mapplethorpe cover image of an androgynous Smith standing in monochrome, jacket flung over her left shoulder, to the suggestive lyrics of opening track 'Gloria' ("I look out the window, see a sweet young thing humpin' on the parking meter... ohh she looks so good, oh she looks so fine"), a teenage Stipe may have found refuge in the non-committal sexuality writ large across the record.

He maintained a scrupulous public silence on the subject of his own sexuality until the 1994 promotional tour for *Monster*, when he decided to confirm to an interviewer that he did not define himself as gay or straight and that he was attracted to and had had relationships with both men and women. He further clarified to *The Observer* in 2011 that, "on a sliding scale of sexuality, I'd place myself around 80-20, but I definitely prefer men to women" - however, one assumes that such confident and clear-minded assessments required a great deal more life experience than Stipe had acquired by 1975. He has since spoken of having an "inkling" of his sexuality in his teenage years, but whatever the case, it seems clear that anything that seemed to celebrate a blurring of such lines, especially if it was as poetic and anti-establishment as *Horses*, was likely to set his mind ablaze. Against a diet of Hall & Oates and Foghat, two other records that Stipe bought that same day, *Horses* rocked Stipe emotionally, intellectually and spiritually.

Energised by the experience, Stipe was now fully equipped for the punk explosion to come. He expanded on his *Village Voice* reading by buying regular copies of *Rock Scene*, a magazine that routinely profiled the new bands coming through the CBGB scene in Manhattan's East Village and he began to pour his energy into records by Television, Wire and the Ramones, whilst catching up on the scene's founding fathers The Velvet Underground (their John Cale had produced *Horses*) and The Stooges.

Upon graduating in 1978, he stayed behind while his family upped sticks once more and moved to Athens. An enrolment at Southern Illinois University at Edwardsville was relatively short-lived, as was a spell living with a real-life punk band in the nearby Granite City. Stipe's money soon ran out and he was forced to swallow his pride and scurry south to join his family, tail between his legs. By early January 1979, he was queuing in the same line as Mike Mills and Bill Berry to enrol at UGA, in Stipe's case for a course in photography and painting, with the idea that his artistic interests could carry him into a future life as a visual artist.

For the first time, all four quarters of R.E.M. were living in the same town, albeit separately. However, it was during these first months in Athens that Stipe's tendencies toward insecurity and low self-esteem escalated to perhaps their most alarming heights, and he has often claimed that he spent his first twelve months in Georgia not speaking to a single soul. A typical slice of Stipean hyperbole it may be, but the spirit of the sentiment is no doubt true.

Music continued to provide solace though and he soon began to familiarise himself with the record stores of Athens. When he strode into Wuxtry one afternoon, a sparkling young woman on each arm, he caused the clerk behind the counter to do a double take. Peter Buck wasn't to know that Michael Stipe's two female friends were his sisters Cindy and Lynda, nor that his new customer was far more introverted than his first impression indicated, he just knew that an interesting new force had entered his store, and indeed his life. Stipe's musical selections that day cemented Buck's intrigue and it did not take long for the two to strike up a casual friendship.

Buck asked Stipe to join him for drinks after his shift working at a local steak bar and that night they were astonished to find that they shared a love for the discordant joys of The Velvet Underground's 1969 live album. Buck's impatience behind the counter at Wuxtry had built to such a point that he was at last itching to find a creative outlet of his own and, just like Craig Franklin before him, he set about down the winding path of talking Stipe into believing that he was born to take the stage.

Meanwhile across town, Mike Mills and Bill Berry had begun their respective UGA courses. Bill Berry had caught the eye of a certain Kathleen O'Brien in the mail room of Reed Hall, where they both lived, and although they spent the early months of 1979 doing little more than exchanging precious glances, they had firmly lodged themselves into each other's consciousness. O'Brien, another of Athens' premier music obsessives, had her own new wave show, *Purely Physical*, on the campus radio station WUOG and as a spin-off played in a ramshackle band The Wuoggerz from time to time as an excuse for a good time.

The Wuoggerz' first show had taken place back in October 1978 opening for The Ashcan Cats, but they were angling for a bigger platform and through her increasingly friendly relationship with Bill Berry, Kathleen reckoned she knew just the spot. The Police were coming to town and being aware of Berry's association with Ian Copeland, she convinced Bill to put in a word for her. Sure enough on 1 May 1979, The Wuoggerz bagged the opening slot for The Police, one of the fastest rising bands on the planet, at the Georgia Theatre in Athens. What's more, O'Brien asked Berry to fill in on drums – there was nothing so much as a regular line-up in this band – and he obliged, picking up the sticks for the first time since the Shadowfax days back in Macon.

Whether the show went well didn't seem to matter to anyone. With O'Brien on vocals and tambourine, they blazed through covers of 'Like a Rolling Stone', '(What's So Funny 'Bout) Peace, Love and Understanding' and 'Do Anything You Wanna Do' to a doubtless

uninterested crowd, but they enjoyed it and the spark between O'Brien
and Berry was now too bright to ignore.

Kathleen O'Brien knew everyone worth knowing in Athens. With the
summer over and having outgrown Reed Hall, she began the search for a
new place and got into a conversation with Wuxtry co-owner Dan Wall.
Coincidentally, the lease on Wall's place was also coming to an end and
O'Brien seized on the opportunity. Wall explained that he had already
lined up a new landlord and gave her Peter Buck's number, entirely
unaware that Buck and O'Brien were old friends. The two had spoken
many times during Buck's previous stint at the Atlanta branch of Wuxtry
and Buck had found in her a rare cultural ally in a city that had otherwise
disappointed him. They both rejoiced in the serendipitous circumstances
and moved into their new home together within days.

And what a home it was. Referred to with some affection as the
Steeplechase, it was in fact an old converted Episcopal church, its ornate
exterior more or less intact with a large open space remaining inside, but
with the front half of the interior stripped and remodelled into a slightly
dilapidated residential apartment. It was little more than "a rotten, dumpy
little shithole" in the words of Peter Buck, but nevertheless it would
provide the carefree, hedonistic conditions that this swelling group of
friends would need to make their lasting impact on the world.

The $350 rent was Peter and Kathleen's sole weekly reminder of their
real-world responsibilities, so they began to seek roommates to share the
burden. Peter's brother Ken was one willing candidate, as, briefly, was
an unassuming mutual friend Robin Bragg, who quickly found that the
wall-to-wall bacchanalia and promiscuity that came hand-in-hand with
the Steeplechase was not to her speed. In truth, the place's reputation
as the epicentre of Athens' party scene preceded Buck and O'Brien's
arrival, but their tenure did little to change anyone's perceptions. A
brief romantic relationship flickered between the two of them too, but
O'Brien still had her sights fixed on a certain drummer.

Another regular visitor in the late months of 1979 was Michael Stipe.
Buck had by now convinced Stipe to start a band with him and they had
tentatively begun their early attempts at writing together. Jam sessions
would generally constitute Buck on guitar, Dan Wall on bass, when he
was around, and whoever else was at hand filling in the gaps, whether it
was Billy Holmes, who would later play in Love Tractor, WUOG host
Kurt Wood, or Michael's sister Lynda, who would eventually form her

own group Oh-OK. It wasn't long before Stipe was spending more time at the Steeplechase than his own home and he officially moved in before the end of the year.

When not hanging around at the church or doing his studies – he seemed to be the only figure in his social circle to legitimately enjoy attending UGA – Stipe could also be found moonlighting with another hastily formed band named Gangster. They were led by Derek Nunally, who decreed that all members of the band must wear zoot suits whenever in public, and on stage they would play covers of Elvis and the Stones (the irony of this would not have been lost on punk-loving Michael Stipe, who was no doubt aware of The Clash's song '1977' by this point). Gangster's biggest gig was playing a Halloween party; beyond that they went nowhere. Stipe's brief flirtation with the stage name Michael Valentine also ended there and then, as did the band's meagre following. By the time R.E.M. were starting to field questions about their early lives, Stipe had sworn the rest of the band to complete silence on the subject of Gangster.

As Christmas approached, Peter and Michael began the search for a rhythm section for their nascent band. Dan Wall was a handy bassist and was briefly considered, but he was older and had already moved out of Athens. It was therefore decided that the first-choice combination should be the team of Paul Butchart and Kit Swartz, two Steeplechase regulars and soon-to-be founders of the key Athens band The Side Effects, and so an official trial was organised for them. Evidently, the pair were dubious about either the seriousness of the offer or the plausibility of the band's credentials and consequently they failed to show up to the audition of a lifetime, consigning themselves to be unwilling protagonists in one of rock music's most agonising near misses.

Kathleen O'Brien was the one person that may have allowed herself to feel a flicker of relief that Plan A fell through, and it was at one of the Steeplechase's first shindigs of 1980 that she grasped the opportunity to forcefully introduce her erstwhile Wuoggerz bandmate and object of her affection Bill Berry to Peter and Michael, lauding his drumming talents. A few weeks later, during a heavy night at Athens nightspot Tyrone's OC, Bill, having made a good early impression, brought his old partner Mike Mills into the fold and for the first time the four men interacted. Any hopes for immediate magical chemistry were to be disappointed though: Mills was blind drunk and behaving obnoxiously enough that Michael and Peter shut down Bill's suggestion from the off. And anyway, was he really cool enough for their band?

But Bill had been here before, ready to dismiss Mike on unfairly judgmental grounds without giving him his fair chance to impress and he had learned his lesson the first time, so he made Michael and Peter an ultimatum: it's Bill *and* Mike, or it's neither. And so it was, in the early weeks of 1980 in the old converted church that the band called home, that Berry, Buck, Mills and Stipe first struck a sound.

Bill and Mike were the old hands in this quartet, their watertight synchronicity lending the band's earliest jam sessions a greater sense of authority and confidence than most beginners could reasonably expect. Mills was by far the most musically proficient of the four, his classical training and natural flair contrasting starkly with Peter Buck's laissez faire, DIY spirit.

Buck, aware of his technical limitations, offered to swap roles with Mills and to take up bass duties, but that would be to break up the one good thing they had going and the thought quickly passed. That Buck was not your typical guitar nerd with a 'Free Bird' fetish immediately set parameters to the band's dynamic and in that sense, this earliest incarnation already demonstrated one of the central hallmarks of R.E.M. Buck did not make love to his guitar, he fluttered and stabbed at it, playing as part of the group rather than leading it. As he explained to *Trouser Press* in 1983, "If you have good enough taste, you don't have to be a great musician to make great music. When the band started, I knew about five chords and a Chuck Berry lick, I didn't even know bar chords."

Buck knew he was breaking the classic rock rules and that's the way he liked it; Mills, on the other hand, knew how to understand the rules. Without Mills there, breaking them wouldn't have sounded so good.

Mike and Bill moved into the Steeplechase in short order and Kathleen and Bill finally formalised their relationship. Peter settled down into a relationship with Ann Boyles and the non-stop party rolled on. Band rehearsals became a near-daily event, the cold of winter forcing them out of what remained of the church's nave and into their living area. The revolving cast of characters coming in and out soon caught wind of the band's finalised line-up and questions began to be asked about when they might go on display for the first time.

Stipe and Buck staved off the queries for a few days by making a maverick trip, along with Kurt Wood and Paul Butchart, to New York

City, the nominal excuse of which was to see fellow Athenians Pylon play live in a club called Hurrah near Manhattan's Lincoln Square. Pylon were, after The B-52's had departed, the most advanced and sophisticated band to have emerged from Athens so far, their serious, art school aesthetic and wiry, bass-heavy sound reminiscent of British post-punk contemporaries like Joy Division, Magazine and Public Image Ltd. All four members had met at UGA and had debuted live in early 1979, signing shortly thereafter with Danny Beard's DB Records and releasing the superlative debut single 'Cool'. Buck and Stipe didn't need to go to New York to see them play, obviously, but for both it was the first time they had made the pilgrimage to the city that they had both so shamelessly romanticised.

It was a hard-drinking trip that took in a number of other shows, including experimental new wave oddity Klaus Nomi and Circus Mort, a precursor to the noise rock titans Swans. As if the years of reading about sordid NYC underground stories had been a premonition, they also managed to find themselves at the centre of a debauched birthday party that had been thrown for the music critic overlord Lester Bangs. His writings in *Rolling Stone* and *Creem* had loomed large in any rock music obsessive's mind throughout the 1970s and, although he was at his most strung out at the time, Buck was delighted that Bangs would have anything to say to him at all, let alone that it was a sentence as perfect as, "You're a rotten cocksucker".

Back home in Athens, Kathleen O'Brien's twentieth birthday was on the horizon and she had big plans. She wanted every band she could get her hands on to play at the Steeplechase, and that included the as-yet-unnamed group that she lived with. They knew they would have to play soon and in truth, an in-house performance that wouldn't need the rigmarole of booking a venue and spreading the word beyond their friendship group felt both achievable and low risk. The Side Effects also agreed to play and murmurs spread throughout Athens that 5 April was going to be a Saturday at the Steeplechase not to miss.

The band intensified their practice sessions and started to figure out which tracks were robust enough for public consumption. In their earliest days, they had leaned on the primitive pleasures of 60s garage rock numbers when rehearsing, which allowed room for Buck's relative inexperience and gave them the chance to tighten the screws on any obvious flaws in their playing. Their debut gig was going to require more than that, though, so they also started to fine tune some of their better original compositions. At a formal rehearsal the night before the big day, they finished feeling confident that they had twenty tracks under their belt and ready to go.

The 5 April began with a promotional spot on Kurt Wood's WUOG show, which was as good a way to spread the word among your extended social circle as technology in 1980 allowed. Paul Butchart created a set of flyers that were handed out around the Athens campus, curiously listing the band as Twisted Kites, a name that they had been considering but had certainly not settled upon. Five kegs of beer were stocked in the Steeplechase. Anticipation was high and yet, despite it all, the turnout on the night far exceeded expectations. First-hand accounts have placed the number anywhere between 300 and 600.

The attendance figure is not the only aspect of the first R.E.M. concert that is subject to historical speculation. According to some, a band by the name of Turtle Bay were the opening act that night. The ramshackle nature of all Steeplechase events means that there is a certain haziness in the way that events have been recorded for posterity – a situation amplified by the abundance of Quaaludes among the UGA art students of the era – but if Turtle Bay even existed, they left little enough impression on the memories of those in attendance that they might as well not have bothered.

More noteworthy were The Side Effects. Led by Butchart on drums and Kit Swartz on vocals and guitar – the duo that failed to make their R.E.M. audition – they played at a point when the crowd were at their most receptive and still relatively compos mentis. Their spiky, angular set had the Steeplechase bouncing but by the time they made way for the next band, edges were beginning to blur.

All that is known for sure is that the first R.E.M. show opened with covers of The Troggs' 'I Can't Control Myself' and the Sex Pistols' 'God Save the Queen'. From the get-go, Stipe was unexpectedly demonstrative on stage, perhaps over-accounting for his innate shyness by bulldozing through it with a Catherine Wheel-like manic intensity. He was gasping down beers and hauling his rakish body around the stage, on his hands and knees as much as his feet. The set was bursting full with covers: 'Honky Tonk Women', 'Hippy Hippy Shake', 'There She Goes Again', '(I'm Not Your) Steppin' Stone'; if anything, some of the art schoolers in attendance may even have bristled at the abundance of non-original material played, if any of them were still thinking coherently enough to manage such complex thought processes.

According to Butchart, "They sounded more like a real band that was tight. They were really good. I know they were better than us, but that didn't matter at the time." The sheer adrenaline and nervous energy of the occasion got them through, and a sprinkling of original songs saw them over the line, most notably 'Just a Touch', which was finally recorded for 1986's *Lifes Rich Pageant*, and 'All the Right Friends', a song that was considered for all of their first three albums, before finally being re-recorded and included on the soundtrack for *Vanilla Sky* over twenty years later. A track called 'Action', a Berry/Mills tune from the Macon days, and 'Narrator', Bill Berry's love letter to Jacques Cousteau, also made the cut that night, two songs rarely played again and destined for an existence in the annals of R.E.M. ultra-geek trivia.

By the time their twenty rehearsed songs had run out, the Steeplechase was somewhere near a hysterical reverie, the high of the occasion now surpassing the chemical high. R.E.M. were hassled into an encore that they could never have anticipated and Stipe in particular had not saved himself for. Almost helplessly drunk by this point, he leaned over audience members during their impromptu attempts at tracks like 'One Nation Under the Groove' and 'Roadrunner', the front row finishing most of the lines for him.

A willing audience it may have been, but Kathleen O'Brien's birthday party had forced the quartet out of their cocoon and into a brand-new reality. Winning around that first crowd was the first important hurdle of their career, and they had cleared it with ease. More than that, it had left them wanting more. The feeling, it turned out, was mutual.

'Radio Free Europe'

R.E.M. have always scrupulously avoided getting into a conversation about the meaning of their name. Millions of people around the world continue to operate under the assumption that it is a reference to Rapid Eye Movement, the so-called 'dream' phase of the sleeping pattern during which eyeballs dart around uncontrollably. Enticingly, the connection even seems to make thematic sense – the band's early aesthetic could easily be said to evoke the hinterland between the conscious and subconscious mind, the imagery of Stipe's lyrics channelling a style of hallucinogenic, logic-free storytelling that is slightly out of rhythm with the cold predictability of our waking reality. In some senses, it is surprising that the band never retrospectively claimed credit for the connection, even if it would be taking merit for something that may not warrant it.

In truth, they spent the early months of 1980 scrambling for names. At one point, visitors to the Steeplechase were encouraged to write suggestions in chalk on the church walls. Peter and Michael knew that they wanted something without any literal or obvious meaning or real-life connotation, a name or phrase that would only throw images of their band into listeners' minds. It explains why some of the names allegedly taken under review – Cans of Piss, Negro Wives, Africans in Bondage, Slut Bank – were given short shrift.

The one that came closest to materialisation was Twisted Kites, the name that somehow found its way onto the flyer put together by Paul Butchart for the debut show. It is an interesting thought experiment to wonder about a world where one of America's most successful rock bands went by any of these more risqué names, or even if the wrong choice could have been an obstacle on their path to stardom, but ultimately they leaned towards the uncontroversial and easy to remember R.E.M. (always with the three periods).

Michael Stipe pushed for it the most enthusiastically. Short of detailed explanations from the man himself, we are restricted to dealing chiefly in rumour, but as R.E.M. biographer Robert Dean Lurie elucidates in *Begin the Begin*, there may be one very intriguing lead that stands above all others. Stipe was aware of the maverick outsider artist and photographer Ralph Eugene Meatyard, a Kentuckian who passed away in 1972 aged 45, that would routinely sign his prints 'r.e.m.', the same way the band stylised their name in the early days.

Meatyard's style bears undeniable similarities with the band's own visual taste: his photographs capture the twilit wild of the American South, blurring and obscuring images to the point of indecipherability, giving a sense of beckoning the nocturnal spirit and embracing the preternatural. With Stipe at the peak of his artistic studies, it is not too far-fetched to imagine that referencing such an obscure and underground figure would have appealed to his transgressive mindset. The band came to a final agreement about the name on the eve of their second show.

The gigs started to trickle in over the early summer. Dennis Greenia had been at the debut and, happening to live next door to the Steeplechase, immediately invited them to play a fortnight later at his bar in Athens, The Koffee Klub, alongside The Side Effects. In front of around 150 people, they took the stage at 1:45am and were promptly forced back off it again 45 minutes later when police shut the venue down after word reached them that unlicensed alcohol was being sold on the premises.

Another major local hotspot, Tyrone's O.C. became a regular haunt, with R.E.M. opening for Atlanta punk band The Brains one night and by all accounts drawing a bigger crowd than the headliners could manage. "It was generally acknowledged that we blew them away," Mike Mills would later say. When they returned a week later, R.E.M. were the headliners, attracting record numbers for the venue. Within six weeks, they were outdrawing Pylon and were by almost any measure the biggest band in Athens.

The R.E.M. of these early shows were still a brisk, tight and fairly straight-ahead punk-influenced ramshackle. For all of their art rock fascinations, when they played together, they were returning guitar music to its most primal and – let's face it – basic form. Bands emerging in 1960 wouldn't have sounded much different to this nascent band of 1980. The earliest surviving live footage of them, from a pre-show set they played at the Decatur branch of Wuxtry Records in early June, reveals a band still trying to coalesce their divergent tastes into one clear prototype for success. Their sets still largely comprised covers too, in distinct opposition to their crosstown rivals Pylon.

The arch, acerbic cadre of UGA art school alumni that clustered around Pylon would often be a little dismissive of Athens' newest flash in the pan and their unashamed desire for a good time. Pylon, having been established earlier and with record deals and singles under their belts, had the clear credibility advantage. You didn't catch Pylon filling their sets with other people's songs, either, subscribing instead to the age-old self-serious muso notion that auteurship is king. R.E.M. might potentially have had equally if not even more high-minded ideas about art and expression, but they were still learning how to articulate them and, in the meantime, they had somewhat accidentally asserted themselves as the frat boy, boozed-up party band of choice.

By the end of 1980, they had played multiple shows in North Carolina and Tennessee, as well as in every corner of their home state. They saw out the year with by far their biggest gig to date, opening for The Police at the Fox Theatre in Atlanta in front of 4000 people. Not for the first time, Sting's new wave trio found themselves inserted into a crucial moment in the early development of R.E.M., on this occasion turning to them as a last-minute replacement for their original support band XTC. Bill Berry's friendship with Ian Copeland was once again paying off too as the local promotional tactics that Copeland had taught him had now become second nature. Where Pylon would make their money through regular trips to New York, R.E.M. were becoming the masters of making the most out of their local resources. Stipe's antics on stage that night – coaxing audience members out of the crowd, running roughshod over security – did not ingratiate the band to the local bookers, but R.E.M had plenty of time to work on their arena show etiquette.

All the while, the songs were steadily improving. They knew that 'All the Right Friends' was the first truly interesting song they had written, with its grown-up chord progression and segmented structure. It dated back to the earliest Buck/Stipe writing sessions in late 1979 and, while it is an impressive achievement for such inexperienced writers, it bears few of the hallmarks of their great records: Stipe's lyrics are, to be kind, rudimentary, with a fixation on the first person that he quickly outgrew, and the track follows a predictable format. In hindsight, it may have been crucial to prove to themselves that they were capable of building a song like 'All the Right Friends' before trying to subvert the conventions and start building tracks in their own idiosyncratic style.

Their setlists, as 1980 became 1981, included a number of far more audacious originals. 'Gardening at Night' had its origins in a late-night drive home from a show. "Rather than inform me of his desire to evacuate his bladder," Berry wrote about one of his bandmates in the liner notes to *And I Feel Fine...The Best of the I.R.S. Years*, "he instead suggested that I pull over so that he might engage in the task of roadside 'night gardening'. To four guys in their early twenties, this was a glaring catalyst for a new song." The track leaned heavily on Peter Buck's rippling guitar lines, inspired on this occasion by Neil Young's 'Cinnamon Girl', and Mike Mills' melodic bass part, but above all it marked a quantum leap forward for Stipe's writing.

"I thought it was the first real song we did," Stipe said in Marcus Gray's *It Crawled from the South*, and you can see why. For the first time, the lyrics have no immediate literal sense. References to Christian telephone prayer lines are just about the only concrete, real-world matters addressed in the lyrics. Rather, this was the moment that R.E.M. consciously severed their ties with convention and clarity. Rock lyrics are not designed for the page but for the ear and with this breakthrough, Stipe started to appreciate the way words *sounded* in connection to each other rather than what they meant.

"We echoed up the garbage sound
But they were busy in the rows
We fell up not to see the sun
Gardening at night just didn't grow".

You could pore over it for hours and never grasp a truly satisfying meaning. Or, you might fill the gaps it leaves with your own answers and arrive at something that intuitively makes sense only to you. Or, due to Stipe's mumbled, high-pitched, inexact pronunciation, you may listen to the song for decades and never strive for meaning from it but instead simply revel in the music of Stipe's voice. By divorcing himself from the need for literal or even poetic truth, Stipe had exploded the possibilities of songwriting wide open for himself. He had found a way to short circuit language, to throw off the shackles of syntax and grammar. If each word had meaning, it was not necessarily in relation to the words on either side of it. 'Gardening at Night' is a collage, offering an impressionistic sense of meaning rather than anything more specific.

More often than not, the results would not be as muddled or opaque as 'Gardening at Night', but even if they were, it tended to work.

Other songs from the period included 'Pretty Persuasion' and 'Sitting Still', among the more driving, forwardly mobile numbers in their rapidly growing catalogue. And then there was the one true outlier.

When friend of the band Ingrid Schorr left the Athens scene to re-join her family back in Rockville, Maryland, it seemed to wound Mike Mills more than anyone else. He took to his guitar and started translating his unrequited separation anxiety into something precious. '(Don't Go Back to) Rockville' was, by this band's standards, a straight-ahead pop song, boasting a chorus that would make Paul McCartney blush. It was thoroughly atypical of their output at the time, or indeed for many years to come, but its presence did prove that should events ever call on them to do so, this was a band capable of writing hits with the best of them.

For now though, the leftfield compositions were winning the day, and the most esoteric of the group went by the name of 'Radio Free Europe', a song they quickly promoted to either the opening or closing spot at their live shows.

Radio Free Europe was a real thing, an organisation funded by the US Government to broadcast news into parts of the world that the US perceived to have a free press deficit, which in the early 1980s was primarily Eastern Europe. But make no mistake, the song was not some early veiled stab at lyrical activism. Stipe liked 'radio free Europe' as a word bunch and the mystery that it suggested. Everyone who has ever thought about the song's lyrics has ended up with a different conception of what it is getting at; when pressed, Stipe has always responded with words such as "babbling" and "nonsense" to describe the lyrics. But nevertheless, there is something compelling about the song's composition, with its nuanced, irregular vocal melodies and bustling, borderline manic energy. It even had a mad, brief but eminently sing-able chorus to boot. It was, they couldn't deny, destined to be their first single.

And so it was that R.E.M. made their first foray into a professional recording studio on 8 February 1981. The location was Bombay Recording Studios in Smyrna, Georgia, a short drive from Atlanta, where the band were introduced to its owner, the producer Joe Perry. R.E.M. understandably knew nothing about how to conduct themselves in such a situation and made the blunder of booking only six hours to record eight songs: 'Sitting Still', 'Gardening at Night', 'Radio Free Europe',

'Shaking Through', 'Mystery to Me', '(Don't Go Back to) Rockville', 'Narrator' and an instrumental called 'White Tornado'.

It would have taken far more experience than R.E.M. had at this stage to pull off the type of story one hears of the classic bands recording entire albums of material in single recording sessions and when the band listened back to the tapes at the end of the day, they were bitterly disappointed. Buck later described them as "flat and dull", admitting that "I didn't know what I was doing". They abandoned hopes of using them as promos to send out to labels and left them with Perry. Needless to say, these recordings would now be hugely valuable, but Perry, with some nobility, has resisted all offers to release them and they remain unheard by the public.

If nothing else, the experience gave them the sense of having taken the next step as a professional band. Within a few weeks, they made another stride by appointing Jefferson Holt to the position of R.E.M. manager. Holt was a native of Chapel Hill, North Carolina who had moved to Athens in late 1980 in order to start up his own record store. The venture failed to take off, but Holt was a hustler and after attending a few R.E.M. shows, he forcefully ingratiated himself into the band's inner circle. Holt's can-do attitude impressed the band right from the start. Bill Berry, because of his experiences at Paragon, had been dealing with all of the band's bookings up until then, but he was more than happy to pass that duty onto Holt when he volunteered his services. Holt expanded the reach of the band's live show circuit almost immediately and, even better, he drove the van to get them there too.

It was also through Holt that the band were able to book their next recording session. Holt knew the band The dB's from back in North Carolina and their guitarist Peter Holsapple recommended another North Carolinian, Mitch Easter, as a producer worth his salt. Easter was an accomplished musician in his own right and, in contrast to Perry, he was a studio nerd. He loved the potential that recorded music offered, embracing the embellishments and accentuations that can be added when not simply capturing a straight live performance. His studio, The Drive-In, was set up in his parents' garage in Winston-Salem, and when R.E.M. arrived there on 15 April, they immediately felt more at home than they had at Bombay.

They decided to focus on just three tracks: 'Radio Free Europe', 'Sitting Still' and 'White Tornado'. This time, it sounded good. Buck's arpeggiated Rickenbacker notes tickled the air, the rhythm was tight and the vocals, although unintelligible, were high in the mix and drew the listener in. The meticulously structured vocal harmonies, with Berry on baritone, Mills on the high end and Stipe in between, were also incredibly well-defined even by this stage. The first R.E.M. miracle was performed that day as the band formally graduated into the musicians they knew they could be. They labelled the recording the *Cassette Set* and made 400 copies for distribution, complete with hand-drawn illustrations and a cover that read, 'DO NOT OPEN'.

At around this time, the band had also become acquainted with another ambitious local music promoter by the name of Johnny Hibbert. He was an Atlanta law student who fronted the band The Incredible Throbs in his down time and had been impressed by the passion R.E.M. were able to stir in a crowd when he caught a couple of their shows. After he got his hands on a copy of *Cassette Set*, he reached out. He had set up his own record label, Hib-Tone Records, and wanted to know if the band would be interested in signing a one-year deal in order to release 'Radio Free Europe' and 'Sitting Still' as their debut single. The band liked the idea of being associated with a local DIY label and agreed almost immediately, even acceding to Hibbert's condition that he would retain sole publishing rights to anything released on Hib-Tone.

Another of Hibbert's demands was that he would be able to supply his own mix of the songs, and so in late May, he joined the band when they returned to The Drive-In. Hibbert's contributions to the recordings were to add overdubs to the guitar parts, the effect of which he liked because he felt it invoked Roger McGuinn's style in The Byrds' music, a comparison that would follow R.E.M. around forevermore. A similar effect was used for the vocals on the 'Radio Free Europe' chorus, with Hibbert adding his own voice to echo Stipe's and fill out the sound.

Mitch Easter caught wind of Hibbert's involvement and was not thrilled that the work he had done – and that he and the band had been happy with – was now being tampered with. He had only become fonder of the session over time, and in late April he had even remixed the 'Radio Free Europe' masters into a playfully bizarre 'Radio Dub' version that is now easily found online. Strange, distorted electronic effects, wavering sound levels and murky, echoey atmospherics may not a dub remix make, but it is without question one of the great sonic curios of the entire R.E.M. legacy.

More seriously, Easter made a concerted effort to compete with Hibbert's new mix by mixing an updated master version of both 'Radio Free Europe' and 'Sitting Still' in early June. The band now had a decision to make, and they went back to Bombay Studios with Hibbert to settle the matter. The band actually preferred the Easter mix, but Hibbert was adamant. His feeling was that it was his money on the line and he needed to be able to stand by the final product. He had, in effect, pulled rank on Easter, and arguably on the band too. Some reports even suggest that Hibbert had already sent his version off to be mastered before the meeting even took place. Either way, Peter Buck in particular wasn't thrilled with the turn of events and his relationship with Hibbert was irrevocably damaged.

Easter's version would eventually show up on the 1988 compilation *Eponymous* and in truth, listening to them back-to-back decades later, there is not a vast space between the two. The Easter mix may just have the edge in urgency and sense of band cohesion, but Hibbert's overdubs do lend a touch of grandeur. Ultimately though, whichever version had been chosen to unveil the band to the world would have had exactly the same effect.

With a single release now imminent, the band had the wherewithal to realise that they would need somebody with legal expertise to look after their affairs. Bill Berry had come across Bertis Downs while working for Paragon and coincidentally Peter Buck had also befriended him at Wuxtry in Atlanta, bonding over a shared passion for Neil Young. Downs had remained in the group's orbit, even attending their second show, and they were aware of his credentials as an entertainment lawyer. They approached him once the single had been finalised, only for Downs to be shocked by the deal they had agreed with Hibbert.

The fact that Hibbert had manoeuvred the band into allowing Hib-Tone to retain sole publishing rights did not pass the smell test to Downs. He instructed the band not to make such a deal again and from that point on, the band never made a major decision without Downs' say so. He would go on to be credited as the band's 'advisor' and he quickly helped them set up their own publishing company, Night Garden Music (named in reference to Downs' favourite of their early compositions). He also started talking to Hibbert himself, and struck a deal whereby Hibbert agreed to reduce the contract from a one-year deal to one single. On the advice of Downs, the band also later bought back the rights to the single, in an early signifier of the ambition and pragmatism that would become a hallmark of the R.E.M./Downs partnership.

Furthermore, Downs helped establish the band as an official government entity, R.E.M./Athens Ltd., with five equal members, including manager Jefferson Holt. It meant that Holt was entitled to an equal share of every dollar that the band made, even if the tax sheets would remain largely empty for a little while longer. Holt was headstrong, the band's adventurous, make-things-happen guy, while Downs provided the grounded legal counsel they also needed. With those two in place, R.E.M. were finally set.

On 8 July 1981, a 7" single was released on Hib-Tone Records with 'Radio Free Europe' on the a-side and 'Sitting Still' on the flip. It featured cover art to match the music: a blurred, ambiguous, mysterious photograph taken by Michael Stipe, an image even more avant-garde than something Ralph Eugene Meatyard might have come up with. Out of roughly a thousand initial copies, 600 were sent to the press and college radio and it quickly went into heavy rotation on campus stations across the US. As Peter Buck later told *Rolling Stone*, "We sent promo copies literally to any magazine we thought of. We sent one to *Women's Wear Daily*, I swear to god."

For such a small debut release, the responses were off the scale. Tom Carson of *Village Voice* called it "one of the few great American punk singles", while Robert Palmer of the *New York Times* included it in his Top Ten Singles of 1981, alongside the likes of Prince, Yoko Ono and Chic. It took Hib-Tone by surprise most of all and Hibbert quickly channelled all the resources he could gather and ordered a further 6000 pressings.

The Hibbert version remained exclusively available on those original 7" records for the next four decades. Together with the re-worked version included on *Murmur*, however, 'Radio Free Europe' continues to stand alongside the most loved and respected songs ever recorded by the band, having been included on '500 Greatest Songs of All Time' lists by publications from Rolling Stone to NME, Pitchfork to the Rock and Roll Hall of Fame. The true Hibbert mix was eventually made commercially available again through an official 40th anniversary re-release in May 2021, a turn of events that was entirely incomprehensible to anyone associated with those ragged, haphazard Smyrna and Winston-Salem recording sessions.

'Chronic Town'

The months that followed the release of 'Radio Free Europe' were among the headiest of the whole R.E.M. tale. It was the summer of their lives. Buoyed by the positive reaction to their debut single and bolstered by the sense of achievement that comes with the first major breakthrough of one's career, they were overcome with new opportunities. The burdens of the future were nowhere to be seen – this was no time for worrying about fulfilling contracts or serving their legacy, nor were they under immediate pressure to force their way through unnatural writing sessions in order to produce new material. They were unrestricted, and what's more they were being offered money to go to the places they had always wanted to go in order to play alongside musicians they had always wanted to meet.

The first R.E.M. show in New York was at the Ritz in the East Village on 17 June 1981, supporting Gang of Four. Jefferson Holt gladly bundled the four boys into his van for the journey, alongside their sound guy of choice, Patton Biddle. Gang of Four were just the kind of arch, artsy post-punk band that Peter Buck and the rest of R.E.M. idolised, and even though they had already shared a stage with them in Atlanta the previous year, being invited to support them in the city of their dreams was a different matter altogether.

By the end of the year, they had found themselves sharing bills with several other of the major movers from the touring British alternative scene: XTC, The Psychedelic Furs, Bow Wow Wow, Siouxsie and the Banshees. With just one single, R.E.M. had already established themselves on the lower rungs of the ladder, and if they were hoping to emulate the musicians they admired, it seemed to be coming relatively easily to them.

The best evidence of the sense of freedom that the four men were enjoying is found in how they filled their non-R.E.M. recreational time.

Michael Stipe, still enrolled at UGA as an art student and eager to put his newfound confidence to use, experimented with a series of other live music projects. He made an appearance or two as a part of a performance group by the name of Pre-Cave, an eardrum-scraping *musique concrete* outfit led by fellow art schoolers Mike Green and Carol Levy, before mustering the courage to put together his own solo headline show at Athens' 40 Watt Club on 6 May.

That night he went by the name 1066 Gaggle O' Sound. It was, by all accounts, a formless, improvisational set of music, with Stipe focusing on drawing inharmonious drones from his Farfisa organ and using a primitive tape recorder to cut and slice sound loops of guitar parts and spoken word. It was a gig aimed at the hardest of hardcore art schoolers, but it also happened to feature the debut performance of opening band Oh-OK, featuring Linda Hopper on vocals and Michael's sister Lynda Stipe on bass.

It was through Oh-OK drummer David Pierce that Michael's more regular extra-curricular musical activities developed. Pierce was friends with UGA alumnus William Lee Self, a prog and Krautrock junkie, and together they had started a band called Tanzplagen. Depending on your tolerance for self-indulgent, freeform experimental rock, their name either translates as Dance Mania or Dance Torture, allegedly derived from pointing randomly at two words in a German dictionary. Pierce brought Stipe and his Farfisa into the Tanzplagen fold and they became a regular presence in the Athens live music calendar.

Tanzplagen's goal was to only play on nights with a full moon, but with Stipe in tow, their options were limited by his R.E.M. schedule. They did, however, still find time to tour the state and to record tracks for a single. Stipe suggested they use Bombay Studios and Joe Perry and two songs were recorded, 'Meeting' and 'Treason', with Lynda Stipe singing alongside her brother. The plan was for the 7" to be released on a new label Dasht Hopes, the brainchild of David Healy, who had recently moved to Athens from his native New Jersey and, like Johnny Hibbert before him, was eager to ingratiate himself into the Athens scene. The single, for reasons out of Tanzplagen's control, was never released on Dasht Hopes, but it was eventually picked up by Strangeways Records in 1991 and lives on for posterity on streaming services now. Self eventually relocated to Germany in 1982 after Tanzplagen were officially over, while Pierce went on to form the band Buzz of Delight with Matthew Sweet.

Stipe wasn't the only one looking to scratch an experimental itch. Bill Berry had caught wind that another of Athens' most eminent outfits, Love Tractor, were looking for a new drummer after Kit Swartz – he of the missed R.E.M. audition – had left the band, preferring instead to focus on his frontman duties with The Side Effects. Berry, having played on multiple bills alongside Love Tractor and being a fan of their material, jumped at the opportunity.

A group of UGA students had formed Love Tractor in early 1980 and there was a mutual appreciation between them and R.E.M. Berry began playing shows regularly with both and, according to Love Tractor guitarist Mike Richmond, he preferred his newest project out of the two. It might have simply been because there was more for a drummer to do in Love Tractor, with their more advanced instrumental structures, but it should also not be forgotten that from day one, Berry had been the most doggedly business-minded of R.E.M. and he may have started to detect an element of complacency seeping into the band's dynamic.

Richmond insists that at one stage, Berry had resolved that he was going to quit R.E.M. and become a full-time member of Love Tractor. Whether or not Stipe, Buck or Mills were ever aware of how close they came to losing him, it was nonetheless clear that Berry's fascination with the Love Tractor project was real and it likely stirred some tribal juices. R.E.M. had so quickly reached a stage where the potential for serious success seemed attainable that perhaps it seemed *too* easy for them. It was a pivotal moment: a period of coasting and taking the moment for granted now could have seen their window of opportunity quickly pass. They were still unsigned, after all, and could easily dissolve at any moment without the world so much as shrugging their shoulders.

And so, as the summer concluded and September's new raft of students arrived in Athens, the three men redoubled their commitment to the band, convincing Berry that their determination to make a success of it was equal to his, and R.E.M. turned their minds to moving the band to the next stage.

With their relationship with Hib-Tone having ended on a sour note, the most pressing issue was to find the right label. Jefferson Holt had befriended David Healy and they agreed that Healy would fund R.E.M.'s next sessions, whereupon Holt suggested to the band that they return to the place where they were most comfortable, Mitch Easter's Drive-In in Winston-Salem. They committed to three entire days of recording, with Healy clearly expecting that the resulting music would be released on his Dasht Hopes label. As Peter Buck explained to *Trouser Press* in 1983, time was of the essence. "The instruments were recorded on Friday," he said, "vocals on Saturday and it was mixed on Sunday. We didn't have the money to take any longer."

The sessions themselves were joyful. R.E.M. were relaxed around Easter; he indulged their playful, reckless inclinations and rarely kowtowed to business concerns or hard deadlines. Easter's love of Kraftwerk had left him with a thirst for studio experimentation too, and with R.E.M. game subjects, he played around with backwards guitar parts and convinced Stipe to record his vocals outside the studio to distort the timbre. The weekend included the first studio attempts at tracks like 'Carnival of Sorts (Boxcars)', 'Stumble' and '9-9', as well as an avant-garde, proto-industrial mindbender by the name of 'Jazz Lips', which featured Stipe reading beat poetry over garbled, tape-spliced loops and feedback.

The fact that they were clearly working towards an EP only intensified the need for a label. They knew what they wanted, they just weren't sure how to get it: the label for them was I.R.S. Records.

Founded in 1979 by Miles Copeland III, brother of Bill Berry's erstwhile mentor Ian and Police drummer Stewart, alongside Jay Boberg and Carl Grasso, I.R.S. (or International Record Syndicate) were one of the few independent labels in the US that showed an interest in the bands that R.E.M. felt they wanted to be associated with. Through a major distribution deal with A&M Records, I.R.S. were already promoting bands like The Cramps, The Go-Go's, Buzzcocks and Magazine, giving them a path out of the dive bars that were still R.E.M.'s principal domain and into international recognition.

Sure, the major labels could do that too, but in 1981 they showed little to no interest in entertaining small-time, anti-establishment bands from the Deep South, and R.E.M. were sure they didn't want to give away control over their affairs anyhow. It *had* to be I.R.S., and so, knowing Berry's connection with Ian Copeland, they set about pursuing their one promising contact.

Alas, Ian's raves about his old Athens friends fell on deaf ears, with the elder Copeland wary of appearing to favour family friends over more deserving acts. A college radio rep and R.E.M. fan back in Georgia took it upon himself to send a rough copy of the recordings from the recent Drive-In sessions to Jay Boberg out in California, but no response was received from that end either. It seemed that I.R.S. were just not interested.

The one place that did have an appetite in late 1981 for R.E.M., however, was the inner circle of the New York music scene, following on from the press enthusiasm received by the 'Radio Free Europe' single. This included the promoter Jim Fouratt, who was getting ready to set up his own production company and had close contacts with the mighty RCA Records, the grand dame of US major labels, long-time home to Elvis Presley and David Bowie. He was hopeful that if R.E.M. came to play a couple of prestige shows in early 1982 in New York and then came in for a couple of recording sessions, he would be able to convince RCA to take the plunge on them.

R.E.M. agreed to Fouratt's requests. They entered Studio C at RCA Studios in Manhattan with producer Kurt Munkacsi on 1 February 1982 and raced through their repertoire, which now included three new songs: 'Catapult', 'Laughing' and 'Wolves'.

Remarkably, the indication was that RCA, against all the odds, were interested after all. There was the usual toing and froing that one would expect from such a corporate behemoth, but the early smoke signals seemed positive. It was the ultimate test of R.E.M.'s principles, and, under the white heat of intensity, they held firm. RCA was not right for them, they still wanted I.R.S. And so, using RCA's delays as an excuse to move on, they got back in touch with Mitch Easter and he travelled to Sterling Sound in New York City to put the final mastering touches on the five songs the band had chosen for their EP. They were going to do it their own way.

A month later, at a gig in New Orleans, the gamble paid off. The show had been beset by technical problems and the band were decompressing backstage, disappointed with their performance, when in walked I.R.S. co-owner Jay Boberg. He had received the tape from the college radio rep months earlier and after slowly falling in love with it, he had dedicated himself to catching the next R.E.M. show that his schedule would allow. Having finally seen them play, he was ready to commit.

To Boberg, the show had been anything but a disappointment. The R.E.M. that he had already fallen for were on full display: haphazard, unpredictable, a surprise at every corner. He actively liked their weirdness and seemed eager to encourage their most esoteric instincts. The timing could not have been more perfect. In truth, the RCA session the band had recorded also happened to have been their most commercially-friendly performance to date. Perhaps because they were rushing, or perhaps because they were feeling the pressure of the might of the US recording industry, the versions of the songs they laid down that day were more straightforward in their arrangement, with Stipe's vocals far clearer and the playing more crisp. What Boberg wanted was closer to the essence of the band and he wanted to sign them with the expectation that he would get more of it.

The band purred at the prospect. Boberg offered to release the EP and to sign R.E.M. to a five-album deal, a proposal that they did not take long to mull over. The band knew the economic realities of signing with an independent label and backed themselves to be able to make their money on the back end by producing records that would sell by word of mouth. They had the record deal of their dreams.

The big loser in this turn of events was Healy. Having funded the sessions, and with the band having returned from New York without an RCA deal, he could have been reasonably confident that Dasht Hopes was the only likely destination for them. I.R.S. would recompense him for the costs and Healy soon returned back north, his label never having taken off.

I.R.S. formally announced their new signing on 31 May 1982 and R.E.M. were back at the Drive-In the next day to put the final touches on their EP, which would hit stores on 24 August.

It is interesting to consider the decision-making processes behind the five tracks that were chosen for *Chronic Town*. They could easily have led with their most commercially marketable material, with fully written and road tested tracks like '(Don't Go Back to) Rockville', 'Pretty Persuasion' and 'All the Right Friends', but none of those had even made studio appearances yet. Instead, with their tails up after netting the label deal and their self-belief cresting at its highest point to date, they leaned towards the oblique.

'Wolves, Lower' was the last song to be recorded and the first to be heard by listeners of *Chronic Town*. It seems only right that the opening sound of the first side of R.E.M. material should be Peter Buck's rippling, arpeggiated Rickenbacker, with Mike Mill's fuzzy bass notes and Bill Berry's muffled drums barely able to wait for their cues thereafter. Buck later described the track as "head and shoulders above the rest" of their early material, and I.R.S. management were particularly high on it, even though it was a relatively late replacement for the track 'Ages of You', which the band had originally planned for the EP ever since the first recording session in October 1981.

Mills almost immediately assumes the position of melodist, the role that he was born for, on 'Wolves, Lower', while Berry at times sounds like he is kicking the backboard of a wardrobe and Stipe paints a typically obscure word cloud that seems to draw from gothic imagery (listeners would have been encouraged further in that direction by Curtis Knapp's cover art, a photograph of the spitting gargoyle from the Notre Dame Cathedral, lit in a blue, crepuscular hue).

It is, in truth, abundantly unclear what meaning Stipe intends listeners to take from the track, although it hasn't stopped theories circulating in the decades since, ranging from it being a depiction of authoritarian mob rule to a tacit cry for help from Stipe's suppressed sexuality. The latter is depressingly common in speculation around early R.E.M. lyrics and should be treated with a healthy dose of scepticism. It is much safer to conclude that the intention for 'Wolves, Lower' is to engender mystery, intrigue and indeed confusion in the listener's mind's eye. Mood and energy were paramount to R.E.M. in 1982 and in that regard, they were already in a lane all of their own.

As previously discussed, the band had a special fondness for 'Gardening at Night' and in this final version it catapults forward with reckless, fizzing momentum. Stipe's vocals are high and nasal, closer to sighing than singing, even if his obvious love of riding the highs and lows of the song betrays the aloofness that he was hoping to convey.

'Carnival of Sorts (Boxcars)', a lyric from which provided the EP with its name, opens with a warped circus clown march before bursting open into the most singalong-able chorus of their recorded career so far. In 2019, Stipe revealed that the song had been inspired by the carnival scene in David Lynch's *The Elephant Man*, indicating that his mind was indeed focused on the issue of social stigmas at the time. The lyrics tell of a town trapped in a cycle of judgement, with Stipe urging, "Gentlemen! Don't get caught!" Anyone looking for psychoanalytic clues to Stipe's possible inner life are certainly provided with ammunition this time.

Side B of *Chronic Town* (labelled on the sleeve as 'Poster Torn') opens with '1,000,000', which chugs along with a rockabilly flavour to Buck's guitar, a crisper drum sound and a much more animated and intelligible Stipe vocal. It might sacrifice a measure of the trademark mystery, but the urgency itself is compelling.

'Stumble' rounds it out and is as good a snapshot of an early live R.E.M. show as we will ever hear on record. At 5:40, it numbers among the longest tracks they would ever release too, allowing time for the Mills/Berry groove to breathe, as well as making space for a brief descent into a loose, sound effect-filled breakdown during which Stipe reads a spoken word piece that Marcus Gray suggests is taken from a 1957 copy of *Cavalier* magazine, one of the precursors to *Playboy*. 'Stumble' captures a relaxed R.E.M., enjoying each other's company and seeming like they would happily play all night.

Chronic Town sold 20,000 copies in its first year, a respectable number. A simple promotional video was shot for 'Wolves, Lower', directed by Jonathan Dayton and Valerie Faris, the husband-and-wife duo that worked regularly with I.R.S. and would later find success in a different world with their debut feature film *Little Miss Sunshine*. Reviews were broadly positive, with *Creem*'s Robert 'Robot' Hull calling it, "undoubtedly the sleeper EP of the year", while *NME*'s Richard Grabel hailed its "songs that won't be denied", and it was ranked second best EP of 1982 in *Village Voice*'s Pazz & Jop critics poll (behind T-Bone Burnett's *Trap Door,* but ahead of such contemporaries as Meat Puppets, ESG and The Brains).

First time listeners to *Chronic Town*, whether in 1982 or in an era that followed, will almost certainly finish their first run through feeling a little nonplussed. Melodies are there but they are often buried; images are offered but they are out of focus. These five songs take surprising turns to the fresh ear and require time to fully appreciate. But everything that had taken R.E.M. this far comes to fruition on this release: the art college studies, the shared passion for underground musicians and cult outsiders, the dogged determination not to follow the path most trodden, the parties, drugs, sex and touring, the combination of genuine musical talent and a punk DIY ethos. It is all here, writ large across this stunning first statement, in a brand-new font all of their own.

36

'Murmur'

By 1983, music culture had become impatient. New artists were expected to be able to capture their essence in a neat, debut album-sized package, arriving into the global conversation with each foible and innovation fully formed, ready to make their indelible mark.

The early rock 'n' rollers and the British invasion groups got away with little more than slapdash compilations of previously released singles and rudimentary cover versions for their first LP releases, before the album-as-high-art concept was developed in the mid-1960s by The Beatles, Bob Dylan and The Beach Boys. Bands emerging from 1967 onwards were lucky to make it into posterity without a defining debut statement, with *The Doors*, *Music from Big Pink*, *The Piper at the Gates of Dawn*, *Are You Experienced* and *Led Zeppelin* all heralding major arrivals into the annals of classic rock within the space of two years.

More pertinent to the lineage that R.E.M. found themselves a part of were towering debuts of an altogether more visceral, discombobulating kind: *The Velvet Underground & Nico* and Captain Beefheart's *Safe as Milk* gave a secret blueprint to an alternative future in 1967, while MC5's *Kick Out the Jams* and The Stooges' self-titled album catalysed a 1969 that had otherwise started to grow overly serious and introspective.

The New York punk scene that Berry, Buck, Mills and Stipe so idolised had followed step closely with a series of debuts that would mark such seminal highs that the artists in question were never able to replicate the same levels again (*New York Dolls*, *Horses*, *Ramones*, *L.A.M.F.*, *Marquee Moon*), and even the bands that were able to grow later in their careers like Talking Heads, Blondie and The Cramps, only did so on the back of highly praised first albums. The story was no different for the British punk and new wave bands that had become such taste-setters stateside too. Even R.E.M.'s Athens counterparts The B-52's had blown critics and audiences away with their 1979 debut. With a single and an EP under their belts, it was clear that this next step was one that R.E.M. could not afford to get wrong.

They knew that the more they played, the better they got, and so the final months of 1982 were packed with tours ranging from the Rust Belt to the Midwest, as well as their first trip to California. I.R.S. were based in the Golden State and Jay Boberg was keen to invite them to play a few shows to the still-sceptical label staff. A string of gigs were set up with R.E.M. opening for local acts such as The Untouchables and Romeo Void, as well as touring Brits like The Beat and, once again, Gang of Four.

The drive to the West Coast, it was decided, would be best broken up by a gig booking in Albuquerque. Only when the band arrived at the designated venue, however, did they learn exactly what kind of situation they had been suckered into. The promoter took one look up and down at the four college boys from a different world standing on his doorstep and wondered exactly how culturally appropriate they might be for the opening act of his strip club that night. He was looking for a good time band to lubricate his New Mexico crowd as a warm up to the Hot Legs contest he had headlining; the finer details of the advances in the left of the dial college rock of the day were of less interest to him. A happy medium was reached between the two parties and, as much for their own safety as his own business interests, the promoter decided that he would pay R.E.M. *not* to take the stage. The band seized the $500 and bolted straight back into their rusty old Green Dodge and hightailed it back onto the California-bound highway.

Life in the van was thrifty, to say the least. They would regularly sleep in the vehicle, or at best share mattresses in low rent motels, especially if it meant they could save some extra pennies for alcoholic replenishments instead. Life on the road was a romantic endeavour to them, an extension of the Beat dream and they knew they were good at it.

Occasionally shows would go wrong, as in the case of a gig at a military base in Wichita Falls, Texas the following June. The band were simply not macho enough for these army brats, a tension that was so immediately obvious that Stipe and Buck began kissing and rubbing their behinds together during an early rendition of 'Radio Free Europe'. "There were oranges flying out of the audience," Buck later recalled.

"Death threats, notes that came up on stage saying, 'Faggot, you die, we're gonna get you backstage'. There were maybe three or four guys who liked the band, but everybody else hated us so much they started beating up the guys who were enjoying it." Unsurprisingly, the band's response to such an intolerant reaction was to double down, with the exception of Bill Berry, who threw his sticks into the crowd and stormed off, to be replaced by Sara from Let's Active. The crowd booed so loudly when they finished their set that the band couldn't resist coming back for an encore.

Nights like those were very much the exceptions, though. The band were tighter than ever, their repertoire of songs growing all the time, and Michael Stipe in particular was more at ease with his stage persona than at any time before. Those first shows in California, although not a good indication of the buzz they had built up elsewhere, were strong enough to win around the remaining doubters at I.R.S., and just by surviving from gig to gig, they were establishing the college rock circuit that would become the lifeblood of US underground music for decades to come. What's more, and much to their own surprise, they kept running into an emerging generation of other bands that were following similar trajectories to theirs.

The US charts of the day were dominated by synthpop imports like Depeche Mode, Soft Cell and The Human League, dubbed in the press as the Second British Invasion, while hungry young homegrown bands thrashed away in basements and warehouses with little apparent hope of a breakthrough. Peter Buck captured the mood: "You'd see some little twee synth pop band that had one hit for thirty seconds, and they'd get 3000 people in America, and yet a local band that made really good records and worked their butt off would get 200 people. It was really frustrating."

Despite this, R.E.M. now knew from their own experiences that something was indeed bubbling underneath, ready to explode. Eking out an affordable, nomadic existence on the road might be a greater logistical challenge in a country the size of the US than it is in Britain, but the stories R.E.M. had heard from the likes of Gang of Four of covering their entire home country in one tour and picking up new fans each night were intoxicating. As it happened, other young American bands had also been hearing similarly inspiring tales and had already started trying to do it themselves. Before long, R.E.M. were running into their contemporaries on the road on a regular basis and learning of local scenes from up and down the entire country.

The Los Angeles-area punk bands, led by Black Flag, X and Minutemen harked back to the hardcore roots of the movement and had taken it to thrashier and less commercially viable places. The bands from the Minneapolis/St. Paul area like Hüsker Dü and The Replacements, while sharing a lot of R.E.M.'s DIY instincts, were a little too cracked and angry to ever be a possibility for mainstream America, while The Paisley Underground, the neo-psychedelic movement out of Los Angeles that included The Dream Syndicate, The Three O'Clock, The Rain Parade and Green on Red, was just too damn weird and trippy to ever get big. But R.E.M. happened to be writing music that, although still decidedly weird, was at least playable on the more adventurous radio stations that were seeking out material that could straddle the divide between the underground and the charts.

"We were trying to do something original, but not necessarily groundbreaking," Mike Mills would later reflect to *Pitchfork*. "We just knew we didn't want to do the crap that was on the radio at the time."

R.E.M.'s aversion to artistic compromise was now rock solid, but if it just so happened that a small part of America still came to them, they could live with that. As Michael Stipe told *Trouserpress Magazine* in 1983, "If we get mass exposure, it'll be because radio bent to us rather than the other way around. The state of the record industry is such that people are grabbing at straws trying to find something new to play." Characteristically, Peter Buck was well on top of the emerging trends and foresaw his own future with remarkable acuity in the same interview: "A lot of weird things are slipping in the back door. Companies like Slash, I.R.S. and Twin/Tone are going to be the wave of rock 'n' roll future."

I.R.S. knew that if Buck was right, they needed to get the best possible results out of their new signings and as the dates earmarked for R.E.M.'s first album sessions neared, Jay Boberg contacted Stephen Hague to see if he would come in to produce the record. Hague was a curious choice, having done very little production work at the time, but I.R.S. were so keen to tease the commercial potential out of the band that they were willing to take the risk.

A little like the radio stations caught between the two competing forces of art and commerce, Boberg and I.R.S. were looking to have it both ways. Yes, Boberg liked R.E.M. the way they were – that was what he had originally fallen in love with after all – but nevertheless, business is business and he knew this band could be his ticket. I.R.S. in general had not been thrilled about the oft-mentioned 'murkiness' of *Chronic Town* and were wary of letting Mitch Easter continue to produce. After all, the R.E.M. of that EP was not the R.E.M. that was touring the country. Live, the band were urgent, lean and playful, whereas the studio concoction was inscrutable and standoffish.

A demo trial was booked in for December at Axis Sound Studios in Atlanta with Hague at the controls, and R.E.M. recorded a version of 'Catapult'. The band did not enjoy it. Bill Berry was forced to play to a click track and Hague was eager to add synthesisers to the mix. The band felt that Hague was pursuing technical perfection, something which made them bristle, and the final version that he mixed at Syncro Sound Studios in Boston did not please them one bit.

The fact was that R.E.M. loved working with Easter and, in truth, they would probably have figured out a way to make sure that any replacement was not going to work out. I.R.S. agreed to let Easter have one final go at producing a demo and on 6 January he and the band convened at Reflection Sound Studios in Charlotte. The upgrade in studio from The Drive-In was Easter's idea, a way of appealing to the label by proving how seriously he was taking the project. The band recorded 'Pilgrimage', complete with three ringing vocal melody lines and a new measure of clarity in Stipe's voice. It was, by early R.E.M. standards, a pocket symphony and even I.R.S. had to accept that it was markedly superior to Hague's 'Catapult'. Easter offered to bring in his old high school friend Don Dixon as co-producer and I.R.S. finally relented, agreeing to all of the band's demands. (Hague, it should be said, later produced 'West End Girls', 'A Little Respect' and 'True Faith', so Boberg was unquestionably right in identifying him as a producer with a gift for eking out a hit.)

What ensued was a month of recording at the Reflection Studios. The atmosphere was relaxed, with Peter, Mike, Bill and Mitch Easter often sitting around together, strumming on acoustic guitars and patiently awaiting the strike of inspiration. Easter's experimental urge that had so impressed the band remained strong and with the equally open-minded Dixon now in tow too, the bond of trust between performer and producer was unshakeable.

Breaking into R.E.M.'s inner circle took some doing, but for Easter and Dixon, this was as much their one shot at immortality as it was the band's and they gambled on their own instincts to get it right. As Peter Buck later said, "Mitch and Don thought their job was to make us make a good record, and not worry about selling records for record companies. So they were like partners in crime for us; they were protecting us from outside influences or financial influences."

Both songs from the debut single were re-recorded. 'Radio Free Europe' was their most-played song both on stage and in the studio by this point and it had naturally shifted in form during the nearly two years since the original Johnny Hibbert recording. It was perhaps this level of familiarity that made it the track that they were most willing to experiment with. Easter decided to channel the ambient sound of the studio through Mike Mills' bass recording to lend the cut an intangible otherworldliness, while Stipe's vocals were recorded in the stairway outside the studio, away from the rest of the band, the idea being that it would give them an air of detachment and isolation, an idea seemingly influenced by Martin Hannett's extraordinary techniques while working with Joy Division. Both Easter and Dixon have stressed on multiple occasions that they never deliberately muffled or buried Stipe's vocal – that really was just how he sounded.

Stipe, so often reticent to comment on such matters, did offer some form of explanation to *Rolling Stone* in 2021: "My vocal style probably had to do with Mike's love of the Ramones and R.E.M.'s penchant for writing really fast, really frenetic songs. I thought they were too fast, I wanted to slow them down, but they wouldn't play slower – we were all speed freaks at the time. So, I just started singing slower and stretching out my vowels, and I slowed the songs down by making my part much, much slower. That served me well and it evolved into a vocal style, I guess."

The new version of 'Radio Free Europe' was a much more deadly beast than the Hib-Tone original. Where the 1981 version opened with a simplistic, high-pitch, falling electronic pulse before Bill Berry's cavernous, muffled drum beat kicked in, the 1983 version opens with ten menacing seconds that sound like alien interference on a Geiger counter, and when Berry arrives, it is as if he is stamping out the mystery. The tinniness is gone too, the new version making the earlier recording seem panicked and overly hurried by comparison.

The two versions of 'Sitting Still' are less divergent. Peter Buck's crystalline guitar arpeggios ring out even more clearly and Mike Mills' basslines bound and bounce with renewed enthusiasm, but in truth they had all but nailed this song the first time around.

Most of the other songs they had given serious trial runs to during previous studio visits made it onto the album. 'Laughing' dates back to the aborted RCA session and is given a prominent role here. One of the few *Murmur* tracks with a discernible real-world reference in its lyrics, it invokes the story of Laocoön, the priest of Greek mythology who threatened to foil the Trojan Horse ambush and was punished by the gods, who sent giant sea snakes to steal his two sons. Stipe does little to probe the story any more deeply than that, and manages to misgender Laocoön along the way, but the longing he loads into the "lighted, lighted, laughing" refrain is remarkable. The band attack the chorus with real muscular momentum, but instead of a dramatic climax, we get a melancholy lament in its stead. As a listener, we are torn between the gusto of the build and the strangely downturned effect of the payoff, leaving a deliciously bittersweet aftertaste that would become a strength of much of the best R.E.M. music.

'Pilgrimage', the song that won Easter the producing gig, is one of the album's oddest songs. It bears the early trademark of Mike Mills echoing Stipe's lead vocals straight back at him, and Mills' contributions on vibraphone also lend it a distinctive note, but Stipe's lyrics – seemingly about a blind, hopeful journey across an ocean to find one's destiny – do not quite fit into that satisfying-but-inscrutable category that encompasses his best work.

'Catapult', the song that nearly brought the band to war with their label, is trusted to open Side 2 of the album, and is a sultry, low-hanging number that lets Buck's noodling fingers wander free for a few delicious moments, while 'Shaking Through', a track dating back to their very first studio visit for the abandoned Smyrna session with Joe Perry, is a surprisingly upbeat, perky track with Stipe's voice sliding up and down the scales. Tucked away deep into Side 2, the colourful and winning tune also boasts one of Stipe's best opening lines: "Could it be that one small voice doesn't count in the room?"

Among the songs that made their recording session debuts for *Murmur*, two golden gems stand well apart: 'Talk About the Passion' and 'Perfect Circle'.

Michael Stipe's insistence that many of his early works should never be analysed is not to be dismissed, but nobody can deny the clear poetic messaging of 'Talk About the Passion'. A connection is made between the "empty mouths" of the world and the "empty prayers" that go unanswered to help them ("combien reaction?"), later reinforced by repeated references to "the passion", noting that "not everyone can carry the weight of the world". Stipe draws a line between the Passion of Christ and the global hunger that haunts our modern world, and goes further by criticising those in positions of power who pay lip service by acknowledging the problem and yet do nothing to help. Stipe would become a political figure in later life, but the signs were always there.

Musically, the song is perhaps the most conventional on the album, with a clear verse-chorus structure and a relatively uncomplicated arrangement, although a mournful cello part and Peter Buck's plucked acoustic guitar lines give a sense of the 1960s folk influences that are known to have been on his mind during this period. It is a major leap forward for the band in many ways, a sophisticated and mature composition that has the nerve to stand alone under its own strength, with the smoke and mirrors largely stripped away.

'Perfect Circle', on the other hand, is the epitome of all that early R.E.M. stood for. Written largely by Bill Berry, it closes Side 1 in majestic fashion, with two competing pianos driving the melody: one a pristine grand and the other an out of tune upright, itself as ideal an encapsulation of the two opposing instincts at the heart of this band as you could find.

The slowest, most maudlin song on the album, it is a showcase for Michael Stipe's burgeoning vocal talents, pulling enormous emotional resonance out of a lilting, lullaby-like chorus, while backwards guitar parts keep the listener guessing, never resting or fully able to resolve the song's unsolvable riddle. The band members themselves disagree on the meaning of the lyrics: Buck has spoken of how it invokes the innocence of children playing football before sunset, while Stipe points to it being about the longing one feels within the confines of a relationship. Whatever your own interpretation, Stipe says that, "I really like that it can mean different things…it's the exact same feeling, but the details are different." The band would go on to write hundreds of songs across fifteen successful albums, including several major international hits, but few R.E.M. compositions contain the emotional expanse or poetic dignity of 'Perfect Circle', a song they arrived at just two and a half years into their career.

Taken as a whole, *Murmur* does everything that the great debut albums before it had done. Their identity as reluctant rock stars, more interested in the fringes of art than the crowd-pleasing centre ground, clearly shines through. Their sound is their own, entirely developed between the four of them and their chosen producers, and cultivated without an eye on their contemporaries. The album rewards repeated listens, as the counter-intuitive melodies, hidden details and abstract subject matter slowly reveal themselves over time.

As Mike Mills articulated to *Trouserpress*, "We like that the more you listen to it, the more you hear things that didn't pop up the first few times, especially on headphones. It'd be horrible to hear a record once and pick up everything on it, that wouldn't be any fun."

That they should settle on the album title *Murmur* is clearly a sly self-referential joke about Stipe's manner of enunciation, a subject on which the singer later quipped, "It's called *Murmur* because it is one of the six easiest words in the English language to say".

The cover art depicts a field outside Athens that is overrun with the devastating kudzu vine, colloquially referred to in the region as "the vine that ate the South"; the plant typically clambers over all other foliage, growing quickly enough to smother the life out of all that lies beneath it. It serves the purpose of rooting the album firmly in the band's home patch, while revealing nothing of their personal lives and maintaining the air of mystery that the record within works so hard to instill.

Recording and mastering was completed over the following weeks in time for its release to the public on 12 April 1983. As was the custom of the day, the album slowly worked its way up the Billboard Albums Chart, first appearing at #190 in May before gradually building to a peak of #36 in August, an unpredictably giddy height. 170,000 copies had been sold by the end of the summer. A 7" single of the new version of 'Radio Free Europe' was also released on I.R.S. on the same day as the album, peaking in the same August week at #78 on the Billboard Hot 100, a chart placement they wouldn't reach again until 1987.

It would go on to be named as Album of the Year by *Rolling Stone*, ahead of *Thriller*, while Robert Christgau of the *Village Voice* charmingly proclaimed, "They're an art band, nothing more or less – and a damn smart one!"". *New York Times* made the most prescient comment of all, stating, "It will sound as fresh ten years from now as it does today."

Most importantly of all, those radio stations that were scouting for the broadcastable alternative went for it hard, anointing R.E.M. as the ringleaders of a new generation. After a long period of waiting, the audience that had been craving a smart, artful, independent and homegrown riposte to the pomposity of the worst excesses of 1980s commercial music finally had somewhere to flock. For both band and audience alike, their patience was starting to pay off.

'Reckoning'

Things were never again so simple for R.E.M. Their uncompromising stance against the commercial realities of their industry had protected them well so far, but with their debut album in the charts they were now beloved not just by their friends and fellow Athenians, but by hundreds of thousands of young music fans across America. They were now a successful band, albeit modestly, and in danger of being railroaded down the path to greater stardom. Their founding principles, which had remained undefeated up to this point, were set to be thoroughly tested.

There were positives. As they saw it, rising tides should raise all of their contemporaries and so for their spring and summer tours of 1983, they brought in their new friends in The Replacements and The Dream Syndicate as support acts, as well as Mitch Easter's Let's Active. It was, in their view, one of the easiest and most constructive ways to make use of their moment at the head of the new alternative rock table and it helped to foster the growing community.

Peter Buck in particular had grown close to The Replacements, so much so that he had been considered as a possible producer for their third album. Time constraints were a major obstacle, however, and in the short turnaround time that Buck required, the Minneapolis band simply did not yet have enough material and so the plans were shelved. Instead, Buck contributed guitar tracks for the song that would end up as the album's opener, 'I Will Dare'.

That album, *Let It Be*, would live on as one of American punk's finest hours, leading to one of the more under-discussed sliding doors moments in the R.E.M. story. Had Buck produced such a classic record at such a young age, subsequent offers would quickly have become inevitable and difficult to ignore. R.E.M.'s demands on Buck's time were only to become greater as the 1980s wore on and periods of burnout were rapidly approaching. The escape hatch of a secondary career behind the production desk may well have proven irresistible for Peter during the band's more testing moments and could well have slowed R.E.M.'s one-album-per-year ascent. R.E.M. were a tight group, all singularly focused and largely devoid of professional distractions; the innocuous nudge of a competing demand on their guitarist's time may have been all that was needed to throw off their precarious balance.

As it was, after the recording session with The Replacements, Buck took himself to see Prince play at First Avenue in Minneapolis at a concert recorded for the *Purple Rain* film. It was a rare break from the relentlessly hectic touring schedule that lasted for the majority of R.E.M.'s 1983.

The last full support tour that the band would ever play consisted of twenty dates with their friends in The Beat in March and April, before they embarked on an extensive, nationwide headline circuit of America's inner city clubs. More and more new songs started peppering their setlists as the tour went on, indicating that this was more than just a period of hedonistic free living, but an artistically productive time too.

By all accounts, the band still loved touring, especially as headliners and on their own terms. I.R.S., meanwhile, had loftier ambitions than that. Even with roughly 200,000 copies sold, they were less than thrilled with the commercial 'success' of *Murmur*, feeling that the band were not maxing out on their potential. The second single from the album, a Europe-only 12" of 'Talk About the Passion', made no impact at all, compounding the label's anxieties yet further.

Feeling backed into a corner, Jay Boberg grasped the nettle and booked R.E.M. into an eight-date run of stadium dates opening for The Police that August. These were megashows, coinciding with the apex of the British band's bewildering success, taking place just a matter of weeks after 'Every Breath You Take' had risen to number one on the Billboard Hot 100. It was the dictionary definition of the mainstream and R.E.M. were painfully aware that few of the people attending would either know or care who they were.

Due to their long-term association with the Copeland brothers, the band felt they were duty bound to comply, but this could scarcely have been a more antagonistic booking. The final two dates of the run were at Shea Stadium in New York and the JFK Stadium in Philadelphia, both to over 65,000 people, for each of which the band received a hefty

$10,000 payment Bill Berry would describe the shows as, "the most wretched and abysmal experience of our lives. We should've stayed home and got drunk, for all the fucking good it did us."

For Boberg, there were no regrets. "Those shows were probably a lot more successful to their career than they will ever acknowledge," he said years later. Either way, relations between band and label were at a low. To R.E.M., the shows represented everything that made them wary of success, as they battled expectations that they should conform to the trends of the day and appeal to an audience beyond their reach by curtailing their idiosyncrasies. In reality, Boberg believed that it was those very idiosyncrasies that made R.E.M. a good choice for the shows and believed in the band's ability to stick to their guns *and* win over new fans. But R.E.M. were not ready to hear it and they duly retreated back into their shells just at the moment when they could have been blooming, desperate to reassess their situation and eager to wrestle back control.

During their spell of introspection back in Athens, they sought out the least commercial enterprise they could find. Laura Levine was a New York art student that the band had befriended on one of their trips to the city and she had cobbled together enough money to make a rudimentary super 8 film entitled *Just Like a Movie*. It was perfect. Inspired by D.A. Pennebaker's classic Bob Dylan documentary *Don't Look Back*, the film was a black-and-white pastiche of the genre and it featured all four members of R.E.M. making their 'acting' debuts, alongside a number of other selected Athens dwellers, including Michael Stipe's two sisters and the enigmatic Matthew Sweet, who had fled from Nebraska to Athens in search of the now-famed music scene and quickly ingratiated himself into the R.E.M. inner circle. The most enduring part of the film is a version of The Velvet Underground's 'Pale Blue Eyes' with Stipe on accordion and Sweet on guitar, a spare, haunting rendition more akin to modern day DIY bedroom recordings than it is to any mid-1980s fashions.

A few weeks later, having re-energised and cleansed themselves of the stadium show aftertaste, they were back out on the road again, starting this time in New York with a very special date. Until this point, R.E.M. had been limited to local press and radio interviews for promotional spots, but with the positive reviews around *Murmur* came a whole new frontier.

Late Night with David Letterman was barely eighteen months into its original run on NBC, but it was already the coolest talk show in the country. Among the programme's staff were a small group of hip young gunslinging music aficionados who had identified R.E.M. as one of their ideal musical guests for the season. And so, on 6 October, R.E.M. made the journey to the NBC Studios at 30 Rockefeller Plaza in Manhattan for their first ever television performance. The other guests on that episode were Hollywood royalty in the form of Sophia Loren and TV cooking legend Julia Child; if it wasn't already glaringly obvious to the band that they weren't in Kansas anymore, sharing backstage corridors with such household names must have rammed the point home.

It was agreed that they would play two songs of their choosing, between which there would be a brief interview with Letterman. Whether from Stipe's shyness or a studied decision to uphold a certain mystery around their frontman, the band put forward Peter Buck as the interviewee, without realising that it meant that Buck would receive twice as much money.

Letterman introduces the band by citing *Murmur* as having been named as one of the year's five best records by the *Los Angeles Times* and with that, they launch into 'Radio Free Europe'. During the performance, Stipe is restrained and coy, setting the frame for the first image the world would form of him. Buck and Mills, by contrast, are darting and animated, filling in the kinetic void that Stipe had created.

Back home, a group of Athens bands and scenesters gathered at the 40 Watt Club and huddled around the television to watch their friends break through the looking glass. As the romantic cliché goes, this was the chance for these four men to shove it back in the faces of everyone who had ever doubted them – people from their past, whether in Athens, St. Louis or the offices of New York and Los Angeles. Even those who weren't watching knew somebody who was and heard about it in the coming days.

As the studio audience cheers and applauds the end of 'Radio Free Europe', Letterman strides in and shakes each band member's hand, before doing his best to bring a light, fast-paced chat to life with Buck. Intriguingly, it is Mills who chips in and does better with the quick-witted retorts, even if Peter does at least manage to squeeze a name drop of his friends in Pylon, Love Tractor and the Method Actors into the small window of opportunity. Letterman wants to know what R.E.M. stands for and why Athens has built up the reputation that it has, but the band clearly just want to get back to the refuge of playing music. And with that, they introduce their second song as being "too new to be named", before debuting to the world a pristine version of 'So. Central Rain (I'm Sorry)'. Using their biggest ever platform to play a new, unnamed, unreleased song is just about the most quintessential R.E.M. move, one that would not have been common for an established act in that era, let alone one making their broadcast debut.

A month later, they would find themselves back in a high-profile television spot, this time during their first trip to the UK. *The Tube* was the premier new music show in the country at the time, hosted by former Squeeze keyboardist Jools Holland, and this time it found R.E.M. rubbing shoulders with ZZ Top, Wham!, Imagination and Dr. Hook. In this format, Michael Stipe is visibly more relaxed, smiling and at ease, albeit still largely rooted to the spot. Mills and Buck once again bring the spiky, punk energy, but there is a looseness here compared to the *Letterman* performance that speaks to quite how nervous they had been on that first show.

The UK press had been just as gushing about *Murmur* as their American counterparts, if not more so, with *NME*, *Melody Maker* and *Sounds* all lavishing fine praise. With Miles Copeland's familiarity with the UK post-punk scene being as strong as it was, the band were always going to be able to get a base level of attention, and I.R.S. saw fit to put together a run of five European shows, including two in France and one in Amsterdam. After a show at London's Dingwalls venue, the NME wrote, "this is the most vital American group of today". For the band's part, they saw the visit as something akin to that of missionaries, to enlighten a British audience they perceived to have been ahead of the curve so often before that there were new US bands worthy of their attention. As Buck told one journalist, "It's one of our duties while we're over here to say, 'It's not a wasteland over there'."

If life in the outside world was starting to expand in a way that finally suited the band, then life back home in Athens was a little more downbeat. The Athens scene had been rocked earlier in the year by a car accident that took the lives of local musician Larry Marcus and Carol Levy, a close friend of R.E.M., one of their regular photographers and a former lover of Michael Stipe. The tragedy put a hard pause on the ongoing party around the UGA campus and is still seen by many in the inner circles to have been the symbolic end point of the Athens glory period. Stipe even told *Interview Magazine* in 2011 that the shock of the event and losing Levy was his instigation to stop taking drugs.

"I couldn't cry. I woke up the next morning and I said, 'That's it'."

By all accounts, Stipe was the least interested in drug culture of any member of the band, or indeed of almost anyone the band knew. One could not go as far as to say he was healthy in his twenties, as attested by his often gaunt, wiry demeanour that belied an eating disorder he would only open up about decades later, but this event drew a line under his involvement with the speed and meth that were so prevalent around the band's friends.

If the sense of an ending was beginning to percolate around Athens in the summer, then it was palpable after R.E.M.'s return from Europe in November, culminating with Pylon playing their farewell show on 1 December at a bar called The Mad Hatter. Everyone was there to see them off and Mike Mills and Peter Buck joined Love Tractor on stage during the opening set for a rendition of ZZ Top's 'Sharp Dressed Man'.

R.E.M. may have had cause to reflect at this point that their break had come just in time. With the party coming to a close, the dream appeared to be dying for Athens' other would-be stars, with many of the other bands folding or carrying on solely as a pastime as the thudding demands of real life became too pressing to ignore any longer. The whirlwind, quixotic circumstances that had allowed for R.E.M.'s emergence seemed to be dissolving away. Had Berry, Buck, Mills and Stipe arrived even three years later, the assorted characters that had flocked to the city just to be a part of the scene – the likes of Johnny Hibbert, Bertis Downs and Miles Copeland – would not have been on hand to facilitate those formative early steps. The only bands that become successful are the ones with the lucky breaks early on and R.E.M. were certainly in the right place for lucky breaks in Athens in the early 1980s.

The band wanted to wait no longer to record their second album. They had been writing so prolifically during the summer that they were even considering making it a double album, with Peter Buck pushing particularly hard for this. In early November, they made the unusual decision of booking studio time with a new producer. They were in California for a string of shows and while there took the opportunity to make use of the Rhythmic River Studios in San Francisco. Exactly how the band perceived this session is unclear: it could have been intended as a warm-up for the real thing back home, an experiment to see how their sound translated to other settings, or most likely of all an excuse to work with Elliot Mazer, the classic rock producer behind many of Neil Young and The Band's finest records. Whichever, it was a mammoth day, with the band laying down no fewer than 22 tracks.

The feeling was that the album would benefit from verging closer to the faster, rockier version of the band that appeared on stage as opposed to the baroque men of mystery that inhabited *Murmur*. I.R.S. certainly felt that way but for once the band tended to agree, perhaps enthused by how tightly honed their live show had become after such intense touring. The Mazer sessions confirmed that this could work well and, satisfied, the band booked in two weeks either side of Christmas with Mitch Easter and Don Dixon at Reflection Studios in Charlotte.

Exactly how many days the sessions took is subject to debate, with the band eager to accentuate in one direction and the producers keen to exaggerate in the other. Peter Buck stated with some pride in interviews that they got it done in eleven days, taking days off to shoot videos and watch movies. Easter, perhaps protective of how hard he and Dixon had been working, claimed that the whole process stretched out over twenty eighteen-hour days. Whichever way you cook it, they were not dilly-dallying.

Easter was in lockstep with the view that something tighter and faster was what the band needed. "We knew that [trying to emulate *Murmur*] was the worst thing we could do," he later said. "The minute you start to get into deliberate music you screw up, I think. That live sound always appealed to them back in those days and so I thought, maybe we can get that on record."

It allowed the sessions to have a clearer focus. A lot of the intricate arrangements and studio wizardry were dialled back while the folksy influences and acoustic guitars receded into the background. Much of the complexity that those elements brought had been subsumed into their songs organically anyway; the vocal harmonies, for example, had evolved and become much more sophisticated since *Murmur*, with Mike Mills often singing one melody and playing an entirely different counter-melody on his bass, both majestic.

The material itself was of the highest order. At one end of the scale there is the song that Stipe had written for Carol Levy, 'Camera', a heart-rending ballad that tells of Stipe's sense of responsibility for keeping her spirit alive – he feels he must be her camera and see the world for her, just as she had done for the band. You hear Stipe longing for answers and struggling to find them, although his curiously disaffected vocal lends the song a certain numbness. Was the pain too overpowering to express, or too painful to go near in a recording studio? Is what we hear the result of a necessary self-defence mechanism, or was his strength of feeling so overwhelming that in fact it is all there in front of us, but it just *seems* underplayed to us?

It is the credit built up with restraint like this that makes the moments when Stipe lets rip all the more special. The chorus of 'So. Central Rain (I'm Sorry)' sees him hit huge, visceral notes of authentic emotion for the first time in his career. The track pops, ringing out clear and true, with Mike Mills' fingers dancing down his fretboard during the glorious post-chorus bass fill like he's John Entwistle. We seem to catch Stipe in mid-sentence at the song's start as he tells an unusually clear story of a boy longing to apologise to a girl, only for the lines to be down, which leaves him waiting impatiently for her to call him back. Stipe finds the right balance between storytelling and expressionism here: the narrative is clear enough, but his words seem to be chosen as much for their percussive rhythm as their definitions. At track three, it is the moment the album takes flight, but as a standalone slice of pop music, it is incendiary.

That is not to look past the quality of the songs that precede it. 'Harborcoat' must rank among the most inscrutable of all R.E.M. songs, its opaque swamp of undulating, overlapping voices in the chorus impossible to pick apart. Peter Buck's licks have a rockabilly skip, the effect of which is uncannily similar to what Johnny Marr was doing thousands of miles away at the very same time. Michael Stipe said in 1991 that the song was "a rewriting of *The Diary of Anne Frank*", which is a beguiling idea. Looking through the lyrics, there are recurring references to Lenin's Red Terror campaign and even a callback to the Laocoön story he referenced on 'Laughing', but linking it to Anne Frank is a push. Stipe further obfuscated things on stage in Dublin in 2009 when he claimed that in fact the song was written in tribute to Lillian Hellman, the blacklisted, Communist-sympathising screenwriter and playwright best known for writing *The Little Foxes* and being the lover of Dashiell Hammett. If it makes a little more sense of the Lenin links, it does little else to offer an understanding of the story at large.

Just as confounding is '7 Chinese Bros.', which seems to reference *The Five Chinese Brothers*, a 1930s children's novel by Claire Huchet Bishop. In it, each brother has a special power, and for one, his power is the ability to swallow the ocean. One day, this brother is accompanied by a young assistant who realises he can grab the stranded fish whilst the brother holds the water in his mouth, but as folk tales are wont to do, there is a moral: the assistant gets greedy and drowns, leaving the brother in some trouble with the authorities. If any of this seems to explain the inner meaning of the song, then Stipe once again is on hand to muddy the waters. He told *Spin* in 2008, "It was about me breaking up a couple – and then dating both of them, a man and a woman, which is a terrible thing to do, but I was young and stupid."

Easter and Dixon were frustrated with Stipe's quiet, unenthusiastic early takes on the track, to the point that Dixon eventually stormed off up into the attic in a huff. Upon his return, he came brandishing an old dusty copy of a rare gospel record – 'The Joy of Knowing Jesus' by The Revelaires – and told Stipe to read its odd liner notes for inspiration. To his surprise, Stipe didn't just read them, but started singing them, and loudly. Somehow, Dixon's madcap idea had succeeded in opening him up and after that he was ready for the take of '7 Chinese Bros.' that we hear. Incidentally, the recording of Stipe reading the liner notes over the backing track has been preserved for history, released under the title 'Voice of Harold' and available on the 1987 compilation *Dead Letter Office*.

The album's riches keep coming. 'Pretty Persuasion' is in many ways the manifesto for the early R.E.M. sound, with Buck's arpeggios rippling by at a speed that is almost too fast to listen to. 'Time After Time (Annelise)', meanwhile, is a bewitching and exotic song that serves as a showcase for Bill Berry. He starts on a set of bongos, which in concert with Buck's strange, circular guitar loops are redolent of Indian classical music, before transitioning to his full kit after the first chorus, when he seems to start invoking some kind of ritual march.

'Little America' is the most playful song here and has the band cutting loose with Stipe cracking jokes about the mundanity of their new touring life ("Another Greenville/Another Magic Mart"). The lyrics make reference to manager Jefferson Holt and, like 'We Walk' on *Murmur*, offer a peppy, jaunty break from the seriousness elsewhere.

And then there is the inclusion of '(Don't Go Back to) Rockville', the song Mike Mills had written during the band's earliest days back at the Steeplechase. His tearstained letter to Ingrid Schorr had not been a regular presence in their setlists in 1983, but it was a personal favourite of Bertis Downs and the band decided to give it a whirl in the studio just for him. As something of an in-joke, they opted to play it in a slowed down, country-tinged version, an impromptu decision that would have lasting implications. It just worked. Even in its original form as a fast-paced rocker, it had still been a clear outlier in the R.E.M. catalogue so far, with a dramatically different lyrical flow and a chorus that finds multiple voices not harmonising, but singing the same melody line in one choral voice. At this new pacing, it was an even more obvious winner and one can easily imagine Jay Boberg's eyes rolling with dollar signs when he first heard it. As fate would transpire, the eventual single release failed to chart in either the US or the UK, but the song's pure and simple accessibility has seen it live well beyond its contemporaries on this album.

All in all, *Reckoning* is nothing but a masterpiece of a guitar pop album. *Murmur* has the mythos, intrigue and unknowability, but *Reckoning* sheds a lot of that and showcases the band in their most bare and honest form. Yes, Stipe spends much of the record hidden behind a shroud, still resistant to the idea of becoming a conventional frontman, but otherwise R.E.M. succeed in making an album that captures a perfect snapshot of who they are at this moment in time. The songs are now only occasionally baffling and the arrangements only sometimes throw you off the scent. This is, after all, an album with '(Don't Go Back to) Rockville', 'So. Central Rain (I'm Sorry)' and 'Pretty Persuasion'. It swings from shining, glorious wonder to pained, tender fragility with such confidence, not unlike the albums they would be making less than a decade later that are now perennially hailed as among rock's greatest ever works. Say it quietly, but isn't *Reckoning* actually a little superior to those? Is it, perhaps, their finest hour?

Michael Stipe collaborated with Howard Finster on the cover art, an animated image of a snake with a head at each end and the song titles scrawled along its belly. It is not the most sophisticated sleeve you will find, but it maintains the rule of not including any image of the band. Once the final details of the album had been sorted, the band, exhausted, returned home to Athens for a very well-earned break.

A period of calm played out between January and April, the first such stretch since the R.E.M. ball started rolling. The band had been good at managing their stresses until now, but for the first time, signs of fatigue had begun to show. After just a few weeks of rest, however, their old selves began to re-emerge. Without anywhere to be, they started to find playful outlets for their creativity again, with the side project band Hindu Love Gods suddenly appearing at clubs around Athens. Bill Berry, Mike Mills and Peter Buck would be joined on stage by Oh-OK's Bryan Cook for the performances, largely playing cover songs such as 'Personality Crisis' and 'Needles and Pins'. Nobody was taking it too seriously; this was simply a reminder that when left to their own devices, these young men just loved to play music and would always find excuses to do so for their own amusement.

It was a good job that they used their down time to unwind. Life was not about to get any more straight-forward.

'Fables of the Reconstruction'

As the clocks struck thirteen on the final night of 1984, R.E.M. were midway through a major homecoming show at the Atlanta Civic Center. The final chorus of 'Gardening at Night' drew to a close, chimes began to ring out and the thousands-strong crowd filled the air with the familiar strains of 'Auld Lang Syne' to usher in 1985. It was a night of well-earned celebration, the band's 117th show of a gruelling year, and they kicked back with crowd-pleasing covers of Donovan's 'Atlantis', Pylon's 'Crazy' and The Troggs' 'Wild Thing'. With fellow Athens scenesters Guadalcanal Diary (technically Atlantans, but you can forgive their PR decision to blur that line) and Love Tractor also on the bill, emotions were understandably high. By the time the bunting had been cleared though, a different story began to unfold.

The success of *Murmur* and *Reckoning* had changed more than the band could reasonably have predicted. The constant touring, a financial necessity for a band without a major label deal during that era, had strained their enthusiasm; remarkably, with only one exception, January 1985 was the first month without any live performances by any members of the band since their debut back in April 1980. Theoretically, that might have allowed for a window of recuperation, but their indomitable work ethic soon forced their idle minds into developing arrangements for a set of new songs they had been road-testing during the previous six months.

I.R.S. was in favour of capitalising on the momentum by releasing their third album in time for the summer and with a college tour booked for April and May, there was little time for manoeuvre. In addition, the band's growing ambition had encouraged them to consider alternative options for the role of the new album's producer. Mitch Easter and Don Dixon remained on good terms with the band, but they had inevitably become highly requested studio helmsmen themselves and both were keen to develop their own recording careers. Peter Buck, as R.E.M.'s resident music historian, overflowed with dream collaborators, and though many were discussed, one name rose above all others.

Joe Boyd had lived many musical lives: in 1966, he was co-founder of the UFO Club, the venue at the epicentre of the London psychedelic scene, and had a hand in several of the movement's key studio recordings, including Pink Floyd's 'Arnold Layne' and the astonishing 'Granny Takes a Trip' by The Purple Gang. He later returned to the States to work as an in-house producer for Warner Bros. Studios, contributing to the soundscapes of films as iconic as *A Clockwork Orange* and *Deliverance*. Of more interest to R.E.M., however, was Boyd's close association with the British folk music community: he had produced multiple records by The Incredible String Band and Fairport Convention between 1966 and 1970 as well as Nick Drake's masterpiece *Five Leaves Left*. Buck, perhaps animated by his frustration that the band's folk influences had been hitherto under-appreciated, had found his man.

In February, a planned project with Mary Margaret O'Hara fell through for Boyd, opening up his timetable for the spring. Aware of the band's interest, he swiftly flew into Georgia to meet them and discuss the demos that would become *Fables of the Reconstruction*, before catching their 18 February show at Atlanta's Moonshadow Lagoon. Barely a week later, R.E.M. found themselves on a flight to England.

If the burnout at the end of their spell on the road had had an impact on their psychological well-being, then this sudden decision to up sticks and decamp to an unfamiliar place only compounded their anxieties. Much has been made of their unhappiness during their weeks in London, with reports varying from trivial details (Bill Berry and Mike Mills, pining for the basketball, found only snooker for 'entertainment' among the UK's four television channels) up to serious rumours of the band's impending split.

R.E.M. were speedy operators from day one when it came to recording, so the temporal pressures were one problem from which they were immune. Boyd's choice of studio, however - the venerable Livingston Recording Studios in North London's Wood Green – was an awkward commute from the band's hotel in Mayfair, whilst the typically dank and sodden British weather added another contributing factor to the band's malaise. Much more than any superficial discomfort, these were creeping, insidious reminders that they were so far from home, so far from the one place most likely to re-connect them to their original passion.

What's more, the songs weren't ready. "It's the only time we've walked in and didn't have a clue," Buck would later tell Tony Fletcher for his book, *Perfect Circle*. "We forgot some of the things you have to remember, like you have to know what you're doing." It was a rare moment of self-doubt for R.E.M. up to this point, and they discussed cancelling the entire ordeal and postponing the album in favour of taking some legitimate time off. It took a pep talk from manager Jefferson Holt to shake the doubts out of them, or at least enough for them to stumble on far enough to complete the album's recording.

It was a particularly distressing time for Michael Stipe. For a long time, he would only speak about this period in calculatedly vague terms, but as he finally admitted in 2011, "I went through this difficult time when we were making our third record where I kind of lost my mind. That's when the bulimia kicked in." He claims to have eaten little other than potatoes during his time in England, during a period when he was experimenting with vegetarianism. But, as he would later explain in the same interview, there was a more existential crisis playing out in Stipe's mind: "I was afraid that I was sick with AIDS."

He remained carefully non-committal about his sexuality throughout the 1980s, but his retrospective admission of this terrifying anxiety is no surprise. The epidemic had undoubtedly affected people close to the band (B-52's founder and guitarist Ricky Wilson would die from the illness later in the year), and it goes some way to explaining Stipe's erratic behaviour. He had adopted a hairstyle somewhat akin to a monk's tonsure around the time and he would reputedly only listen back to the day's studio recordings whilst lying underneath the mixing desk.

What he was hearing vibrating through the studio floor was not like anything the band had created so far. For the first time, outside musicians were enlisted, from the string section employed on the climax of 'Feeling Gravitys Pull' to the Stax-indebted brass interludes on 'Cant Get There from Here'. Mills' basslines did the work of carrying the songs' melodies less frequently, whilst Buck's trademark jangle was used more sporadically, with several tracks allowing him to flex his imagination with flashes of dissonance, chromatic scales and post-punk clangs. Even Stipe's vocals emerged, albeit timidly, from the mix at times, in a sly nod to the very different future that awaited him. The growing pains that the band were experiencing – all too literally were written large all over this markedly darker third album.

Not that it was all "dark, dank and paranoid", as Stipe once described it. 'Cant Get There From Here' (an early trademark of the band's aesthetic was always to leave out apostrophes) is a booster shot of a lead single, closer to the *Reckoning* mould, which conjures the bounding stage energy of Buck and Mills, whilst also channelling the spirit of displacement and feeling lost that was undoubtedly at the forefront of the band's mind at the time. That particular tone is also struck on the album's other standout pop moment, the wistfully romantic 'Driver 8'.

Written largely by Bill Berry, the song is sung from the perspective of a lonesome passenger train driver, specifically of the Southern Crescent, a beloved locomotive that ran from Washington D.C. to New Orleans (that is to say, straight through the heart of Georgia) until 1979. It is a rare full-blown character portrait for R.E.M. at this point and it pulls at a core emotional connection that the band and others from the region felt for the historical romanticism wrapped up in the train's symbolism. "When you think of trains in the night, that tugs at your heart," Mills once explained.

"We can reach our destination/But it's still a ways away," Stipe sings from a sodden, unfocused and depressed studio in England as he thinks of what he had hoped for his band to be. The light/shade contradiction in that lyric is a typical R.E.M. trait (think of "Follow me/Don't follow me" or "Fall on me, don't fall on me", or even "He's not to be reached/ He's to be reached" on this album's 'Maps and Legends'), but here it preserves the quiet dignity of work in much the same way as Jimmy Webb's timeless 'Wichita Lineman', whilst offering a potent evocation of the Southern Gothic style that is written large across *Fables*.

These truly are fables. The driver is only one of countless characters that populate the album, some fictional, others very much not. 'Maps and Legends' is a tribute to Stipe's fellow UGA art student and friend Howard Finster, designer of the *Reckoner* sleeve and a future Talking Heads collaborator, while one of Finster's former assistants is immortalised in the wittily written 'Old Man Kensey', which commemorates him as an Athens character that allegedly stole other people's dogs and collected the ransoms in order to fund his drinking habit.

The maudlin 'Wendell Gee' was woven out of a misty memory of a Wendell Gee's Autos that caught the band's eye on a journey south of

Athens during their early days together, but most offbeat of all is the tale of 'Life and How to Live It'. Brivs Mekis was another local eccentric – it's remarkable how many a town the size of Athens could supply – who lived between two homes that were joined together by a hole in their shared wall. Legend has it that Mekis would sporadically tire of one home and pack up his stuff and move entirely into the other. When he died, a towering pile of an unpublished book bearing Mekis' name was found in the basement of one of the homes, titled *Life: How to Live It*.

Stipe is easily in his strongest storytelling mode to date here, reflecting the nature of the band's home. This might be an album recorded thousands of miles away, but it is very much a love letter to the South and its famed hospitality. As Peter Buck said in a 1985 interview, "[The South] is the last place where the old tradition really exists. People pass stories down. There's more of a feeling of place on this record, a sense of home and a sense that we're not there."

Stipe and 10,000 Maniacs singer Natalie Merchant had become friends during a period of touring together in 1984 and they had made a pact to both write a song that addressed the genocide of the Native Americans on their respective new albums. The result for R.E.M. was 'Green Grow the Rushes', which speaks of the owner of some pristine new buildings being "haloed and whitewashed" while they skip off to "find a cheaper hand" to do their dirty work. The song clearly invokes the Christian folk song 'Green Grow the Rushes, O', referencing the stalks of the rushes plant that were used by some Native American tribes to weave baskets. It is an elegant piece that shows Stipe as not just a sensitive writer but as a lyricist that could ably weave grounded meaning into his work without sacrificing any of his trademark mystery, but it also fits the gently downbeat nature of the album that surrounds it.

"It's the most dense record we've ever made," said Buck. "And if you take the stance that a record is supposed to show where a band is at, that does it perfectly."

The material on *Fables* is still incredibly strong and the guitar innovations in particular are intriguing and, in hindsight, an important break for the group's development, but some of the band's strongest cards are still underplayed. Mills' contributions are sidelined too often and the melodies that demand time to be discovered are simply not there. The highs remain gloriously high, however, and to compare this third album to its predecessors only further highlights how great R.E.M. were out of the gate.

For Joe Boyd's part, it remains somewhat unclear exactly how much impact he really had. The band were morphing independently anyway and they were notoriously sceptical about letting outsiders into their tight, trusted group. Their unconventional mindset jarred somewhat with Boyd's more establishment-friendly ways and Boyd himself admitted that he felt more at home when outside musicians were in the studio with them. "With most bands," Boyd said, "everyone's saying, 'I can't hear my guitar or my voice – turn it up!' With R.E.M., everyone was saying 'No, there's too much of me in there, pull it down'."

Nevertheless, *Fables* sold well, easily racing past *Reckoning*'s figures and quickly becoming the most played album in the history of US college radio up to that point. The reviews remained supportive, albeit with the superlatives dialled down a little. Suddenly there were mentions of murkiness and it no longer seemed to be the compliment that it once was. Others even started to say that the band were becoming predictable, an accusation that, however unfair, is to be expected with one's third album in just over two years.

The band were back home as quickly as air travel would allow. Only a few weeks later, a show by a mystery band going by the name of Earnest T. Hemingway was advertised at the 40 Watt and the scuttlebutt around town was that it was a pseudonym for R.E.M., who it was thought might be using the gig as a tune-up for the long stretch of touring ahead of them. Athens was full of multiple new age-groups of students for whom R.E.M. were already more a local myth than a band you could pop down to the local club to see and unsurprisingly the 40 Watt was absolutely under siege that evening as stage time drew near.

Those people had reason to jump to conclusions, as R.E.M. had used alternative names multiple times already. Their last gig before the trip to London was at Athens' Uptown Lounge to trial run a number of the newly penned *Fables* songs and that night they went by the frankly obnoxious moniker of Hornets Attack Victor Manure. On top of that, there were the numerous Hindu Love Gods shows that had taken place around town over the previous couple of years, and even that band had been known to go by the name It Crawled From The South on occasion, so you had to be on your toes. As it transpired, Earnest T. Hemingway was in fact a short-lived band that featured Michael Stipe on drums, but when word got out of the huge turnout, Stipe got cold feet and decided to pull the plug on the whole thing.

There was a two month period of calm before the serious touring began and the band took this opportunity to embark on their first bespoke music video shoot. Even though R.E.M.'s emergence tallied closely with the rise of MTV, their early videos had been spartan affairs. The Jonathan Dayton/Valerie Faris directed lo-fi promotional piece for 'Wolves, Lower' was a simple live shoot, while Howard Libov's 'So. Central Rain (I'm Sorry)' was shot inside Reflection Studios for an even more authentic snapshot of the band at work. The latter was particularly curious as Stipe insisted on recording an original live vocal take for the video, which deviates from the recorded version enough to make it an essential R.E.M. obsessive's token.

The closest they had come to a fully-fledged concept video was in the aftermath of the release of *Reckoning*. The idea was to make a longform piece that would accompany the entirety of the album's side one and they recruited Athens artist Jim Herbert for the job. One of Stipe's oddball bohemian associates, R.A. Miller, owned a farm just north of Gainesville, Georgia and they all decamped there to make what would eventually be called *Left of Reckoning*. Herbert clearly appreciated the disjointed, narrative-averse nature of Stipe's writing and created a film-making technique that attempted to mirror it. Through a process known as 'rephotography', he sequenced photographic frames of the band playing and prancing around the whirligigs on Miller's farm in an illogical order and panned and zoomed at his own will to accentuate the disorder. The result was a hypnotic, if not entirely satisfying, short film that received little to no airplay on any substantial platform.

Much more successful was the promo for 'Cant Get There From Here', which was by anyone's standards a real music video, worthy of the more frequent rotation it received on MTV. Directed by Stipe along with Aguar Brothers Films and Hartley Schilling, it sees the band going to a drive-in cinema, throwing and spitting popcorn at each other and frolicking in the hay bales on the way home. It captures a quasi-ironic fun and upbeat version of R.E.M. and most intriguingly of all features some of the song's lyrics on screen, in a dramatic move away from the mystery that was usually attached to Stipe's delivery. The MTV support helped spur on radio plays, allowing the song to far outstrip the spread of any of their previous singles.

R.E.M.'s association with MTV had blown hot and cold up to this point. The station was notoriously slow at adapting to new musical trends, although they did run a late night series named *The Cutting Edge*, which was a largely I.R.S. production with direction from Dayton and Faris and featuring presenting contributions from Jools Holland and The Fleshtones' Peter Zaremba, which gave R.E.M. a competitive advantage in getting a foot in the door. The most visible payoff arrived one day in June 1984 when the station were assembling a series of shows called *Rock Influences*, each one focusing on a different chapter of canonical rock history. When it came to the 'Folk Rock' episode, after perhaps a little nudge from the I.R.S. staff, MTV opted to go with R.E.M. as the house band for the episode.

Peter Buck definitely loved the 1960s folk rock bands and felt their impact on the R.E.M. DNA was underappreciated, so the band jumped at the invite. They travelled to the Capitol Theater in Passaic, New Jersey and recorded a substantial set for broadcast, which included very early live performances of tracks that would later be included on *Fables*, namely 'Driver 8' and 'Old Man Kensey'. More memorable, however, were the final three songs of the night. John Sebastian, erstwhile lead singer of The Lovin' Spoonful, joined them for a rendition of their 1965 smash 'Do You Believe in Magic', a childhood favourite of Buck's, while none other than Byrds frontman Roger McGuinn guested on performances of 'So You Want to Be a Rock 'n' Roll Star' and 'Gloria'. The former was a track that had been appearing sporadically on R.E.M. setlists for some time anyway, although in rehearsals with McGuinn they learned that they had been playing a version of the pre-chorus bridge with a bum note. McGuinn, perhaps grateful for such adulation from the hot young things, agreed to play it R.E.M.'s way for the cameras.

That R.E.M. had been handed such a hefty slice of television exposure so early was somewhat unnatural, given their songs had barely featured on MTV up until that point and even 'Cant Get There From Here' a year later was hardly competing with Janet Jackson or Madonna's omnipresence. However, this didn't worry the band; they knew how to spread the word of their new records in the way that suited them and when June 1985 arrived, all that was on the horizon was touring, touring, touring.

They were back in Europe to start the ball rolling on a tour that included a date at the Milton Keynes Bowl on 22 June at a personal invitation from U2. It was another megadome show, this time with 50,000 in attendance and Billy Bragg, Ramones and Spear of Destiny also on the bill. Their previous experience with The Police had been marred by the band's anxiety that they would be rejected, even though in truth they were treated with indifference. This time, however, their concerns were realised, with Stipe having to dodge bottles of warm urine at the front of the stage, a bracingly obnoxious form of expressing displeasure for which the British had a reputation at the time.

By now though, R.E.M. were battle-hardened. Naturally spiky and quick to leap to their own defences, they had heard it all before and were largely unfazed. Another prickly encounter occurred at a show in Ottawa later that summer. Opening their first encore with 'Moon River', an audience member near the front bellowed, "Fuck off!" as loudly as he could muster, triggering first Mills, then Stipe and finally Buck. The latter kindly invited the gentleman onto the stage so that they could walk through the finer details of his request, but alas the man's nerve failed him at the crucial moment. The band, unimpressed, launched into a too-perfectly-timed-to-be-coincidental version of 'I Can't Control Myself', before continuing to play no fewer than fifteen further cover versions, many of which had not had an outing since the band's earliest gigs. They had apparently decided to hold a grudge in the most passive aggressive way imaginable; on this night, some fifty nights into their tour, their integrity mattered more to them than their dedication to fan service.

It was, of course, an exception. R.E.M. bootleggers will point to this period of touring as one of the tightest, highest calibre versions of the band that ever existed. They were still at the apex of their subculture too, as evidenced by their success at the annual College Music Journal New Music Awards show. Hosted by Cheech and Chong, it was a celebration of homegrown independent music and R.E.M. were winners of Best Album for *Fables*, just as they had been a year earlier for *Reckoning*. Alongside Run-D.M.C., who were also present, they were presented as the most essential new artist in America and as such were invited to play live to close the show.

They were joined by Susanna Hoffs and Michael Steele from The Bangles on backing vocals, but after a successful acoustic set, the full band part of the show had barely got started before, after a version of 'Cant Get There From Here', Peter Buck hurled his guitar at one of the television crew and stormed off set, never to return, frustrated that they were not being given help with the sound. As it transpired, the band had only agreed to play an electric set once the television broadcast had ended, by which time the union crew on site had evidently decided that their day's work was done. Whatever the root cause for the misunderstanding, the music press were quick to pick up on the kerfuffle and, understandably, some considerable heat fell on Buck's head. Even now, with three albums under their belt and awards and radio success all theirs, the show business side of the band's existence clearly still rankled Buck and every instinct in his music purist body convulsed against it.

For the final leg of their Reconstruction tour, support switched from 10,000 Maniacs to the hard-edged Californian trio Minutemen for a stint of shows that would prove to be their last. One of the most respected and enduring names in US punk, Minutemen were known for eclecticizing hardcore music, introducing elements of jazz and funk without compromising the urgency and brevity of the form. They were natural philosophical bedfellows for R.E.M. at this point, even if there was clear water between them musically, so when news arrived of Minutemen frontman D. Boon's death at twenty seven in a car accident, just nine days after the last of their shows together, it was a profound shock. Minutemen dissolved and later reformed as Firehose, while what had already been a difficult chapter in the life of R.E.M. was now touched by tragedy. For a leader in their peer group, so close to them in age, worldview and adoration, to be taken so suddenly brought the absence of control over their lives and careers that had haunted them from day one back into focus. 1985 had been their most challenging year and it was agreed, once again, that a break was badly needed.

'Lifes Rich Pageant'

Rock music survives on second hand mythology and the rumour that the moment you just missed will never be achievable again. Greatness is rarely captured live, much less documented in real time, and those caught up in the heat of a great music scene tend not to realise how fortunate they were until the dust has long settled.

Like a character from Woody Allen's *Midnight in Paris* or Edgar Wright's *Last Night in Soho*, it is the people who arrive in the aftermath that romanticise an artistic movement the most, imagining implausible heights of glamour, danger and possibility, while simultaneously resigning themselves to having missed the boat. It is the particular masochism of the music obsessive to behave this way; the unspoken truth is that by doing so, there are no limits to how great a classic record can be, or how incendiary a performer once was in their pomp.

Few American music scenes have been mythologised more than Athens in the late 70s/early 80s. The ripples lasted for decades, with an entirely separate second scene sprouting there in the mid-90s when a Generation X wave of new young voices flocked to its hallowed ground, desperate to somehow rekindle the magic, which resulted in the Elephant 6 Collective and bands like Neutral Milk Hotel, of Montreal and The Olivia Tremor Control.

The first genuine attempt to make a substantial document of the original Athens scene came in early 1986 from an out-of-towner named Tony Gayton, a Los Angeles-based film student looking for an excuse to flex his skills. He travelled to Athens to record as much material as his limited resources would allow, interviewing current and former members of local bands and hunting down the various eccentrics and fringe characters that gave the town its unique flavour. The result was *Athens, Ga: Inside/Out*, a documentary feature film that did the festival and arthouse circuits in the spring of 1987.

The film is necessarily retrospective in scope; as discussed, the energy in Athens had somewhat dampened a year or two earlier, and many of the film's talking heads speak in just the sort of *"You had to have been there"* tone that has made rockumentaries so ripe for pastiche. It is almost sentimental about its matter-of-factness, simultaneously arguing that the Athens scene was little more than just some kids hanging out while also expecting the audience to believe that a film about this was both worth making and worth watching.

Gayton captured live footage of as many of the contemporary bands as he could – the likes of Time Toy, Kilkenny Cats and Squalls – but these were very much the second generation of Athens acts and few would survive for long. R.E.M. were considered almost too big to even be involved, and at first they were reluctant, but all four eventually relented and their charisma lifts the film into a higher category, as does the inclusion of an acoustic version of 'Swan Swan H' and a spellbindingly charming version of The Everly Brothers' 'All I Have to Do is Dream', one of the true hidden pearls of the R.E.M. portfolio. In addition to its limited theatrical run, *Inside/Out* received support from the Athens-friendly late-night MTV shows, and Gayton continues to work on the fringes of Hollywood, including a co-write on the 2010 Dwayne Johnson action vehicle *Faster*.

Filming for the documentary aside, the first quarter of 1986 was largely dormant for the R.E.M. machine, once again allowing the band's members to indulge in their extra-curricular interests. Busiest of all was Peter Buck, who was still showing some beginner's interest in work behind the production desk. A trial run with the band Reaction in Atlanta the previous autumn had given him an early taste, and when his own side project Full Time Men sought to venture into a recording studio a few weeks later, it was naturally Buck who took the reins.

These proved to be the baby steps that paved the way for the bold strides Buck took during the R.E.M. break. Cult New Jersey jangle poppers The Feelies had been a Buck favourite during the period when Buck and Stipe were becoming friends, so when a reformed version of the band reached out to him when they were preparing to record their long-awaited second album *The Good Earth*, Buck snapped at the opening. Likewise, upstart Athens band Dreams So Real braved their arm and asked Buck to be the producer for their debut album, *Father's House*. In both circumstances, the bands approved of the guidance and simplicity that Buck brought to the sessions and were able to maintain lasting friendships with the guitarist.

It may be that Buck was desperately trying to stay as busy as possible; in addition to losing his father in the early months of 1986, his long-term relationship with Ann Boyles had also recently come to an end. Aside from busying himself with the camaraderie of his friends' bands, he even found himself back behind the counter at Wuxtry Records once again, taking his pay in vinyl and reconnecting with happier, simpler times.

Conversely, Bill Berry became the first band member to get married during this time. Since breaking up with Kathleen O'Brien, he had been seeing Mari for some two years and was becoming more and more attracted to the appeal of a homely, rockstar-free life. Indeed, Athens was still very much seen as home by all members of the band, as Buck confirms in *Inside/Out*. Stipe and Buck had even both quietly amassed a decently sized portfolio of real estate properties around town with some of the first hefty paychecks that their day jobs had earned.

Michael Stipe filled his down time with musical friends, too. As well as hanging out in John Keane's Athens recording studio with his friends in the band Hugo Largo, he became a semi-permanent touring member of the band The Golden Palominos. Spearheaded by drummer Anton Fier and New York avant-garde jazz-funk genius Bill Laswell, formerly of Material, the Palominos are the R.E.M. side project that has best survived the sands of time. Their atonal, dub-influenced sludginess possibly sounds more at home thirty years on than it did at the time and Stipe's vocals, which dominate the first three songs on their second album, 1985's *Visions of Excess*, fit neatly alongside other guest contributors John Lydon, Richard Thompson and Jack Bruce. Stipe's part-time ventures were always the most out there of the R.E.M. quartet, dating back to the Tanzplagen days, but this project found him working with elite musicians and composers and to this day remains sorely under-appreciated. Stipe not only joined them on a springtime nationwide tour, but even enjoyed a three-day jaunt to Europe in July, which included the glitz of the Montreux Jazz Festival.

Record store shifts, marital bliss and European jazz festivals are all well and good, but eventually the jollies had to come to an end and focus had to turn to album number four. Upon reconvening, the band found themselves in the jaws of a mini-crisis regarding their putative producer. It was broadly agreed that the Joe Boyd decision had been arrived at in haste, so a certain amount of deliberation was taken. Between the Jonny Hibbert fiasco with 'Radio Free Europe', the aborted Stephen Hague plan for *Murmur* and the leaden London experience for *Fables*, the band can be excused for developing a certain neurosis about the importance of getting this bit of personnel recruitment right.

One thing that had been unanimously agreed by all members of the band and their management was that the rockier, live show-centric aesthetic that they embraced on *Reckoning* had worked really well and so they decided that perhaps the new record would also benefit from a move in that direction.

The name of Don Gehman arose organically. This Pennsylvania native was best known as the man behind the clean, driving, heartland sound on John Cougar Mellencamp's hit records in the early 1980s, most notably the AOR staple 'Jack and Diane'. To put it conservatively, he was associated with music that was a quantum leap away from *Murmur* and quite what the band identified in his signature that they thought would resonate with their own still remains something of a mystery.

Gehman himself caught wind of the band's interest and quickly got his hands on a copy of *Fables*, which he struggled with greatly. Even when he caught an R.E.M. show in Virginia at the tail end of the 1985 Reconstruction tour, a combination of bad sound, overcrowding and an all-acoustic encore left him less than infatuated. If this already all made for a frosty start, then a double no-show from Michael Stipe for their first two official meetings only compounded the problem. Whether or not that was an indication of the frontman's wariness to make this gesture towards a more mainstream-friendly producer, it didn't stop the rest of the band from entering some early constructive talks with him and a demo recording session was booked at John Keane's in Athens.

As Gehman later told Tony Fletcher, "I wanted to make records that were more clearly focused...The idea of being able to hear and understand the words that Michael was saying...To make a commercially viable record."

This was not at all the same goal that the band had worked towards on *Reckoning*. That album still celebrated its songs' aloofness, mystery and internal complexity; what Gehman was suggesting was an altogether different proposition. Nevertheless, the band welcomed him in and the original sessions went swimmingly. A set of new and old songs, which were all made available as part of the 25th anniversary re-release in

2011, they sounded great to the band and Gehman was officially hired as the producer for the new album. It has been suggested that it was his ability to tease the intrinsic poppiness of their stupendous new song 'Fall on Me' that sealed the deal and I.R.S., it is needless to say, were delighted by the more accessible move and agreed to financially support the album's production.

Recording took place at Mellencamp's studio in Bloomington, Indiana in April and May and band and producer immediately got along like a house on fire. Gehman set strict disciplinary rules and a tight schedule, while the band merrily brought the energy and enthusiasm. An engineer dusted off an old pump organ that was lying around in the innards of the building and it spontaneously became an integral part of the album's sound, such was the band's openness to the new settings. The tracks they were laying down most definitely bore the fingerprints of a big-time rock producer: Berry booms like never before, Buck rings out and blazes and Stipe is enunciating like he's teaching phonics to pre-schoolers.

Gehman made Stipe's vocals his pet project, working hard to get him into a place where he was comfortable to break free from what Gehman felt were bad habits. "Don was the first person that hauled me aside and questioned what I was doing," Stipe would later say. Gehman, for his part, has a slightly different take: "We'd run around the subject four or five times and come up at the same place we started. There's no way to manipulate Michael," was his modest reading of the situation.

It seems that in Gehman, R.E.M. had finally run into an elder that they actually respected and responded positively towards. He instilled a new confidence in Stipe, in particular with regard to his vocal talents, and in this respect, Stipe never looked back. From his early years as an overly exuberant, drunken stage performer, through the 1982-84 period of portraying the withdrawn, frozen figure that had appeared on *Letterman*, he was now undergoing a further evolution, into a more expressive, confident, politically awake figure. This Michael Stipe was taking the stage emblazoned with slogans, going out of his way to make a stand for issues that moved him and proudly letting his lyrics sing for themselves. He arrived at these sessions ready for a significant change and in Gehman he found just the right amount of encouragement.

The same seemed to apply to the rest of the band. "Don helped me question why I play at certain places," Peter Buck explained in an interview at the time. "If he had done this on the last album, I would have said forget it, but this time we wanted it to be more dynamic." These are especially intriguing and revealing comments, signalling a major shift in philosophy for the most idealistic and doggedly underground member of the band. The *Fables* experience evidently still stung the band quite sharply, for them to embrace change so wholeheartedly.

For the first time, they entered a recording session at a time when they were not drowning in new material. Looking for ways to fill out the list of contenders, they circled back to a few discarded numbers from their early days, with 'Just a Touch' and 'What If We Give It Away', which had previously been known as 'Get On Their Way', both eventually making the cut, and 'All the Right Friends' once again just missing out. 'Hyena' is a track they had considered for *Fables* but had dismissed as being too fast; this time around they included it, and, symbolically, sped it up even further. They also relied, for the first time, on a cover version to round out the tracklisting: 'Superman' was an obscure b-side from the Texan one-hit-wonder band The Clique, a favourite of Buck's, and it featured a debut lead vocal from Mike Mills, supposedly because Stipe was significantly less enthusiastic about its inclusion than the rest of the band and opted to take the day off.

"Let's begin again" sings Stipe as the first chorus lurches in on *Lifes Rich Pageant* opener 'Begin the Begin' and listeners begin to draw their own conclusions. Make no mistake, this is a brand new R.E.M. straight out of the blocks: clean as the driven snow, boldly unobscured, shorn of the nuances that had made them what they were. Of course, Stipe is not actually singing about his band's new sound though, he has bigger ideas on his mind.

"The insurgency began and you missed it," he sings, nothing short of a call to arms, before invoking the name of Myles Standish, the English military advisor for the Plymouth Colony who arrived on the Mayflower and was known for his pre-emptive attacks on Native American lands. The plight of the indigenous people of his home country is a subject Stipe had already explored on 'Green Grow the Rushes' and it is a recurring theme throughout *Pageant*, just one of multiple political motifs running through the record. "Life's rich demand creates supply in the hand of the powers," he continues. "The only vote that matters, silence means security, silence means approval." There is absolutely no ambiguity here, these lines read like an introductory slide for a seminar on anti-capitalist political theory. He points to Martin Luther as a possible model for radical social change and proof of the benefits of active protest. What's more, Stipe elocutes these lines like an aging thespian, and in fairness why would you still want to blur the edges when the entire point now is to send a clear message?

'Fall on Me' introduces the album's other key theme of ecological anxiety. Michael Stipe, predictably, has repeatedly issued denials that the song is merely a cry of anguish triggered by the emerging panic surrounding acid rain, which is fair, but it would also be absurd to pretend that it is not intended to be at least one of the threads weaving the song together. "Buy the sky and sell the sky" is Stipe's bridge into the chorus, harking back to a famous speech by Chief Seattle, the 19th Century Suquamish leader and statesman, which beseeched the authorities of the day to respect the sanctity of the resources that are shared by everyone. Stipe also appears to be reaching back into themes first raised on 'Talk About the Passion', namely a frustration with the inaction of the people in power, the intransigence of political change and the nature of Western civilisation to trap itself inside a system where caring is secondary to succeeding.

Beyond the subject matter, what we have in 'Fall on Me' is R.E.M.'s most spectacularly finely crafted song to date. It is the *ne plus ultra* of the melody/counter-melody vocal interplay that had been Mike Mills' speciality since the band's early days, an early apex in his ongoing search for harmonic perfection. Stipe introduced it during the band's 1991 *MTV Unplugged* show as "maybe my favourite song in the R.E.M. catalogue", a perfectly reasonable choice.

The Native American theme is most directly addressed on the haunting 'Cuyahoga', named after the river that runs through Cleveland, which Stipe describes as a "river red" in a beautifully elegant double metaphor that neatly captures both of *Pageant*'s dominant lyrical themes: red both with the blood of the slaughtered tribes and from the flames that engulfed the river in 1969 as a result of dangerously high levels of pollution.

The album's other explicitly political track is 'The Flowers of Guatemala'. After the Eisenhower-backed CIA overthrew a democratically elected government in the Central American nation, human rights-abusing dictators were upheld by successive American regimes, in the knowledge that American businesses operating there would not be hit by corporate restrictions. The most notorious beneficiary of these waived sanctions was the United Fruit Company, which held a decades-long monopoly over the country, a practice from which we now derive the concept of the banana republic. Genocide befell the country's Mayan indigenous population in the 1970s and early 1980s, with up to 110,000 reportedly killed. Stipe and Buck had been haunted by an article documenting these events after their return home from England and were moved to put the song together, with the flowers of the title being a reference to the Amanita Muscaria, a flowering, hallucinogenic mushroom that is known to grow over the graves of those killed by the Guatemalan death squads. Stipe would regularly introduce the song on stage by quoting David Bowie's song 'Future Legend': "This ain't rock 'n' roll, this is genocide".

The socially conscious nature of the material on *Lifes Rich Pageant* represents a major growth in the band's writing, but musically, this is not their strongest set of songs, 'Fall on Me' aside. With nowhere to hide in the crystalline, gleaming palace of the record's production, the tracks' relatively mid-range pacing and familiar structures have a tendency to meander and although it has always been held in high esteem by the R.E.M. fanbase, in retrospect it can be seen as falling between the two stools of the band's twin career peaks either side of it. Gehman's touch offered a bridge out of the band's self-created wilderness, and it may well be that without his unlikely involvement here, the global recognition that was now just around the corner would never have flickered on their radar. However, in the end, *Lifes Rich Pageant* does indeed sound like an R.E.M. album produced by John Mellencamp's right hand man, with all that that entails.

Stipe for his part was now close to pulling through the period that he later described to Pitchfork as a "profound depression and a nervous breakdown", dating back to the *Fables* sessions in London. This downward spiral hit a particularly scary nadir at a gig in Europe where the singer managed to lacerate his eyes with a pair of gritty contact lenses, one of the aspects of his self-care that he had been letting slide for some months. "I accidentally blinded myself, I had to wear bandages over my eyes for ten days," he said in 2021. "I'm an extremely visual person and during that time I had these crazy dreams. [*Lifes Rich Pageant* album tracks] 'I Believe' and 'These Days' were basically written as a way for me to remember what those dreams were."

The health scare abated after he was able to remove the bandages on the other side of a transatlantic flight, and with the relief of regaining his sight came a final turnaround in his psychological fortunes. "I'll never forget looking out the window onto the street in Seattle and feeling this elation," he said. "Something had happened. I had this turning point that was deeply profound and important. I took those bandages off my eyes and came out of the depression. I felt emboldened and strong enough to carry on, I was a different person from that day forward."

For all of its very sober themes, the fact that the album's title was taken from an Inspector Clouseau line in 1964's Pink Panther sequel *A Shot in the Dark* is just about as jarring as the band's choice of producer, but it amused them. Final recording and mastering touches were made in Los Angeles in May, during which time the band took the opportunity to check in with some of their friends: Buck joined The Dream Syndicate on stage at UCA for renditions of 'Cinnamon Girl' and 'Papa Was a Rolling Stone', while Stipe sang vocals on 'Eight Miles High' with Hüsker Dü at the Roxy.

Lifes Rich Pageant, with its cover art of Bill Berry in the top half and bison in the bottom (is this a Buffalo Bill reference, or some more obscure environmental allegory?) was released on 28 July, becoming their first gold album, denoting sales of over half a million, and peaking at #21 on the US charts. The accompanying single release of 'Fall on Me' reached #94 on the Hot 100, lower than either 'Radio Free Europe' or 'So. Central Rain (I'm Sorry)', despite clearly having more mainstream appeal and arriving at a time of higher profile for the band, such is the opaque nature of chart mathematics. There were not ninety three better singles released in the entire 1980s, let alone on that one week in the summer of 1986.

As was now customary, only a few weeks passed after the album's release before a lengthy national tour began, this time a three-month jaunt around the theatres and arenas of America's metropolitan hubs. Just days after the tour's three blow off shows back at the Fox Theatre in Atlanta, a weary-legged R.E.M. were back in the studio to record a track for the soundtrack to the light-hearted fantasy comedy film *Made in Heaven*. They opted for a song they had trialled in 1982 but never seriously considered for any of the albums, 'Romance', and booked a couple of days in Atlanta's Soundscape Studios to get the job done. Gehman, a meticulous planner, could not make himself available at such short notice, but he did know somebody else who was free.

'Document'

A founding principle of pop music folklore dictates that a great producer can stamp their signature not just on an individual record, but across an artist's entire career. The long-term effect of Jerry Wexler on Aretha Franklin, Quincy Jones on Michael Jackson or George Martin on The Beatles, to name just three, went far beyond tinkering with sound levels and drum snares; these producers were able to fundamentally alter the aesthetic directions of these musicians, forging a vision for their legacy that teased the artists a little further outside of their comfort zones than their instincts might have preferred.

Such influential producers have typically established their elite reputations before embarking on the collaborations that would come to define them. Martin had masterminded an entire cottage industry of novelty records with the British comedy elite before The Quarrymen even formed. Wexler had been a sought-after producer at Atlantic Records in the 1950s while Franklin was still touring gospel churches in a caravan with her father. Jones' heavyweight jazz and film score credentials made him a veritable elder statesman compared to Jackson. Some of R.E.M.'s own musical heroes had turned to producers with cherished recording careers of their own, from Patti Smith's work with The Velvet Underground's John Cale to Talking Heads' decision to turn to former Roxy Music space traveller and ambient innovator Brian Eno.

Scott Litt had no such resumé. His greatest claim to fame at the time that he first met R.E.M. was his work as "additional producer" on Katrina and the Waves' 1985 smash hit 'Walking on Sunshine'. As credentials go for the role of taking the reins of America's number one cult band of the day, that was thin gruel. He was, however, friends with Don Gehman, with whom he shared management, and had also previously worked with The dB's and Matthew Sweet, musicians close to the R.E.M. fold.

All had spoken well of Litt's likeability and competence, so the band happily agreed to give him a whirl for the one-off session for 'Romance'.

Their two days at Soundscape Studios in Atlanta were creatively unremarkable, but they were casual and convivial. Litt, who was barely five years older than the band, was an easy figure for them to connect with and if anything, he seemed a more natural bedfellow for them than Gehman, if dramatically less experienced. In truth, Gehman did not anticipate great things for R.E.M.'s future and was relatively relaxed at the time about letting his connection with the band slip away. Buck would later describe a conversation between the two parties: "He was saying, 'I really want to make a record that's a huge commercial success and much as I like you all as people, and I like the band, the way you work I can't hear that you're going to have a huge hit'." Gehman would later admit that not going out of his way to cultivate a longer-lasting relationship with R.E.M. was "the biggest mistake of my life".

It is abundantly clear that nobody involved would have guessed at this point that the R.E.M.-Litt connection would last for six albums, but there may well have been a tacit understanding that the constant switching of studio personnel had not been ideal for the band so far. The Mitch Easter/Don Dixon team had been the perfect foil for the first incarnation of R.E.M., but as proven by *Lifes Rich Pageant*, the band was now a markedly different animal with very different needs.

Before they had the chance to reconvene, there was some other business to attend to. With a growing fanbase came extra demands and I.R.S. felt that this was the right moment to offer the die hards something to satiate their ravenous appetite for more material. The winning idea was *Dead Letter Office*, a collection of b-sides and other assorted officially-released studio artefacts. There was no succumbing to temptation to spruce up the bootlegged live recordings that had been doing the rounds, nor renewed attempts at recording discarded demo tracks – this was strictly a compilation of the bits of the band's material that had been exceedingly difficult for most fans to get their hands on, including the entirety of the *Chronic Town* EP, released here on CD for the first time.

Peter Buck took it upon himself to put together the liner notes, a job he lovingly executed, eager to impress upon the buyer that this was a more thoughtful piece of work than the contractual obligation release that bands so often find themselves having to promote. He likened the experience of listening to *Dead Letter Office* to "browsing through a junkshop" and indeed it does have a ragtag unpredictability to it when listened to as a piece. More than a third of its original 15-song tracklisting is comprised of covers, three of them Velvet Underground numbers. Also included are 'White Tornado', the whip-cracking surf instrumental that had been a part of all of their earliest recording sessions, and 'Voice of Harold', the whimsical recording of Michael Stipe reading the liner notes of a gospel record aloud during the making of '7 Chinese Bros.'. The latter's inclusion speaks to the band's ability to at least occasionally avoid taking themselves too seriously, the sort of detail that can be the difference between an act that is able to make a special connection with its core audience and one that is not.

Dead Letter Office hit stores on 27 April 1987, near the end of the band's month-long recording sessions for album number five, *Document*. This time recording took place in Nashville's Sound Emporium and from the outset, the band insisted on being credited as co-producers, another sign that they felt the bouncing from one helmsman to another could be curtailing their progress. It transpired that Litt's sensibility was in fact very similar to Gehman's: he preferred clarity and boldness and records that were proactive about seeking out and capturing the passing attention of an audience. R.E.M.'s early albums required that their listeners leaned in closer to catch their hidden details, whereas Litt wanted the band to do the reaching themselves.

There is a lazy tendency to assume that the band were naturally wary of such transitions, but all of the evidence suggests otherwise. Litt has said, "We talked about pop songs when we were cutting the record – they wanted to hear their stuff on the radio too." The most significant shift in their attitude had occurred between *Fables* and *Pageant* and this time around the album-to-album development is more granular, with Stipe's voice rising yet further up through the layers of recording to the point that it is now completely dominant. Both band and producer have commented over the years that these were not premeditated decisions, but rather organic processes that fell into place in such a way that all parties were left content.

Stipe in particular had taken the major gamble to put himself out on the wire both vocally and lyrically on *Pageant* and, in as much as he needed validation, the shift had been received very positively. The figure that attacked the *Document* sessions, consequently, is a writer and singer even more emboldened and ready to knock the world off its axis. "The whole album is about chaos," he said in a television interview around the time. "I've become very interested in chaos and the hypothesis that there is order within chaos, so I guess that kind of carried over into the recording."

The same sense of wild abandon animates the rest of the band here, too. There is life to R.E.M. on *Document* that was not as natural or clear on *Lifes Rich Pageant*; they are now virtually a full-time campaign band and the anger is palpable throughout. And yet, crucially, this record is playful and easy to digest at the same time. If *Pageant* may occasionally have strayed into po-faced territory, then any lecturing has now been replaced by the kind of energy that The B-52's first brought to Athens nearly a decade earlier. *Document*, especially in its first half, flies along, a colourful trip of a listening experience and much closer to the mould that would guide the band into the heartland of American mainstream culture over the following few years. If Don Gehman was needed to get them over the bridge to the next step, then Litt had the ultimate destination in sight from the get-go.

R.E.M. treat side one of *Document* as their battlefield. The US was a year out from a presidential election that many at the time considered to be a struggle for the soul of the country, and Michael Stipe for one had a lot that he wanted to say about the matter.

"The American work ethic can be a very ugly thing. Some of the songs on the album deal with a misunderstanding of work as a replacement for feeling, or repression of feeling," Stipe explained in an interview around the album's release. In many ways, he was one to talk, given how seriously he was now taking his role as a public thought leader, but it certainly explains opening track 'Finest Worksong', a blisteringly spirited anthem propelled by a siren-like one-note guitar riff from Peter Buck that seems to embody the quotidian churn of working life. Each note the same, in endless supply. "What we want/And what we need/ Has been confused," goes the refrain from Stipe and how could you not feel its truth.

'Welcome to the Occupation', like 'The Flowers of Guatemala', reflects Stipe's preoccupation with US interventionism in Central and South America, both of the officially declared variety and otherwise. "Fed and educated, primitive and wild" are lyrics that give us insight into how Stipe perceived the Reagan regime's colonialist arrogance to be playing out. The line "hang your freedom higher" had originally been penned as "hang your freedom fighters", but Bill Berry felt that this was too strong and urged Stipe to change it. The freedom fighters in question were the right-wing, anti-communist Contra fighters in Nicaragua that Reagan had been assisting in their struggle, although Stipe goes on to offer his explanation for the US government's real motives ("Sugar cane and coffee cup/Copper, steel and cattle"). "Listen to me," yelps Stipe at the song's climax, his throat clenching tighter with each repetition; of course, it had never been easier to listen to him and he knew it. It might have been a slyly self-referential line, but behind it lay a genuine plea for the people listening to pick up what he was putting down.

The opening triptych of political grenades concludes with the furious 'Exhuming McCarthy', an attack on the American thirst for personal gain and consumerist, free market aggression. Opening with the sound of a typewriter, a surefire way to invoke a sense of McCarthyism-era paranoia and Orwellian distrust of the written word, it goes on to include an audio sample from the McCarthy hearings, where Army counsel Joseph Welch is heard reprimanding McCarthy: "Let us not assassinate this man further, Senator, you've done enough. Have you no sense of decency, sir? At long last, have you left no sense of decency?"

Stipe is known to have been voraciously consuming books on McCarthyism during his time in Nashville recording *Document*, and his discontent with his homeland was more than shared by the rest of the band. Peter Buck went so far as to say, "America would be a nice piece of land, if you could wipe out most of the people." 'Exhuming McCarthy' also invokes Reagan's famed 'Buy American' slogan with the lyric "by jingo, buy America", words that would have resonated loudly in 1987. George H.W. Bush's resounding victory over Michael Dukakis the following year dealt a hammer blow to Stipe and Buck's generation of young progressives, who were condemned to suffer a third consecutive Republican administration for the first time since the war.

'Disturbance at the Heron House' is much less clear in its messaging, but is nevertheless cut from the same political cloth – the ghost of *Animal Farm* seems to lurk in its shadows – but after all the grandstanding, this elusiveness is welcome. It is also one of the record's most straightforwardly beautiful compositions, with a gently rolling melody and a wild, angular guitar solo at its heart. A cover of Wire's 'Strange' follows with a thrusting energy that more than justifies its leftfield selection and a few lines that fit in very nicely ("There's something going on that's not quite right"). The only previous cover version to make the cut for an album tracklisting had been 'Superman' on *Pageant*, but where that had been tacked onto its album's back end, 'Strange' is thrown right into the heart of the action, with very satisfying returns. The song that closes side one, however, no R.E.M. fan could have been prepared for.

In 1985, Michael Stipe answered his front door to be met by the intrusive lens of an overbearing fan's camcorder. It disturbed and ultimately fuelled him to write an anxiety-filled song called 'PSA', in which he shout-sang a litany of rapid-fire, seemingly unrelated exclamations in a triple-speed, tat-tat-tat delivery. 'PSA' would later be rehashed into 'Bad Day' in the early 2000s during a time when the US was toiling under the stewardship of a different President Bush, but the writing experience left an impression, kicking open a creative pathway that would ultimately lead to one of the band's most indelible contributions to pop culture.

'It's the End of the World As We Know It (And I Feel Fine)' is *Document*'s deus ex machina, a composition with no relative in the R.E.M. catalogue to date and few obvious comparisons in any band's repertoire (the band have pointed to Dylan's 'Subterranean Homesick Blues' as a distant family member). A 600-word, vitriolic, bile-filled stream of consciousness, Stipe is borderline maniacal during its three hysterical verses, each one laced with humour in the same way that one might lace one's foe's whisky with strychnine. Every line is meaningful, but taken in concert they are too disparate to tell a coherent story; instead, we have a deluge of incomplete thoughts, splurged out virtually all at once.

It scoops together the themes that are strewn all across *Document* and forces them into the same verses and often the same lines. All of Stipe's recurring anxieties are there: ecological panic, governmental corruption, the futility of violence, public apathy, personal disappointment. He expressly references the Iran-Contra Affair ("Wire in a fire, representing seven games/And a government for hire and a combat site") and the Iranian hostage crisis ("Six o'clock, TV hour, don't get caught in foreign tower"), and by bombarding the listener with too much information to process, he somehow captures the anger and despair of the political zeitgeist more acutely than the more straightforward protest songs that precede it on the album.

'Document'

Stipe and Buck's maiden voyage to New York City in 1981 had evidently made a lasting mark on Stipe, with that debauched party that they had accidentally stumbled into making a memorable appearance near the song's climax ("Lester Bangs, birthday party, cheesecake, jelly bean, boom!"). Bangs is the last of the famous four LBs that come all in a row, probably the most quoted Stipe lyric to date. Critics have bent over backwards trying to forge links between Leonard Bernstein, Leonid Brezhnev, Lenny Bruce and Lester Bangs, all equally unconvincingly. Stipe insists the idea came to him in a dream in which he found himself stuck at a dinner party populated only by people with those initials, a dream he argues pre-dates the real 1981 event. Whatever the truth, randomness often works well in pop music – consider the following year's surprise Prefab Sprout hit 'The King of Rock 'n' Roll' and its chorus of "hot dog, jumping frog, Alburquerque" - and it is the bizarreness of the LBs lyric that helped the song latch onto its listener's consciousness.

The song continues to have one of the longest tails of any R.E.M. composition, despite its relatively modest performance as the album's second single. Memorably featured during the band's guest appearance on *The Simpsons* and continually spliced over apocalyptic predictions of the future and nihilistic political campaign videos, its title, message and remarkable structure make it distinct enough to continue to be ripe for pastiche and re-writes.

If it's 'End of the World' that continues to live on, then it was *Document*'s first single that first truly set their career ablaze. 'The One I Love', it turned out, proved to be an absolutely perfect fit for the daytime radio playlists of 1987. It hit all of their soft spots: a quick and easy melody, a clear, repeated verse/chorus dynamic, no unnecessary frills or complications. That is until, of course, you start to think about how the naïve simplicity of Stipe's first two lines ("This one goes out to the one I love/This one goes out to the one I've left behind") is savagely undercut by the third ("A simple prop to occupy my mind"). Even now, in this brave stride into the lives of millions of new listeners, Stipe is subverting. Indeed, the implications only get darker later into the track with the "another prop" sentiment, a callous touch. It is no more than one might expect from the classic songwriters, perhaps, but it is a measure of the sure-footedness of Stipe as a writer that he had already become this good before his

83

arrival at the big table. It is also, deliciously, the first R.E.M. song to feature the word 'love' in its title.

Released one week ahead of the album in August, it surged up the Billboard Hot 100, smashing through their previous ceiling of #78 within weeks. Legend has it that Scott Litt and Bill Berry had made a private bet in the studio over whether 'The One I Love' would be a top ten hit; by early December, they had their answer, the single peaking at #9 in a top ten that also included 'Heaven is a Place on Earth', 'Faith' and 'So Emotional'. That same week, the band graced the cover of the *Rolling Stone* under the headline 'America's Best Rock & Roll Band'. It was a vertiginous rise.

Over seven years had passed since their formation, the steadiest of builds for this eventual payoff. The long days spent establishing a reputation the manual way, cultivating a legitimate word of mouth spread, taking principled stands in the face of major industry interest and staunchly resisting the follies of the day in order to stick to their guns – it just made the satisfaction of the moment all the greater. They knew it would never have happened if they had continued to record *Murmurs* every year. 'The One I Love' may have sounded like a conventional hit, no matter what the context, but R.E.M. were now fully formed artists who knew what they wanted and why. Successful or not, they were on a definite path and, furthermore, they could explain to you exactly why this path was the right one for them. If another band had released 'The One I Love' as their debut release with only a year of playing behind them, they would almost certainly have been threatened by its success, blinded by the lights and pressured into quick deals before they were ready. There is a lot to be said for leaving your breakthrough hit for your fifth album.

It is inevitable for a successful act with such underground credibility to have to face the dreaded questions about 'selling out' at some point and Mike Mills was admirably level-headed in response: "We'll keep a lot of the fans, but the ones that leave us because we've gotten too big are the same ones that will go and find another unknown band and support them, and that's really good. It's kind of a life cycle."

True to form, Peter Buck's attitude carried a little more saltiness. "I figure there's about 10% of people that listen to music that are the ones that get out there and see the bands when nobody else is going to see them and buy the teeny little independent records," he said. "Those are the people that keep this business changing over and keep it interesting. If all people bought was Top 40, then where would the new bands come from?"

"I don't see that there should be a huge backlash," he continued. "We haven't made some glitzy record just to sell records. It's actually a fairly weird record."

Document also smashed through their previous albums' barriers of success, cresting at #10 in the Billboard charts and being declared Platinum, indicating sales of over one million, in January 1988.

"The reason it's called *Document*," said Michael Stipe, "is that it's kind of a shortening of the word documentary, which is a reference to film. I think it's a very filmic album." The visual aspect of R.E.M.'s career was becoming more pivotal each year, with Stipe in particular becoming obsessed with the art of the music video and the creative potential that lay within it. "I'm very visually oriented," he explained in the same television interview. "I've always seen [videos] as a way to get across the more visual part of R.E.M. and if you can make a video without compromising yourself and giving into the look that people want, they may never play it on TV but you've made it and it's there."

Suffice to say, the rest of the band were far more ambivalent about both the process and the artistic value of music videos. "There's something commercial about them, you can't get away from that," was Mike Mills' response to the question. "I wouldn't do videos," said Peter Buck. "I don't see the point of releasing singles either, really, except for people buy them and it's a marketing tool. Writing the songs and playing them, that's what's real." Nevertheless, they recorded three videos in the summer of 1987 for the three *Document* singles and enjoyed the benefits of a legitimate hit by having 'The One I Love', 'End of the World' and 'Finest Worksong' all getting significant exposure on music television.

The 49-date 'Work' tour commenced with four European dates in the middle of September, their first full and proper shows of the year. Europe still allowed them relative anonymity, but their return to touring their home country now elicited a sizeable increase in music press interest and they often found themselves being confronted by journalists a little more intrusively than they would have liked.

The news sections of music papers started reporting on details pertaining to the band members' day to day lives, and took particular interest in the fact that the band were now travelling on two separate tour buses. Gone was the rusty Green Dodge, but the band were still uncomfortable with the image that they now needed two buses between them to survive on the road, despite the fact that it was a perfectly natural and sensible decision that had been mutually agreed. The two buses had been informally dubbed the 'tea-drinking bus' and the 'fun bus', but in reality the former was Stipe's home on the road and the other three band members shared the latter.

Stipe had always been the member most likely to keep to himself, preferring calm isolation, particularly before showtime. The more convivial instrumentalists drew their pre-show energy from the camaraderie of being forced together into confined spaces. The circumstances worked, honed by their now extensive experience on the road, but the press didn't necessarily understand this, or at least saw the professional advantage of choosing not to.

More uncomfortable even than the suggestion that there could be internal tensions within the band was the press interest in the people with whom Stipe chose to keep company. R.E.M.'s primary support band for the US leg of the Work tour was 10,000 Maniacs, whose lead singer Natalie Merchant was already a close friend of the band. It did not escape the press attention, however, that even for good friends, she was spending a lot of time in the 'tea-drinking bus' when the rest of the band were not around. If R.E.M. were sensitive about this kind of fame, the world had plenty to show them yet.

'Green'

The elephant in the studio throughout the recording of *Document* was the fact that this was R.E.M.'s fifth full-length album, and thus the final obligation of the original contract they had signed with I.R.S. Records back in May 1982.

The traditional post-album-release tour that the band had agreed to do was only scheduled to run for two months, whereas I.R.S. had been hoping for something much longer. At the level that they were now operating, two months was more than enough time to cover North America, but the band felt that the rest of the world remained a largely untapped market for them and they had serious reservations about I.R.S.' ability to break that potential open.

For their part, I.R.S. had gone out of their way to prove to them that they really could put together a world tour that would satisfy their demands, but the band's resolution was firm. They had already done five European tours and they had not seen the growth over time that they had hoped for. The world tour plan was ultimately rejected. In the words of Peter Buck, "I wasn't sure I wanted to be on the road all that year when we'd been over [in Europe] a lot and spent weeks and weeks and weeks beating our heads against the walls, playing to nobody. And we didn't have that much fun anyway." The vast majority of R.E.M.'s European shows had actually been sell outs, often turning people away, but the bulk of his point stands.

Needless to say, Miles Copeland and Jay Boberg were eager to re-sign R.E.M., and they were prepared to break the bank in order to do so. Discussions had been ongoing for years, at least since the run-up to the release of *Fables* in 1985, but the band were consistently reluctant to be drawn on the subject. The capacity to provide international exposure was one of the most noticeable distinctions between an independent like I.R.S. and the major labels and R.E.M. now knew that they would be able to approach even the entertainment industry's most towering institutions and be taken seriously.

The deal R.E.M. and I.R.S. had was unique in regards to the extent to which the band were given artistic freedom, even in the independent music world. If R.E.M. were to make the jump into the mainstream, they were going to find it difficult to give up on the luxuries they had become used to. Boberg and Copeland left them well alone during the creative process, seldom interfering during studio sessions and only really having their say with matters such as single releases and promotional work. With *Document* storming up the charts and 'The One I Love' a bona fide smash hit, R.E.M. felt that the timing was on their side and they would be able to approach the majors with a legitimate request to maintain these terms and not get laughed out of the building, and they were right. They had earned it, and given that they knew they could re-sign with I.R.S. on the same terms as before – and the majors knew this too – R.E.M. were in a remarkably strong negotiating position.

It was time for manager Jefferson Holt and legal advisor Bertis Downs to earn their stripes. They toured the available options before concluding that the realistic choices were A&M, Arista, Columbia and Warner Bros. Records. Of those, one stood out. Warner Bros. ticked a lot of the muso boxes that mattered to the band, and to Buck in particular. They had been the label to jump on The B-52's bandwagon early on with 'Rock Lobster', for example, and R.E.M.'s friends in Gang of Four had released three albums with them. Hüsker Dü had signed with them just a year earlier, while The Replacements had hitched their wagon with Sire, a Warners subsidiary. Warners happened to have high ranking executive staff with strong music credentials, too: co-presidents Lenny Waronker and Mo Ostin, two giants of the American music industry, had overseen a shift in the company's image in the 1960s, taking it from the safe home of the establishment to the platform that launched Jimi Hendrix, Van Dyke Parks and the Grateful Dead. These things appealed to R.E.M.'s music culture romanticism, as did the fact that Warners had hired John Cale as an A&R man.

Reciprocally, Warners were excited by R.E.M. They implicitly understood that the quartet were on the precipice of a new kind of success for their kind of band, and they knew they could provide all of the necessary tools to get them there. They demonstrated enough respect for the band's demands to impress them from the get-go, undercutting any

R.E.M. live in concert in Padova, Italy on 22 July 2003. Left-to-right: Mike Mills, Michael Stipe, Bill Rieflin, Peter Buck. *Wikimedia Commons (photo: Stefano Andreoli)*

Michael Stipe playing with R.E.M. in Vilnius, Lithuania on 14 September 2008. *Wikimedia Commons (photo: Kapeksas)*

Michael Stipe playing with R.E.M. at Glastonbury Festival 1999. *Wikimedia Commons (photo: Charlie Brewer)*

Michael Stipe playing with R.E.M. at South By Southwest Festival 2008. *Wikimedia Commons (photo: Kris Krug)*

Michael Stipe playing with
R.E.M. in Koper, Slovenia in
July 1999. *Wikimedia Commons*
(photo: Les Zg)

Top left: Bill Berry, returning to play with the band in 2008. *(Photo: Mike O'Donnell)*
Top right: Peter Buck, playing in Manchester in 2008. *(Photo: Andrew Hurley)*
Bottom left: Mike Mills, playing in Manchester in 2008. *(Photo: Andrew Hurley)*
Bottom right: Michael Stipe, playing in Naples in 2008. *(Photo: Roberto De Martino)*

R.E.M. play at the Royal Albert Hall in London, 24 March 2008. *Wikimedia Commons (photo: wonker)*

Michael Stipe and Peter Buck on stage in Ghent, Belgium in 1985. *Wikimedia Commons (photo: Yves Lorson)*

R.E.M. photographed before a show in November 1981. *Hank Grebe (original photographer)*

Michael Stipe playing with R.E.M. in 1986. *Dean Brush (original photographer)*

Peter Buck playing with R.E.M. in 2003. *Dean Brush (original photographer)*

R.E.M. in concert in Utrecht, Netherlands in June 2003. *gert74 (original photographer)*

apprehension R.E.M. might have had that they were entering talks with unrealistic expectations. Warners offered R.E.M. essentially the same deal that they had had with I.R.S.: five albums, with a promise never to interfere artistically or aesthetically with any of their creative decisions. It also included complete autonomy with regard to their artwork and videos, effectively surpassing the I.R.S. model. What Warners offered in return, of course, was the sort of industry clout that nobody could compete with. With the stroke of a pen, the band would be waving goodbye to any concern that they were being held back by the limits of their resources. A global booking strategy that was good enough for Prince and Van Halen would certainly meet their loftiest ambitions and with the full flex of the Warners promotional muscles behind them, there was no reason why their expectations would not be met.

They particularly felt that a measure of success in the UK should have been theirs by now; indeed, they had originally believed that it would have preceded any US breakthrough, although it was now clear that this boat had sailed. Partly because of the sheer number of British bands that they had toured with and partly because of their own tastes, they still upheld the UK scene as a progressive, ahead-of-the-curve beacon and they wanted a slice of it. If anything, the Copeland family's connections in the UK ought to have afforded R.E.M. enviable advantages, but while the press had done their part, establishing their cult credentials, and although their albums had slowly and steadily crept up the charts over the years, none of their singles had even come close to making a dent on the UK Top 40 until 'The One I Love' reached #16.

Jay Boberg knew all too well the perception that the band had of his label's limitations. As he put it, labels like his are typecast in their role: "take a baby band, develop them, feed them like a little seedling, give them the space to grow, create that family, and break them." That is to say, they can take you so far, but no further.

What they also couldn't do was meet Warners' most surprising offer to the band: that they would be able to own their own master recordings. This was a highly irregular proposition; labels like to own the recordings that they oversee as a sort of guarantee in case of unforeseen legal or personal differences with the artists in question. In this circumstance, R.E.M. would own the music themselves and effectively lease it to the label for a specified period of time, an agreement that bears the hallmarks of the savvy Bertis Downs. It was a huge, good faith offer from Warners and, taken with all of the other aspects of the contract, R.E.M. had no good reason to turn it down.

The most sordid and endlessly discussed detail of any such deal is inevitably the dollar amount. Both sides insist that money was by no means a driving factor for the band and indeed, it needn't have been. The band knew they would be getting a major upgrade in that respect whatever decision they made, and the other factors in the negotiations were far more likely to undermine their happiness than an extra zero could at this stage. The exact figures remain confidential, although Miles Copeland, who did discuss the matter with the band at the time, is on record as saying that they were due to receive advances of $2-3 million for each of the five albums in the deal, plus a guarantee of over 20% of royalties. It has been reported that there were bigger money offers on the table from other major labels, but their mind was already made up.

Boberg and Copeland were devastated. They would happily have met all of the same demands, even if this meant trying to somehow meet the relatively astronomical advances, but they would legally have struggled to replicate the Warners offer for the band to own their masters. I.R.S. had a pressing and distribution contract with MCA and could not be seen to be in breach of that, as their own infrastructure could not replace what MCA provided for them.

Boberg sought to be as creative with his offer as he could; for example, he had the idea of offering higher royalties for the back catalogue. He threw everything at it, fearing what the future might hold for his label without their darling centrepiece. Counterintuitively, the sheer scale of the I.R.S. offer might only have served to resolve R.E.M.'s minds. The numbers Boberg was promising seemed to be out of his reach and nobody would be winning if it turned out that he wasn't actually able to meet them. Holt, Downs and the band invited Boberg to Athens to break the news to him.

"It was a terrible, terrible day," Bertis Downs later reflected. The team took care to explain that the future was too uncertain for the band to be able to turn the Warners offer down. "If they knew they were going to be doing this until they were sixty," Downs explained, "maybe we would have re-signed with I.R.S. for a few more years."

The band left I.R.S. with an overwhelming sense of gratitude. "There's no label in the world that could have done for us what they did," commented Peter Buck shortly after the move. "What other label would have been able to get us to where we were, trusted us to give us the artistic control? Sometimes you just feel it's time to move on."

From I.R.S.' point of view, it was a bitter pill. "I think injustice occurred," Boberg said after a few months' reflection, "in that the little guy got beaten out for no apparent, no obvious reason." In some ways, Boberg and Copeland were only experiencing the same sour aftertaste of determination and ruthlessness that Jonny Hibbert and Hib-Tone had been on the wrong end of in 1982, or David Healey and Dasht Hopes later the same year. R.E.M. had shown themselves to be canny operators from their infant stages and while their principles had been proven to be hard to corrupt, their single-minded focus on making rational business decisions that preserved their own interests had likewise remained unshakeable.

The official announcement that R.E.M. had signed with Warner Bros. Records was made on 20 April 1988. I.R.S. did indeed suffer a serious blow to their business, although lucrative signings in the form of Fine Young Cannibals and Concrete Blonde staved off the decline in the short term. The label struck a deal with EMI in the early 1990s to distribute their records before finally closing its doors in 1996, although Boberg would later find success as President of MCA Music Publishing.

Ordinary bands would have taken a year off after receiving such a windfall, especially if they had been churning out one album per year like clockwork for half a decade, but the ink was still drying on the contract when R.E.M. were back in the studio once again. They didn't hesitate to ask Scott Litt to return as producer and a couple of demo sessions were booked in for the late spring.

The band, knowing they were at a major crossroads in their career, felt that the moment was right to shake things up in their creative process too. Sensing that their I.R.S. run had produced five broadly similar records – a belief this book hopes to have called into serious question – and that their recording habits had become a little too familiar, they set themselves the task of re-routing the chain of events that led from composition to recording.

The most successful of their ideas was for the three instrumentalists in the group to switch roles. Bill Berry would spend entire sessions playing bass, Peter Buck would sit behind the drumkit and Mike Mills would wander around the studio, playing every instrument to hand at a high level. One was an accordion, which piqued the band's curiosity; another was a mandolin, which Mills naturally excelled at, but which Buck could not resist experimenting with as well. The simple introduction of these new ingredients seemed to not just unblock their brief writing lull, but also to break open new, virgin creative ground for them to play around in.

"We wanted to get away from the whole idea that you have to have bass, drums and guitar to be in a rock'n'roll band," said Buck of this miniature eureka moment. Suddenly, Michael Stipe was taking a more central role in the musical composition of songs too. Traditionally, the band would hand him a draft instrumentation, over which he would write lyrics, but in these early sessions he was often involved in the very genesis of a song. With a newfound spring in their step, they booked in a three month studio stint, half at Ardent Studios in Memphis, the former home of the great band Big Star, and half at Bearsville Sound Studios, near Woodstock, New York.

Three months of recording time was an absolutely mammoth undertaking for R.E.M., doubling the commitment they made for *Document*, which had itself seemed pretty hefty to them. These were the perks of having the Warners accounts covering their costs, and they didn't mind taking advantage. Scott Litt described the period as much more challenging than that of the *Document* sessions, perhaps because a lot of the logistical wrangling of time, organisation and resources was left to him, but for the band, this was a time of creative abandon. The music they found themselves conjuring up marked a borderline radical move towards an optimistic worldview, a reaction to what Stipe described as the "shop-bought cynicism" that he clearly felt had been too prevalent, both in the outside world and quite possibly in his own back catalogue too.

The band was no longer convulsed enough by contemporary politics to write broadsides against US foreign policy or the venality of its Republican leaders (with, admittedly, one glaring exception); rather, they created an album that is bursting with light and colour. From its eventual title, *Green*, to its every musical crevice, this is a glistening, confident statement of an album, a true demarcation from their I.R.S. days, and not in the safe, corporate way that fans of independent music often fear when artists sign up for the big cheques for the first time, either. This is a version of R.E.M. that is still individual, idiosyncratic and highly artistic, but this time they are also brighter and clearer and, yes, more willing to engage with the rest of society.

Green explodes into life with 'Pop Song 89', a candy-coloured, major-key bauble of a song that is almost bubblegum pop in tone. The band had become intrigued by the late 60s power pop of The Monkees and The Archies and set about making their best approximation of it, although their rendering maintains a bold streak of new wave wonkiness too. It's a fascinating detail that some ten years after The B-52's first drew national attention to Athens, R.E.M. were now opening their major label debut with a track that carries a lot of the same frenetic energy that Kate Pierson and her band had originally struck gold with.

"Hello, I saw you, I know you, I knew you/I think I can remember your name," are Stipe's first words, a literal greeting to the mythical new mainstream world that they had just signed up to. The lyrics draw a direct reference to 'Hello, I Love You' by The Doors, with Stipe's awkward, insecure delivery a deliberate riposte to Jim Morrison's cocksure alpha male arrogance, a dissection of toxic masculinity that predates the term by several decades. "Should we talk about the weather/ Or should we talk about the government", Stipe continues, as if he were echoing the questions that fans and onlookers had been asking about whether R.E.M.'s more contentious views would be curtailed given their new corporate backing. Stipe never gets round to actually talking about either the weather or the government in 'Pop Song 89', letting the track's zaniness carry the day in arguably the first fun-for-fun's-sake R.E.M. song.

It sets the tone for the first half of the album appropriately. 'Get Up' follows in its slipstream as another blitz of mad, manic energy, this time written by Stipe about Mike Mills, a notorious over-sleeper, although Mills would only find this out around a decade later when Stipe introduced it as such on stage. 'Stand', meanwhile, exceeds 'Pop Song 89' in the bubblegum stakes and is another of what Stipe has described as his "fruit loop" songs. Modulated choruses shift higher and higher as the song progresses, while in his crackpot solo, Peter Buck makes use of a wah-wah pedal that he had bought especially for the track's recording. The lyrics are gobbledygook, more Barney the Dinosaur than Beaudelaire, and Buck later proclaimed it to be "without a doubt the stupidest song we've ever written," before adding, "that's not necessarily a bad thing, though."

With a band as intelligent and introspective as R.E.M., it is hard to escape the sense that this is more of an ironic take on pop music than an authentic stab at it, a sort of erstatz pop in the vein of Black Box Recorder's 'The Facts of Life' or The Timelords' 'Doctorin' the Tardis', both of which were records created by seasoned observers of pop that felt they had studied and analysed the pop rulebook and solved the formula before making their own successful version. But 'Pop Song 89' and 'Stand' are not as cold or as calculated as all that; this is a much purer take on happy music, albeit with one eyebrow ever so slightly arched at all times. 'Stand' would climb all the way to #6 on the Billboard Hot 100 in the early months of 1989, rubbing shoulders with 'Like a Prayer' and 'Eternal Flame'.

If those songs marked one new branch of the R.E.M. songwriting tree, then the track nestled between them on the first side of *Green* was the first fruit of a new blossom that would become one of R.E.M.'s most precious commodities. Of all of the breakthroughs in sound that had occured so far in the band's development, from 'Gardening at Night' to 'Radio Free Europe' to 'The One I Love', there may be none as important as 'You Are the Everything'. The band's newfound interest in the sounds of the mandolin and accordion from the early demo stages had spawned a skeleton track that Stipe took away and worked on in private, and by the time of its return to the rest of the band, something new had grown.

The band recorded the track with Buck on mandolin, Mills on accordion and Berry on bass, while over the top of them, we hear Stipe, unleashed and in love. It is the first straightforward, uncomplicated love song in the R.E.M. canon, and it opens up a new emotional frontier for Stipe as a singer. The song is far from gaudy, it is not overly simplistic and it refuses to fall into the traps of stadium rock – instead, we hear something immensely personal and fragile, as intricate as Stipe's own fingerprints, a sort of new musical language that he has assembled. It establishes a template where melancholic wonder and romantic longing combine to create a heart-bursting end result, and all from little more than downwardly inflected melodies, feather-light arrangements and Stipe's extraordinarily emotive vocals. The 1990s R.E.M. begins here.

And *Green*'s treats keep coming. 'World Leader Pretend' finds Stipe playing with his role as public performer. "I raised the wall, and I will be the one to knock it down," he sings, and we know the wall to which he refers. Even from their earliest interviews, R.E.M., and Stipe in particular, were expert at keeping the outside world at arm's length, and so it continued as the decade wore on. In the great tradition of pop stars playing with notions of identity, Stipe would alternate between various masks, letting them slip judiciously at times, enjoying the subterfuge and gamesmanship of toying with the audience. Again, at first glance, 'World Leader Pretend' seems to signal some kind of relaunch in this respect, but upon further examination it quickly becomes clear that in fact Stipe is just introducing another layer to the game. How can we know that whatever we will get from now on will be anything other than a newer, smarter, more sophisticated wall? Stipe knows we want to know him and he enjoys the chase. He recorded the vocal take for the song once and was so pleased with the results that he refused to do it again. Lyrically, he considered it a personal triumph too, noting that he was paying tribute to Leonard Cohen in his use of metaphors – in this case military barricades – to express his inner emotional conflict. So proud was he of the lyrics, in fact, that they were the first to ever be printed on an R.E.M. record sleeve.

The formal adventurousness is further expanded on 'Turn You Inside-Out', one of the more underrated R.E.M. songs, featuring percussion from former Sugar Hill Records house drummer Keith LeBlanc that lends the track that crisp, Clyde Stubblefield funk snap, while Stipe clearly inhabits the spirit of Patti Smith with his fluctuating, melismatic vocals. 'Hairshirt', meanwhile, takes up the mandolin/accordion template and uses it to tell a tale of self-care, revolving around the hair shirts that were once worn as religious penitence by the faithful, wherein Stipe states that he longs to remove the item in order to stop abusing himself for losing out on the love that he desires.

The song that the band ultimately chose for their first Warner Bros single, however, was none of the above. 'Orange Crush' was the only expressly political song on *Green*, taking its name from Agent Orange, a chemical weapon best known for being used by the US Army in Vietnam. A herbicide, it is reportedly responsible for as many as three million casualties, despite the fact that US soldiers were assured beforehand that there would be no negative physical effects for them. It is now thought to have been a factor in countless miscarriages and has also been linked with causing spina bifida, hence Stipe's refrain of "I've got my spine" and the response "collar me, don't collar me".

"I've had my fun and now it's time to serve your conscience overseas," Stipe sings, referencing the American government's assertion that the Vietnam War began because they believed it was their duty to intervene in the spread of communism in Asia. A machine gun opening drum beat, the sound of circling helicopters and marching chants and a megaphone lecture only serve to inflame the song's *Apocalypse Now*-like rage, but despite it all, 'Orange Crush' is another sparklingly bright, ear-catching pop song that proved to be a smart choice to launch the album campaign. Only released as a promotional single in the US, it broke records on the Mainstream and Modern Rock Tracks charts, spending eight weeks at #1. Additionally, it reached #28 on the UK Singles Chart, which was enough to earn them their debut performance on *Top of the Pops*.

Altogether, *Green* is not an album that hangs together with the same cohesion as any one of their previous records, but that had been their stated aim from the outset. The band were looking to move past what they had done before, to break free from what Buck described as the "minor key, mid-tempo, enigmatic, semi-folk-rock-balladish things" that they had become known for. In that respect, the album was a major success.

In the respect that mattered the most to Warner Bros, it was also a major success. Released on the 8 November 1988 to coincide with election day, it would go on to be certified double platinum, reaching #12 on the US charts and eventually selling over four million copies. It was critically well-received to boot, and five years later would be named by Kurt Cobain as both his favourite R.E.M. album and one of his fifty favourite records of all time. Cobain had not met R.E.M. yet, but it wouldn't be long before the two were leading a cultural revolution.

'Out of Time'

Now that they had signed the big money deal, R.E.M. no longer had any excuse to avoid a mammoth, no-expenses-spared world tour, and boy, did they not avoid one. The entirety of 1989 was given over to it; 132 shows in seventeen countries across ten gruelling months, with only a few fallow weeks over the summer to allow them a passing shot at physical survival.

The schedule was so intense that the band spent most of their final month of freedom locked away in a prolonged series of rehearsal sessions, complete with Peter Holsapple, co-founder of The dB's, on second guitar and occasional keyboard duties. Holsapple would join the band on stage at every date of the unimaginatively titled Green World Tour, which kicked off in Tokyo on 26 January, and included the band's debut performances in Australia, New Zealand, Italy, Denmark, Sweden and Finland, as well as far more extensive coverage of the more familiar United Kingdom, Germany and France.

The Green World Tour was a quantum leap forward production-wise, with the stage re-tooled and customised to the band's specifications, which included having Michael Stipe's hand-selected range of art films streaming on the backdrop during performances. They had a free choice of all available bands for opening acts, with established names such as The Go-Betweens, Robyn Hitchcock and Throwing Muses jostling with breakout acts like Indigo Girls, The Blue Aeroplanes and Drivin' N' Cryin'. R.E.M. sets would typically include no fewer than three encores, each filled with cover versions of songs by the usual suspects, although one particularly eye-catching choice was David Essex's 'Rock On', a track that it has often been observed bears an unmissable resemblance to R.E.M.'s 'Drive', which the band would write no more than a year later.

Setlist choices for the tour are worth scrutinising; songs from *Green* and *Document* naturally dominated, but even with such long sets, several of the standout gems from the earlier years were surprisingly under-utilised. 'So. Central Rain' and 'Driver 8' only made the cut in one in four shows, and 'Radio Free Europe' and 'Talk About the Passion' barely at all. Indeed, it is a confident band that can play this many shows and never once get around to playing songs as strong as 'Gardening at Night', 'Cant Get There from Here' and '(Don't Go Back to) Rockville', but such was the quality of the band's first decade of output.

A small number of gigs in Germany had to be cancelled in May due to Bill Berry contracting the nasty, tick-borne Rocky Mountain spotted fever, but beyond that every date was met. While in the UK, they made their long-awaited debut on *Top of the Pops*, miming deliberately badly through a performance of 'Orange Crush'; Stipe had spent the 1980s eschewing nearly every invitation to lip-sync, but his frostiness was slowly thawing. As the tour unfolded, two new songs emerged, 'Belong' and 'Low', suggesting that at least early on they were still writing on the go as well.

And yet, as the months wore on, their most strenuous period of touring began to coincide with a difficult sense that perhaps Warners had overstretched in their ambition. Gradually, some of the faceless North American arenas they would show up to were not full anymore. The 'Get Up' single that the label had planned for the fall season to keep the riches flowing had failed to chart, and the band's fatigue was now echoing and multiplying. As Bill Berry said, "We were so burned out by it, we were just on stage going through the motions. We really felt we were robbing the audience of what they deserve. We were playing in arenas a little larger than we were comfortable with and the whole thing was pretty depressing."

Luckily, there were always half-committed side projects to keep them distracted during their days off. Peter Buck was especially keen to find ways to reward himself with recreational live music spots, whether it was guesting on a track or two during an afternoon solo show by Holsapple, or as part of a band named the Chattahoochee Coochie Men, led by Buren Fowler, Holsapple's predecessor as R.E.M.'s unofficial fifth member and now the frontman of Drivin' N' Cryin'. Buck was the Coochie Men's regular guitarist and mandolinist, striking up a relationship with the band's singer Kevn Kinney that in 1990 would result in the two men conducting a mini-tour around the Northeastern United States. In turn, those dates saw them befriend Nikki Sudden, erstwhile frontman of the eccentric English post-punk noiseniks Swell Maps, with the result that Buck would be heavily involved in the 1991 recording of his own solo album *The Jewel Thief*. T Bone Burnett, the grand duke of modern American blues and roots music, known for masterminding the soundtracks to *O Brother, Where Art Thou?* and *Walk the Line* among others, was yet another musician that became ensnared in Buck and Kinney's web over those weeks. It all speaks to the sheer caliber of musicians with whom the R.E.M. guitarist was now associated, a very far cry from the fumbling, self-taught novice that first strummed his way through those early Steeplechase sessions.

By the time that the Green World Tour concluded in Atlanta at the end of November 1989, the band had already decided that it was finally the time for R.E.M. to take a sustained breather, a culmination of a decade of unbroken work. Stipe, like Buck, found that not having the day job pressing on him did not mean that he stopped enjoying the thrill of performing live and made a string of appearances alongside his friends Natalie Merchant and Billy Bragg that evolved into a quick jaunt around Europe with them the following summer. Having made a habit of popping up to perform guest vocals on the Indigo Girls song 'Kid Fears' during that band's spell opening on the Green World Tour, Stipe also took the opportunity to jump into a recording studio with the Atlanta folk-rockers early in 1990, adding backing vocals to the track 'I'll Give You My Skin'. Most surreal of all was his involvement in the Earth Day Rally at the US Capitol in April, a gathering of a half million Americans that was headlined by speeches by the bizarre activist team of Tom Cruise, Kevin Bacon and LL Cool J.

There were still day-to-day band duties to be fulfilled, even in the down time. Word reached them that I.R.S. were planning on a second compilation album of the band's material in less than three years. The first, *Eponymous*, which was released a few weeks before *Green*, had been warmly signed off by the band as a parting gift to the label and their first official greatest hits collection. Notable for its inclusion of the original Hib-Tone version of 'Radio Free Europe', it was a brisk, twelve-track run through of their I.R.S. years, with the added inclusion of 'Romance', the first Scott Litt collaboration, as an extra. This latest release, however, seemed a little harder to justify. Simply titled *The Best of R.E.M.*, it performed essentially the same job and was once again strategically released to coincide with the release of the next new R.E.M. LP. One would struggle to blame I.R.S. for eking out the value of their former darlings, but if the band had considered the parting amicable, then perhaps they were learning that there was still something of a grudge being held on the other side.

The other notable between-albums release of the period was *Tourfilm*, an avant-garde, black-and-white VHS production assembled by C-00 Film Corps, the film-making project of Michael Stipe and Jim McKay, an old friend from the road who had recently moved to Athens. The band did not like the idea of live albums, but *Tourfilm* fell into none of the genre's typical traps; instead, this was a spliced-together amalgam of several different experimental DIY film-makers' footage of four dates from late in the Green World Tour where handheld shots crossfade with stock footage and incongruous crowd reactions. It was the first real test of Warners' commitment to the band's most subversive instincts, and they happily released it on their Warner Reprise Video label.

Only one R.E.M. show occurred during this eight-month period of rest, a sweet-natured gesture on the occasion of the tenth anniversary of the band's first ever show. On 5 April 1990 at the 40 Watt Club in Athens, the four men appeared as the unannounced, unnamed opening band for two unassuming local bands, Beast Penis and Jarvik 8. It was a beautiful touch, and a reminder of how much they still loved being R.E.M. By the time that the demo recording sessions for album number seven rolled around in July at John Keane's Studio in Athens, they were hungry again.

"I stayed away for a month and a half and let them get to it," Michael Stipe said about the band's initial return to the studio. "And when I came in, they had this group of songs that were unlike anything I'd heard from R.E.M. It was classic R.E.M., but the instrumentation was skewered, completely different from what we'd done in the past."

It was true, and it all came about as a result of their decision to shake things up during the *Green* sessions, most especially for that seismic sonic breakthrough, 'You Are the Everything'. The bolt of fresh energy that had liberated them in those months may now have seemed like a while ago, especially as the long, hard year on the road had forced them back into their set roles within the band, but in those early sessions after reconvening, they could not wait to explore a little more of that virgin territory once more. Buck in particular was tired of being stuck in the electric guitar ghetto and craved some acoustic variation, not the least of which involved becoming re-acquainted with the mandolin. If anything, Buck was hungrier than before, believing that they could push things much further still; he was fond of the idea of creating full string sections and mini chamber arrangements, akin to those by bands like Love and The Zombies in the 1960s. Before long, Mike Mills' keys or organ parts were sitting in for what they imagined would be more sophisticated string ensembles further down the line. Possibilities were opening up everywhere they looked.

"We just thought, we're going to make a record that's going to destroy our career," remembered Buck decades later, "and it'll be cool. And then we'll make another record and it'll be fine. I think that we wanted to put a full stop to one part of our career and then start the next part."

Recording in earnest began back at Bearsville Sound Studios in New York State in early September 1990, with Peter Holsapple still highly involved. With the band now freely roaming the studio, it was useful to have an extra musician in the room, ready to hold down a guitar or bass line if Mills felt like tampering and improvising on some third instrument. Recording was a dream, all members now supremely comfortable in their roles and excited by the fact that their skills were at such a level as to make every experiment if not worth releasing, then at least worth exploring. Many core parts were laid down in one or two takes, with as full a band performance as possible captured to ensure that sense of cohesion.

They had already determined that they would not be touring after this album's release, so gone were any concerns about having to be able to actually replicate these tracks immediately on stage. Not unlike The Beatles' golden period after they withdrew from touring in 1966, R.E.M. were unbound, ready to push the envelope of what they could achieve with sound. "We will miss playing live," said Bill Berry at the time, "but the only alternative is to go out and beat our heads against the wall for another year, and we're just not prepared to do that."

Mark Bingham was brought in to work alongside Mills in creating the string arrangements that would ultimately adorn eight of the album's eleven tracks, while the beloved New Orleans horn player Kidd Jordan came in to add saxophone and clarinet parts. String parts were recorded by the Atlanta Symphony Orchestra at Soundscape Studios in Atlanta, and final mixing took place at Prince's iconic Paisley Park Studios in Minnesota, in a week of studio time that also included early run throughs of future favourites 'Drive', 'Try Not to Breathe' and 'Nightswimming'.

The most surprising guest contributor to the album was without doubt KRS-One, of whose work as MC with Boogie Down Productions Stipe had been a fan. His additions to album opener 'Radio Song' were admittedly little more than a sprinkling of extra flavour and a brief rap cameo over the outro, but even this was seen as a leftfield move in its day. Rock and hip-hop artists had been collaborating for some time, but more often in the sphere of hard rock and metal, whereas aside from Chuck D's memorable feature on Sonic Youth's 'Kool Thing' the previous year, bands from the indie and alternative space had not been known for it.

"When we wrote it out, we only had acoustic guitar, bongos, bass, organ and a 12-string over the chorus," remembered Buck. "When we got to the studio, we added drums and I put down some funk guitars and we thought, 'Well, gee, now it's kind of a funk song." It was Stipe's suggestion to bring in KRS-One, having worked with him on a short film project as part of C-00 Film Corps, and the energy he lent made it an easy choice to open the record.

Lyrically, the track is another case of Stipe tapping into the post-modern absurdity of being a singer with enough self-awareness to realise that he is trapped inside a radio pop song, not unlike the "Should we talk about the weather, or should we talk about the government" conundrum of 'Pop Song 89'. "It's that same sing-song on the radio/It makes me sad," he says this time around, lamenting how disposable the commodity of popular music has become, a point made all the more amusing as the track is one of R.E.M.'s most stylistically divergent recordings to date.

For the long-term fans, 'Radio Song' would have been quite the attention-catcher. As Peter Buck put it, "It blows people's mind, and gets them thinking, 'Woah, what's the rest of the record going to be like?' But then we go into 'Losing My Religion,' which is probably the most typical R.E.M.-sounding song on the record."

To lose one's religion, if you come from the South, was a once common phrase meaning to feel at the end of one's tether. Almost one billion YouTube views and more than 750 million Spotify plays later, nobody thinks of it that way anymore.

The mandolin composition that lent magic to 'You Are the Everything' had lingered with Buck, inspiring him to spend a lot of his spare time over the next two years practicing and teaching himself the instrument's foibles, to the point that he was now competent enough to conjure up melodic lines like the central strain of 'Losing My Religion' almost absent-mindedly in the midst of a personal jam session. He immediately recognised that the melody had an infectious quality to it, finding his fingers returning to it time and time again. It was only a year later that he realised the riff closely resembled a melody line from 'Merry Christmas, Mr. Lawrence', Ryuichi Sakamoto's acclaimed theme to the 1983 war film by Nagisa Oshima, but all he knew at the time was that he needed to bring it to the rest of the band.

"You can't really say anything bad about E minor, A minor, D and G – I mean, they're just good chords," a self-effacing Buck later said of his day's work. "We were trying to get away from those kinds of songs, but like I said before, those are some good chords."

Upon hearing them, Bill Berry's instinct was to preserve their fragility and "play it soft, give it a Latin feel", but eventually, "the general consensus was that it could do with a little more oomph", and so his full drum part came together quickly. Mike Mills landed on a characteristically melodic and counterintuitive bassline, which the man himself would describe as "a little mysterious and kind of disturbing, and you don't really know why".

From there, Stipe took the demo recording away and, in his usual way, allowed himself time to process the music, alone, with little more than a typewriter, a Dictaphone and the space to prowl. He began to formulate ideas.

"I don't remember having to write 'Losing My Religion', so that's a good sign," Stipe later said. "It indicates that it kind of just flew out of me."

The song's lyrics are legendarily inscrutable. In rare moments of weakness, Stipe has at least conceded that his relationship with the song bears some association with his relationship with the song 'Every Breath You Take' by The Police, a track notoriously misunderstood by the mass public, most of whom don't realise that it is about what can only be described as an obsessional stalker. "I wanted to do the same thing," said Stipe, "but I flipped it and made it about the vulnerability, and I created a character that is calling out to someone, and we don't know if that someone even knows if that person exists."

Whatever your personal interpretation of the song, the protagonist has to be considered as insecure, Stipe argues. "As a shy person," he says, "it's about the feeling of rejection when you have a massive crush on somebody but you don't know how to tell them, and you're not sure if whatever's happening is a friendship that's developing, or something more. You want to say something, but you don't know if you've said too much or if you haven't said enough."

Stipe has repeatedly insisted that he meant to infer no religious meaning to the song whatsoever, although in fairness, his history is brimming with things that he has insisted are not actually things. It is at the very least an inevitable consequence of his tendency to write in obtuse terms that people will arrive at their own conclusions, and it is certainly no surprise that after its period of global domination, the possible sacrilegious subtexts inflamed some of the planet's more conservative forces; its video, for example, would go on to be banned in the Republic of Ireland, a country at the time still very much in thrall to the power of the Catholic church.

The band were proud of the way the final recording came out and demanded that it should be the album's first single. When the label voiced their concerns about such an unconventional piece of music being the launchpad of a new album campaign, Buck summarised the band's response neatly: "No, we're going to do that."

Mike Mills at least understood Warners' concerns, even if he did not share them. "Think about it," he said, "you've got a five-minute song with no discernible chorus and the lead instrument is a mandolin – why would anyone play that on the radio?"

Trying to understand why they not only wanted to play it on the radio, but why they continue to do so with the kind of never-ending rotation that R.E.M. could never have imagined back then, is not easy to parse out. From the way the sashaying drumbeat crashes straight in at full stride to the helpless addiction of the mandolin tune; from the way that Stipe's bold vocals have the knack of catching the ear with the most unlikely repeated phrases to the way that the song's unconventional structure dares you to attempt to memorise the strange pattern of the verses; most invisibly of all, the way that the first-person lyrics invite you to apply your own secrets to their tale, it is an odd song. Whichever way it stands out to you, there is a great deal to love about 'Losing My Religion', and as the decades roll by, the song's legacy continues to grow exponentially.

"'Losing My Religion' is kind of a mistake," suggests Stipe. "It's a song that should never have been a hit single, it's so weird the way that it's put together. The fact that it became what it became is still puzzling to all of us."

Certainly, one major contributing factor to the runaway success was the song's video, directed by the relatively unknown Tarsem Singh, who claimed that he wanted to film it "in the style of a particular kind of Indian movie in which everything is melodramatic and very dreamlike." In it, Stipe, who is almost alone, but for the apparitions of the other band members, appears to be captured in the frame of a Caravaggio masterwork. He flails as he acts out the song's lyrics, while allusions to Biblical imagery, Greek mythology and the films of Andrei Tarkovsky charge proceedings with the suggestion of hidden subversions. It is a highly artful video, laser-designed to tease out the latent mystery in the song's writing and it struck a major chord with audiences. It is no exaggeration to say that it is hard to imagine 'Losing My Religion' having even a fraction of its initial success – and therefore overall success – without its video, such was the prominence of music television channels at the time.

The band won the tussle with Warners and the single shot to #4 on the Billboard Hot 100, one of the forty biggest hits of 1991. It remains by far the band's most played song around the world, with nearly ten times the number of Internet video hits as its nearest contender, 'Everybody Hurts'.

Within weeks, the band realised that the song had changed their lives. "I was walking up 5th Avenue in New York and every single person I was walking by recognised me from the music video," Stipe later recalled. "I was suddenly really famous." Mike Mills remembers being an hour outside of Asuncion, Paraguay a year later and the car radio tuning in and out of frequency, and all they could hear were snatches of 'Losing My Religion' between the hisses of static.

If Warners were initially wary of the marketability credentials of 'Losing My Religion', then their doubts could only have been heightened once they got their hands on 'Shiny Happy People', which was any record company's dream for a lead single. "Can you imagine that 'Shiny Happy People' and 'Losing My Religion' are even on the same record," Stipe once quipped. "It's almost schizophrenic."

An almost ludicrously joyous, frivolous, throwaway slice of treacle, 'Shiny Happy People' is still considered contentious in the R.E.M. catalogue. For many of the fans that appreciate the band primarily for their extraordinary power of nuance, 'Shiny' is just too bold and obvious for their taste. It was this album's equivalent of 'Stand', although notably more complex, with its sudden switch to a 3 / 4 signature after the second chorus. It also features the first female voice ever heard on an R.E.M. song, with their old friend Kate Pierson from The B-52's joining a three-way dance with Mills and Stipe in the chorus, bringing muscle memories of the great heights of her own band's pop nuggets and adding spring to the song's already bounding step. All art is subjective, but few could deny the song's parasitic qualities as an earworm.

Even in this most surface level of songs, though, there is hidden depth. Its lyrics were inspired by a Chinese propaganda poster that was published in the wake of the 1989 Tiananmen Square Massacre, designed to promote China as a utopian workers' paradise. The slogan had been cackhandedly translated as "Shiny Happy People Holding Hands", a preposterous enough phrase to match the giddiness of the composition.

"The challenge for me was to write a song that was as happy as the music," Stipe explained. "It's so much harder to write a happy song than it is to write a sad song. It's so easy to think sad thoughts...happiness is not something you can really define."

Although evidently happy to put their name to the song, the band were still reluctant for the whole album to be defined by its intense saccharine sweetness. They blocked an approach for it to be the theme song for *Friends*, for example, with only the unaired pilot ever using it before Warners turned to The Rembrandts instead. They played it on two television appearances around its release, but it never once graced any concert setlist and it was left off several future compilation tracklistings. Buck would later say that he was the only band member that was not embarrassed by the song, while Stipe, for his part, would say, "If there was one song that was sent into outer space to represent R.E.M. for the rest of time, I would not want it to be 'Shiny Happy People'".

Striking a diplomatic midpoint between the two singles is 'Near Wild Heaven', a charming, open-hearted letter of broken love from the pen of Mike Mills, who also takes the lead vocal, something he had only previously done on the 'Superman' cover on *Lifes Rich Pageant*. Like his other notable solo composition for the band, '(Don't Go Back to) Rockville', the song shows Mills to be as sweet a writer as he is a melodist, with a set of lyrics that talk directly about the subject on the writer's mind, which is a contrast to Stipe's typical style, even if he worked alongside his bandmate here. The song has just as hummable a tune as either 'Losing My Religion' or 'Shiny Happy People', but it was crowded out of the field and never managed to make its date with chart destiny.

Elsewhere on the album, the mood tends to turn inwards, with the pace set by the pair of compositions that had broken into setlists in 1989. 'Low' is a lurking, strung out piece where Holsapple's blunt staccato bass stabs set the tone and Stipe's lyrics suggest sensory burnout where low and high, day and night and fast and slow are barely distinguishable, while true love and depth is dismissed as "silly" or "shallow". It is hard to escape the idea with 'Low' that we are framed within a depressive mindset where the ability to feel anything has been robbed from the narrator. 'Belong', meanwhile, finds Stipe trying something new, using the spoken word to tell the mysterious tale of a mother imploring her child to "belong" while she watches an unnamed band of creatures "clearing the barricades" and "heading for the sea". Howling, wordless choruses seem to pull at primal, parental longing and the agony of possibly knowing that at some stage you must let your child leave and join their tribe.

The formal experiments continue with 'Endgame', where strings, clarinet, saxophone and flugelhorn combine to create a picturesque, baroque instrumental, very much in the vein of Paul McCartney's 'Singalong Junk' or Curtis Mayfield's 'Think'. R.E.M. had expanded their repertoire enough now to be able to assemble these kinds of compositions without them seeming out of place, with some prime Beach Boys vocal harmonies gracing the track's high end for regal decoration.

Two beasts of R.E.M.'s career hide in the album's home stretch. 'Half a World Away' returns them to the mandolin motherlode, the richest seam they had found, this time accentuated with harpsichord and organ. One of the true magical highs of the band's catalogue, it once again demonstrates their ability to elevate heartache, anguish and pain to something astoundingly beautiful and multicoloured, or as Stipe puts it in the track, a state of being "high-alive". Like the character of Joy in Pixar's *Inside Out*, R.E.M. had grown to understand that it is only by allowing sadness into the heart that you finally begin to enjoy the full spectrum of emotional possibilities and with 'Half a World Away', they were now able to elicit wondrous riches from what others would dismiss as unhelpful negativity.

'Country Feedback', often quoted by Stipe as his proudest work, is just as powerful. Tapping into that Southern roots storytelling rhythm, the song uses the cry of John Keane's pedal steel guitar to express the emotion that Stipe himself is refraining from. There is an observational, almost stoic quality to both his words and his delivery; clearly the character in the song is at a crossroads in their relationship, but the scale of a major life transition weighs so heavily on him that he is reduced to sharing glimpses of reflection before getting stuck on a note of stagnant self-pity ("It's crazy what you could have had"). It could easily be read as an analogy for the band's growing pains, with the seductress that comes to him with a bone in her hand and her hair curled tight representing the promises of success, or more pointedly the empty promises of the people with the power to hold success away from them. Whatever the intentions were, they arrived in the spur of the moment, as Stipe turned up for the recording with nothing but a hastily scribbled note that, depending on who you believe, consisted either of "a few words" or "two little drawings". He improvised a set of lyrics and left, returning the following day to find that everyone was more than happy with his solitary take. No further vocals were ever recorded.

With the album complete, the band needed to come up with a title, but when deliberations spilled over into four entire pages' worth of suggestions, Warners started getting antsy. Mike Mills, stressed, came off a phone call with their front office and moaned aloud, "Well, we're out of time." Of course, it is too neat a story to have happened as cleanly as that, but nevertheless, they realised that *Out of Time* worked in a pleasing way, in the sense that it presented the music as somehow not belonging in the era that it was being released into. At the time, Stipe could often be found talking about how he felt that the material on the album was a bolt from the blue for the pop music of 1991, but then this is where the two-and-a-half-year gap between albums had left a lasting impact. For each of their first six albums, they had existed in a communal space, as a pivotal part of a scene of like-minded bands making loosely similar styles of music. With the transition into the 1990s, not only had that scene largely dissipated and been replaced with the much gnarlier grunge or the slicker funk rock, but the band themselves had left that style behind too.

Stipe had changed the demeanour that he sent out into the world. The goonish, almost jester-like figure from the 'Stand' and 'Shiny Happy

People' videos did not seem so out of keeping with Stipe the interviewee in 1991, and it was all a very far cry from the painfully shy frontman that couldn't even bear to talk to David Letterman nearly a decade earlier.

Out of Time was released in March 1991 and by May it was the number one album in America, selling over three million copies by the end of the year. As a knock-on effect of this level of success, sales of their previous albums enjoyed major spikes, with *Reckoning* and *Fables of the Reconstruction* both being certified Gold that summer.

A mammoth promotional tour spanned several weeks either side of the release, much of which was conducted from a series of hotel rooms around Western Europe. From CNN to KCRW, BBC2's *The Late Show* to *Rolling Stone*, everyone wanted a slice of R.E.M. The band were known inside the business for being unusually, even unnecessarily, courteous with journalists and producers, no doubt thanks in part to their slow ascent to the top and their years of relying on the good will of others to hold their fledgling career together. They played two shows at the Borderline, a tiny venue in West London, under the name Bingo Hand Job, in the same week that 'Losing My Religion' made the UK top 20. They could not have expected the secret to be kept under wraps and indeed it was not, but with Billy Bragg and Robyn Hitchcock joining them on stage for covers of songs like EMF's 'Unbelievable' and Madness' 'Baggy Trousers', the shows lived on in word-of-mouth glory for years. When they returned home, it was to record a stunning episode of *MTV Unplugged*, followed later in the same week by their musical guest spot on *Saturday Night Live*, hosted by comic actor Catherine O'Hara, where they played 'Losing My Religion' and 'Shiny Happy People' with Kate Pierson.

They were suddenly in contention for the music industry's most prestigious awards too. At the MTV Video Music Awards in September, they won six, all for the 'Losing My Religion' video. Tarsem, Berry, Mills and Stipe were all there to collect, with the latter wearing a series of slogan t-shirts, including 'Love Knows No Color', 'Wear a Condom', 'Alternative Energy Now' and 'Handgun Control', just to make it clear that even if *Out of Time* was a largely apolitical record, the band's interest in current affairs had not waned. Stipe told *Rolling Stone* that the feedback he got for the t-shirts that day dwarfed anything he had ever done.

When the Grammys rolled around the following February, R.E.M. won three of the seven for which they were nominated: Best Alternative

Music Album, Best Pop Performance by a Duo or Group with Vocal and Best Music Video: Short Form (the latter two both for 'Losing My Religion'). In a year when Natalie Cole's mawkish album of duets with her late father Nat 'King' Cole swept the board for the biggest gongs, it was a reminder of what that most loaded of qualifiers, *alternative*, actually encompassed. With *Out of Time*, R.E.M. had proven that the term did not mean an alternative to success. If anything, in the context of the Grammys, it appeared to mean an alternative to everything that the establishment was currently churning out with its eyes closed. A decade of tussle and turmoil had led them to the big table and they were still manifestly who they had always been. That's why the slogans at the VMAs resonated – it was a giveaway of their personal truths, which had remained unchanged. R.E.M. had swapped chart placings in 1991 with New Kids on the Block, Mariah Carey and Vanilla Ice, and they had done so by being themselves. If 'Shiny Happy People' or 'Near Wild Heaven' didn't sound incredibly alternative to the ears of music fans who were well attuned to such distinctions, then Stipe and Buck's public behaviour certainly still did.

Perhaps it should have been considered a new form of alternative, one able to sit right at the heart of mainstream cultural life, but which espoused a set of virtues and values that were decidedly more progressive and subversive than the institutions were used to broadcasting. And yet, across those same channels as 1991 became 1992, a brand new explosion was starting to beam out. When Nirvana's *Nevermind* topped the Billboard Albums chart early in the new year, alongside Skid Row, Billy Ray Cyrus, Van Halen and Michael Bolton, it sold twice as quickly as *Out of Time*. But *Out of Time* ran so that *Nevermind* could fly.

If R.E.M. were being questioned about whether they had held onto their underground roots while topping the charts, nobody could listen to 'Smells Like Teen Spirit' and wonder the same thing. Between the two albums, a barrier had been breached. No sooner had the burden fallen on Stipe than it had been passed onto Kurt Cobain, seven years his junior and clearly more in touch with a new wave of young disaffection. In the public sphere, the two frontmen believed they were fighting the same fight, but privately, Cobain was dialling Stipe's number, seeking advice for how to be the biggest rockstar in the world.

'Automatic for the People'

Stardom was always going to sit awkwardly with R.E.M. The prevailing sense was that their choice lay between presenting a clean, sanitised version of themselves – or, to put it another way, to start pretending to be something they were not – or to stick to their guns and confuse a conservative public. Choosing not to tour off the back of the success of *Out of Time* and then disappearing off the national scene as soon as they had arrived confirmed that they were choosing the latter path, and so their war with the mass media over the control of their image began.

Far from spending the second half of 1991 mingling in the Hollywood fast lane, they happily occupied themselves by playing one-off live spots with their friends' bands and hosting screenings of their latest video ventures for their Athens friends. Occasional radio interviews were the closest they came to stoking their career momentum, as well as a brief trip to London early in the new year to collect their first Brit Award for Best International Group.

In truth, there was barely a gap between the end of the *Out of Time* process and the beginning of *Automatic for the People*. The three playing members of the band first entered their home studio at West Clayton Street in early June 1991, assembling semi-regularly thereafter for several months, and swirling through as many new song ideas as their time would permit. The original intent was to emerge from the period with a set of songs that were harder rocking than the songs on *Out of Time*, a natural response given how much that album had shifted them from their roots, but their tendencies only seemed to be taking them further down the same line. They still preferred the freedom of wandering between instruments, often leaving percussion out entirely, while the mandolin was very much still Peter Buck's number one choice. As before, Michael Stipe chose to leave the rest of the band to it, preferring to hear the songs for the first time in their completed demo version.

Someone else who was absent from the sessions was Peter Holsapple. His contributions in studio and on stage had been so substantial over the last three years that any newcomer would have assumed him to have been as much a member of R.E.M. as any of the others but while the friendship remained tight, R.E.M. were not about to destabilise the band from a business perspective by opening up their split of the royalties. The agreement they had made in their earliest days to split the money equally among the four members, regardless of the actual share of the writing, plus the deal to include Bertis Downs and Jefferson Holt as equal members in the band's legal income, had served them excellently during their rise through the ranks, but as much as they appreciated Holsapple, it simply could not extend to his becoming an official fifth member. Holsapple, understandably, was disappointed by their decision and chose to pursue his own career instead, releasing more music but never enjoying the riches that playing with R.E.M. would have afforded him.

By the end of 1991, the demos were ready to hand over to Stipe. "Very mid-tempo, pretty fucking weird. More acoustic, more organ-based, less drums," were Stipe's exact words as he described them to *Rolling Stone* at the time, and he was right. The band had returned to their conventional instruments to record the demos and the result was a deeply textured, sensitive collection of tracks that compelled Stipe to reach further inwards into his own emotional reserves to meet the challenge.

The album was recorded in five different studios in five different states. They first settled down at New Orleans' Kingsway Studio, the home of producer extraordinaire Daniel Lanois, where Scott Litt had his first chance to hear the new material. The band loved the "magical and mercurial" spirit of New Orleans, as Stipe described it. "When you're there, you know that you're there and when you're not there, you miss it", he said. If anything, the celebratory air of the city became detrimental to the band's workrate, with one particularly late Mardi Gras night out leading to a prolonged day of hungover, repetitious and ultimately fruitless attempts to record the song 'Drive'.

Sensing that the distractions were becoming too problematic, they relocated to the now-familiar Bearsville Studios in Woodstock, New

York. It could not have been more different: secluded and remote, the band not only could not indulge in late night activities, they could barely remember that there was a busy world out there beyond the trees. It certainly focused their minds, with most of the album's twelve tracks now beginning to advance to their final form, even if the studio notes reveal that many of them were still in search of permanent titles ('Monty Got a Raw Deal' was still just referred to as 'Bouzouki Song', for example, and 'Ignoreland' was listed as 'Howler Monkey').

After a period cooped up in upstate New York, they once again sought the polar opposite conditions and as May signalled the beginning of summer, they decamped to Criteria Studios in Miami. With the bulk of the music now laid down, the band took out beach houses and while his bandmates chose to indulge in the perks of South Florida, Stipe, the least beach-natural member of the band, remained inside, slaving over strange new lyrical turns of phrase. Peter Buck fondly recalls meeting Jimmy Page during one hazy afternoon, but it was one of Page's former bandmates that would become instrumental during stop number four in this recording odyssey.

Over a couple of busy days in late May, back in Atlanta at Bosstown Studios, the band found themselves once again in the company of the Atlanta Symphony Orchestra. The band knew they wanted several of the new songs to have string arrangements, and Scott Litt thought he knew just the guy to help. John Paul Jones may have cemented his legacy in rock history as the bassist in Led Zeppelin, but Litt was a particular fan of his previous work as a string arranger on records such as The Rolling Stones' 'She's a Rainbow' and Donovan's 'Hurdy Gurdy Man'. He sent Jones the recordings they already had and was delighted when Jones very quickly responded that he liked what he had heard and would be happy to help. In many ways, Jones and Mike Mills were perfect bedfellows: both bassists by title but all-rounders by nature, they were able to turn their hand to a miscellany of musical instruments, and after a whirlwind collaborative weekend, Mills was left struck by Jones' contributions. "If you thought about it, you knew that he was capable of that kind of brilliance if you listen to 'Kashmir', but it just didn't occur to us," Mills later said.

The final port of call was in the city that Buck was now calling his semi-permanent home, Seattle. His marriage to Barrie Greene was struggling and Athens no longer held the allure that it once had done. He had already amassed a number of properties around the country, and it was no surprise to those who knew him that he decided to buy a home in the city that was now at the epicentre of the new music boom. Before long, he found himself not just in the right city to be near the action, but on the right block. Kurt Cobain and Courtney Love, already avowed fans of R.E.M. and well acquainted with them individually, caught wind of Buck's real estate purchase and decided to buy the house next door to Buck's, just so that they could be near one of their favourite musicians and spend as much time around him as possible. The two bands became closer than ever.

The four weeks that R.E.M. spent in Seattle were primarily dedicated to putting together the final mixes of the tracks, and by the start of July, they were happy with the final product. The key result of such a drawn-out recording experience was that the songs had ample time to breathe and gestate, with the band keen to distill the compositions to their least cluttered and most direct form. There were little to no musical contributions from outside the band, other than the string players, and while the record would turn out to be full of additional sonic trinkets, it did at least largely mark a return to the conventional band dynamic.

What remained from the *Out of Time* experience was a sense of liberation. The band were now almost entirely secluded; it had been well over two years since they had last toured and no further touring loomed on the horizon. In addition to that, they had long since thrown off the shackles of the 1980s independent rock scene and voyaged out into unknown terrain. They felt they had no peer group to lean on anymore, nor any formula to rely upon. They were lost in an R.E.M. bubble, and it provided the circumstances for something artistically unique and exceptional.

Much has been said about *Automatic for the People*'s preoccupation with death and morbidity and it certainly is a recurring theme, but it is one among many. "We had lived through our twenties," Michael Stipe would later reflect. "I was 31 when we started writing this record, so that's a time of life when you start re-examining who you are as an adult, who you are as a younger person, and I think all of that went into the mood and the themes of this record. It's about mortality, death, but also transition and shifting from one thing into another."

If it seems like the album has the weight of the world on its shoulders, then it is worth remembering how difficult a period it had been. Like

Green, this album was being released in an election year, after twelve exhausting years of Reagan and Bush, and at a time when the shock of the HIV/AIDS pandemic was still reverberating. Stipe, in particular, had felt first-hand the horrific consequences that the illness had inflicted on the New York artistic community that had welcomed him in and it is no surprise that such existential matters would spill over into his writing. As Mills put it, "there was a weird confliction between the fact that we were in a pretty good place as a band, but there were a lot of darker things happening in our country."

If anything underscored the album's inclination towards the dark light, it was the song that was selected not just to be its opening track, but most telling of all, its lead single. A surly, prowling track that simmers without ever boiling over, 'Drive' must have been considered by Warners to be an even more surprising choice to lead off the album campaign than 'Losing My Religion' had been. Unobtrusive, borderline tasteful accordion tones and the lightest touch of strings, restrained and far from schmaltzy, add depth without building height, while Stipe's vocals remain sombre with a vice-like solidity.

"Smack, crack, bushwhacked," goes the opening line. In 1988, Stipe had taken out newspaper adverts during the election campaign, using the phrase, "Don't get bushwhacked, get out and vote", referencing the Republican candidate. Here, two albums and one presidential cycle later, we hear the same derogatory term, but this time with a hidden confidence that Bush was almost certainly on the way out.

As already mentioned, 'Drive' shares more than a strand of DNA with David Essex's 'Rock On' from 1973, a link that did not come about by accident. Stipe has pointed to 'Rock On' and Elton John's 'Bennie and the Jets' as two singles from his formative years that left an indelible stamp on his emerging self-consciousness. "They were both very oddly produced singles," he once said. "They were beacons of light to me as a young man discovering as a teenager that I was different to everyone else. And not just in terms of my sexuality – I am an outsider and my father was a bit of an odd guy and I got that from him, that darkness, that humour, that not-quite-fitting-in, a square peg in a round hole. Those songs indicated to me a direction that I might want to go in."

In turn, Stipe uses the opportunity on 'Drive' to dole out the kind of spiritual guidance that he himself received from those singles. "Hey kids, where are you? Nobody tells you what to do, baby," he sings, an elder statesman figure sticking up for the new generation's rights to follow their own path, listen to their instincts and not let the old folks drum the life out of them before they even get started. It is strikingly redolent of David Bowie's 'Changes' in that regard, and fits Stipe's vision of the album as representing life transitions, in this case the shift into adulthood, or at least away from adolescence.

A very different transition lies at the heart of the song that follows, 'Try Not to Breathe'. Although the music does not betray the full scope of the song's tragedy, bearing a less morose tone than several other tracks on the album, the lyrics carry a tremendous emotional weight. Our narrator has resolved to end her life and above all longs for her most cherished ones to understand how and why her decision has been made ("I will try not to breathe, this decision is mine, I have lived a full life, and these are the eyes that I want you to remember"). The song is the antithesis of the ignorant, uncaring attitude that still pervades about people who choose to take their own life, that considers it to be a selfish or cowardly act. This character has done their best to persevere, trying not to worry those around her, trying not to be a burden. Stipe's writing is incredibly evocative and moving, as he carefully considers a transition out of suffering.

With such a one-two punch at the start of *Automatic for the People*, Warners might have started to worry. But their patience was rewarded; the album includes some of R.E.M.'s most instantly welcoming music too, including the exceedingly radio-friendly 'Man on the Moon'. With Peter Buck's new Seattle neighbours now part of the band's social circle, songwriting competitiveness came to the fore. Stipe was an admirer of Cobain's, but could not help but be amused by the preponderance of a particular vocal tick of his, and made a bet with himself that he would be able to write a song where he sang "yeah" more times than Cobain did on Nirvana's 'Lithium'. What started as a joke became a useful framework for the song, although the remainder of the lyrics took so long to come together that the days of allotted studio time were starting to seriously dwindle before Stipe finally landed on something that he was happy with.

He knew he was intent on writing an homage to Andy Kaufman, one of American comedy's most mystifying and subversive geniuses. A surrealist and a deconstructionist, Kaufman, best known for his regular appearances in the early seasons of *Saturday Night Live* and for playing the role of Latka Gravas on *Taxi*, enjoyed playing with the notion of performance more than he enjoyed the performance itself. Stipe had form in that regard too, dating back to the self-referential singer role he had played on songs like 'Shiny Happy People' and 'World Leader Pretend', and, like many with an outsider perspective, he was acutely drawn to the strange grey areas that Kaufman played around in.

Kaufman had a predilection to take these games to darkly extreme ends, including having sketches descend into excruciatingly awkward installation pieces, or creating a seedy nightclub singer alter-ego in the form of Tony Clifton to add a fractured mirror effect to the audience's sense that the dizzying layers of pretence were too many to keep up with. The notions of real and fake were central to everything he did – was he really so close to the Latka character? Was he really caught up in a blood feud with Memphis pro wrestling legend Jerry "The King" Lawler that spilled over into the talk show studios? Were those appearances with Lawler initially scripted one way, but his desire to make it real resulted in him legitimately provoking Lawler into attacking him on live television? Or was that also written into the act in a maddening game of bluff and counter-bluff? Were his wrestling matches real and was he really inviting women from the crowd into the ring so that he could beat them in a fight to remain the Intergender Wrestling Champion of the World? When he began a stand-up set by declaring that he was going to read *The Great Gatsby* in full, was he really going to do it? (He did). When he fell ill in his mid-thirties and died, was he making that up, too? Or was, as many believed, he actually hiding in premature retirement, and occasionally still performing live as Tony Clifton?

This is what lies at the heart of 'Man on the Moon'. People really did believe that Elvis was still alive, and they really did believe that man never landed on the moon, just as they believed the things that Andy Kaufman was telling them. The song becomes a treatise on how we can't really be sure about anything in life when there are so many competing messages in the ether, albeit written in an era before the true sociopolitical danger of conspiracy theories had taken its terrifying grip on modern life. It is no surprise, then, that Stipe could not resist throwing in biblical references to boot – the net can be cast as wide as you like when it comes to pressing down on the nature of faith and truth. However deep one chooses to get with 'Man on the Moon', though, one thing remains unalterably true: it contained 56 yeahs to 'Lithium's mere 42, so it was a win for Stipe.

Exactly how all of the song's other litany of cultural references play into the theme can be somewhat unclear: Stipe has admitted, for example, that he has no idea why Mott the Hoople make their appearance in the opening line, other than that they might have entered his own life at roughly the same time as Kaufman. He lived with the demo recording for several weeks, during which time it was known only as 'C to D Slide', allegedly because when Bill Berry was playing his guitar part, he reached for a beer and his finger slipped on the fretboard, creating a change that the rest of the band insisted should remain as part of the song's structure. Stipe would put on his Walkman and walk around downtown Seattle, waiting for inspiration to strike, not unlike the wanderer he portrays in the song's video, until the lyrics we are now familiar with landed in their rightful place.

If 'Man on the Moon' came as some relief to Warners, then 'The Sidewinder Sleeps Tonite' would have been a cause for high fives all around. The band generally sensed that there would probably be no need for a 'Shiny Happy People'/'Stand' kind of number on this record, and sure enough when they detected one emerging – it went by the demo name of 'The Fruity Organ Song' and boasted Farfisa organ and playful, bouncing basslines – they stamped it out fairly early on. But Peter Buck was uncomfortable with the abundance of slow material that was coming to define the album and strongly felt that something different was needed to break up the pacing.

"It was not my choice to put it on the record," said Stipe. "I have to say, there are songs where I feel that I was lyrically lazy; on this one, I think I might have been lyrically a little too over-caffeinated. I didn't think too hard about it, I just let it come out of me."

Every bit as catchy as 'Shiny Happy People', 'Sidewinder' is a joyous slice of power pop that takes its name and Stipe's opening wordless vocal melody from 'The Lion Sleeps Tonight', a 1920s composition by South African songwriter Solomon Linda under the original title 'Mbube'. That song took a circuitous route to global fame, being interpolated by many a folk act in the 1950s, often under the title 'Wimoweh', a mishearing of the original chorus of "Uyimbube", before translating into a major US hit by doo-wop band The Tokens in 1961, and later a global hit for Tight Fit in 1982. Adding to the ridiculousness is the barely suppressed giggle that follows Stipe's mention of Dr. Seuss; Mike Mills had spent all afternoon lecturing Stipe that he was mispronouncing Seuss as Zeus, but Stipe wasn't budging. As deeper meanings of the song go, good luck finding one, but the sidewinder of the title that "sleeps in a coil" certainly seems to suggest the tightly wound cord of our central character's public telephone that Stipe implores his loved one to contact him on, day or night. If it's nuance you want from a song about waiting impatiently by the telephone, though, maybe try 'So. Central Rain (I'm Sorry)'. Like 'Shiny Happy People', 'Sidewinder' never once made its way onto a regular R.E.M. setlist.

The track that has most outgrown *Automatic for the People*, though, is 'Everybody Hurts'. "You never really know how songs are going to go over with people," says Mike Mills. "We knew it was beautiful and it had some connectivity, but it reached a lot more people than we thought it would." Mills can rarely have been more understated. After 'Losing My Religion', it is easily the band's second biggest song, fuelled by perhaps their best-known video. Directed by Jake Scott, son of filmmaking great Ridley, the video made manifest the song's profoundly empathetic content by depicting a cross-section of everyday American life at an enormous traffic jam. Characters are shown during an unexpected pause in their daily proceedings that forces them to reflect on their lives, which offers hope and contentment for some, but frustration, dissatisfaction and pain for others. We see subtitles that represent the inner monologues of these people, some of which seem to contravene what the characters are choosing to put on display, in a nod to Federico Fellini's *8 ½*.

The video struck the same tone as the song. Rarely if ever had Stipe written so unambiguously, nor the band composed so open-heartedly. 'Everybody Hurts' has taken on such an unpredictable life of its own that it has not just left the band's possession, but it exists now as a self-help ballad for the sort of audience that R.E.M. would not typically call their own. In hindsight, it could just as easily have been the song that Bridget Jones wails along with in her moments of despair, instead of Eric Carmen's 'All by Myself'.

Its uncommon blend of an electronic drum beat, complete with the strange popping sound of a beatbox, surging strings that for once let the sentimentality take hold, and soaring, skyscraping vocals put it in a category all of its own in this band's catalogue. "It's a very strange combination of complete sincerity and a little bit of silliness," Mills would concede.

Once again, a comparison should be made with David Bowie, in this case 'Rock 'n' Roll Suicide', which not only contains a very similar guitar phrase to that which opens 'Everybody Hurts', but which also leans on the phrase "you're not alone" as a reassuring hand on the shoulder of its audience. It had briefly been considered as a duet between Stipe and his teenage idol Patti Smith, and while the timings did not fall in the right place for that, it at least allowed the band to learn that Smith was not only aware of their existence, but a fan of their work, having seen their videos on MTV. Even better news was that Patti Smith's husband, the MC5 guitarist Fred "Sonic" Smith, referred to Stipe as "your boy" whenever his face would appear on their TV, such was Patti's fascination with him. The two singers had yet to make their connection in real life, but there was still time yet.

'Sweetness Follows' returns to the recurring theme of transition, this time into a life spent managing grief. The band hired a cellist, Elizabeth Proctor Murphy, to augment the track and while warming up, she played a hook that caught the ear of the band, who immediately had her repeat it, so that they could loop it and use it as the backbone of the song, in lieu of a bassline. The track tells of the grand tide of pain that can "pull you under" when you lose someone, but Stipe, as always, is on hand to remind that a sweetness follows the hurt, even if it is the bittersweetness of fond memories, or that twang of realisation that the moments that should have mattered the most were taken for granted.

The story of Montgomery Clift, the Hollywood A-lister whose matinee looks were damaged in a car accident at the height of his success, requiring extensive facial surgery that caused him psychological trauma and an eventual slide into addiction and depression, forms the basis of 'Monty Got a Raw Deal', a track powered by Mills' bass with rubber surgical tubing substituted for its strings, and Buck's kooky turn on the bouzouki. The Clift tale had fascinated rock writers before, notably The Clash on 'The Right Profile', the rarest of cases of a fable that played out in real time on a global platform. When Stipe was invited to Elton John's fiftieth birthday party at Hollywood's Chateau Marmont, Courtney Love coaxed him into approaching Elizabeth Taylor to tell her that he'd written a song about her friend and that she made an appearance in it too. Taylor was one of the first to find Clift after his accident, even pulling a tooth from his tongue to stop him from choking. She told Stipe, "That love we shared had no name then, and it has no name now, it's the most eternal love that I have ever experienced."

The most nakedly angry song to appear on any R.E.M. record so far is 'Ignoreland'. Gone are the attempts at veiling their political fury – as Mills put it, "sometimes you have anger and you have to let it out, and thank goodness we have music for that outlet". Some of the pre-chorus splurge of animosity ("brooding, duplicitous, wicked and able, media-ready...") seems to recall the blistering outrage of John Lennon's 'Gimme Some Truth', both songs expressing sentiments that seem more relatable by the decade. The song also includes only the second f-bomb on an R.E.M. record (after 'Country Feedback'), but its thunder is soon stolen by the following track, 'Star Me Kitten'. Only going by that title thanks to the threat of a 'Parental Advisory' label that could have stopped some under-18s from purchasing the album, the song's true name is 'Fuck Me Kitten', with the band opting for the word 'star' over a string of asterisks. Scott Litt and Mike Mills had been locked in conversation about 10cc's stunning single 'I'm Not in Love' and chose to co-opt its method of recording entire banks of vocals – Mills' own, in this case – and manipulating them at the mixing desk as if they were playing an instrument with them. It is the album's most experimental flourish, and it more than plays its part in creating the song's scorching hot sexual tension.

The final two tracks contain the soul of *Automatic for the People*. Mike Mills was goofing around with a melody that he liked on the piano in the studio one afternoon – incidentally, the same piano on which Jim Gordon had written the coda to Derek and the Dominos' 'Layla', which tickled Mills – and Stipe overheard it and told him to play it on a loop for ten minutes so he could come up with a few ideas. By the end of the day, they had virtually completed the core of 'Nightswimming'. The two would later compose the string part, which John Paul Jones would arrange, but if ever a song existed as a duet between human voice and piano keys, it was this one.

The transition at the heart of 'Nightswimming' is generational. Stipe has said that he thinks of the adolescent memories in the song's lyrics as having a church-like purity to them, and that not only has he lost that, but maybe even more importantly, he believes the generation behind him have lost that too. He views the world as having become too accelerated and unrestrained to truly understand the beauty that he seeks to describe.

The lilting piano notes, the swelling strings, the regretful oboe line, the light croak in Stipe's voice, it's all impossibly romantic, an appeal to your lost innocence, to those first moments of gaping, giddy wonder in your formative years, of lunging at that first grab of independence and pushing the envelope to a slightly uncomfortable degree. Two images endure from Stipe's lyrics. First, the idea of two moons, side by side in orbit, a concept Stipe borrowed from Samuel R. Delany's 1975 dystopian novel *Dhalgren*, the cover of which depicts a city in ruins with a giant blazing sun behind it and two distant crescent moons. "I wondered how humans' mythology would shift if we had not just one moon, but two," Stipe has said. "How the stories we tell and the mythologies we create would be different." Secondly, the photograph on the dashboard that elicits the nostalgia in the first place, which is only visible thanks to the reflection on the windscreen as the streetlights shine upon it. It is the private, tender nature of the observation that reveals how deeply felt these flashes of memory are. These are not just reminiscences of something wonderful, but also of something that is now gone; "these things, they go away, replaced by every day".

'Find the River' closes out the album in even more poignant fashion. Like 'Nightswimming', it came together remarkably quickly, with much of the original demo surviving onto the album version. "It didn't take longer to write it than it does to play it," Mills observed. Mills suggested to Bill Berry that they should not only both contribute vocal harmony parts, but that they should write and record them separately, without hearing each other's. When they were finally combined, it created something slightly uncanny, with Mike's high notes and Bill's low hums creating an alchemical combination that they would never have consciously written, but which had the power to rip a hole in your heart.

Bill Berry's melodica part ushers the song in, its notes somewhere between childlike lullaby and a coded emergency siren, before Stipe's sage, elder statesman monologue arrives. The song's poetry is not immediately decipherable, but once you start to pick at its surface, the lyrics' profound insights begin to reveal themselves. "Hey now, little speedyhead," sings Stipe, addressing some unspecified younger counterpart, before imploring them to cool their heels and stop sprinting their way through life. Stipe is eager to show this person that they have the time to do everything they could ever want, and all will come to them in good order, while in the meantime they are not absorbing the precious moments that are flying past their eyes right now. Similar to the message in 'Sweetness Follows', the worst thing of all is that they don't even know they're missing it.

Meanwhile, our elder character has the opposite problem. His journey is nearing its end, his river preparing to empty into the tide, the one unassailable truth of life. The tastes and flavours that garland the song's lyrics – ginger, lemon, indigo, et al – read like a cavalcading sensory callback of a million simultaneous memories, the full richness of life and the sweetness of its journey flooding his mind as he contemplates what lies ahead. The song hinges on the handover between the two characters – "There's no-one left to take the lead/But I tell you and you can see/ We're closer now than light years to go/Pick up here and chase the ride" - before, as the moment arrives, our elder tells us with heartening reassurance that it is strength and courage that ultimately overcome all else, as he quietly accepts his fate, the ultimate transition.

'Monster'

Automatic for the People was released to the world in October 1992 largely without comment. Given the scale of expectations R.E.M. were now dealing with, their desire to prolong their withdrawal from the publicity circuit, especially given the introspective, cryptic nature of the material within, was a bold move to say the least. Michael Stipe and Bill Berry both declared that they would not be discussing the subject matter at all, and pulled themselves from all major media interviews. Peter Buck and Mike Mills spoke, at best, in general, evasive terms about what it might all be about.

The one morsel of information that did reach the public was the meaning behind the album's title. 'Automatic for the People' is the motto and slogan of Weaver D's Delicious Fine Foods, a well-loved eatery back in Athens that Bill Berry describes as "the best soul food restaurant in the South". It captured the Southern hospitality spirit and rooted them specifically in their hometown once again, just as the kudzu on the *Murmur* cover had done. The star that adorns the album cover represents the record's itinerant recording process and was taken from the Sinbad Motel in Miami, a short hop from the Criteria Studios. The photograph was taken by Stipe and he was proud enough of it to have it pinned upon the studio wall for the rest of the recording, even adopting 'Star' as a working title for the album ('Unforgettable' was also in the running at one point, the name of the Natalie Cole album that had beaten them to Album of the Year at the Grammys, but they got cold feet on that idea, fearing that it would come across as sour grapes). R.E.M. completists should note that the Sinbad Motel stop can now be left off the pilgrimage tour, as the star has long since suffered hurricane damage.

The noblest of all R.E.M. traditions by this point was to dramatically downplay expectations ahead of an album's release, but this time around it would have been reasonable to assume that *Automatic* would follow a different trajectory to its predecessor. "I don't think it's going to sell like *Out of Time*," said Mike Mills. "It's smaller, personal and more intimate. It's not gonna have the splash like the last one did."

Peter Buck concurred. "If this one sells a mere two million – which is one fifth of what the last one sold – that's cool. I think nine million records is a fluke. I'd rather make a record that's a little bit difficult and have it successful on our terms. If we do a million in America and a million outside America, I'll still be happy."

The album went double platinum domestically within two months, had sold three million copies in the US within a year and went on to shift fifteen million more copies over the next three decades. It was held off the US number one spot by Garth Brooks' *The Chase*, but it made number two with ease, as well as hitting the top spot in the UK for the first time. It was, in other words, a resounding success, equalling the global sales figures of its predecessor. What it lacked by comparison to *Out of Time*, though, was a single that reached the heights of 'Losing My Religion', with 'Drive', 'Man on the Moon' and 'Everybody Hurts' all maxing out in the 25-30 range on the Hot 100. 'Everybody Hurts' fared better across the pond, landing at #7, just one shy of their career peak for 'Shiny Happy People'.

The only show to speak of that the band played to mark the release took place at the 40 Watt on 19 November and included the debut public performance of many of the new songs, as part of a series of Athens shows to benefit Greenpeace. The event was powered by a solar generator as part of the charity's Alternative NRG campaign, still considered a fringe interest in 1992, and sound-desk recordings from the night were later used as b-sides, while the whole show is now available as part of the extensive 25th anniversary re-issue release. Meanwhile, the rest of the world still had a while to wait for their chance to catch the band who were now legitimately in the conversation to be the biggest rock act in the world.

The one thing that could coax Stipe out of his seclusion was the feeling that he could in some way be useful in the downfall of President Bush. When the Democrats rolled into town at the University of Georgia in late October, Stipe was more than happy to be asked to introduce Senator Al Gore, the running mate of Bill Clinton. Even Stipe must have cringed, though, when Gore spoke the excruciatingly contrived words that George Bush was "out of time" and that Gore and Clinton were "automatic for the people". Two weeks later, Clinton won a resounding victory, the first Democratic president in the adult lives of R.E.M.

Clinton's music credentials were legendary, and he, Hillary and Chelsea made sure to make an appearance at the MTV 1993 Rock 'n' Roll Inaugural Ball at the Washington Convention Center on 20 January, the day of his swearing in. The roll call of invited guests was a glittering potpourri of the era, with En Vogue and Boyz II Men rubbing shoulders backstage with Don Henley and Soul Asylum. Stipe joined 10,000 Maniacs for a version of 'To Sir with Love' and 'Candy Everybody Wants', while Stipe and Mills joined forces with Adam Clayton and Larry Mullen Jr., the rhythm section of U2, for a version of the latter's 'One'. For one night only, they went by the name of Automatic Baby, marking the first collaboration between two modern rock juggernauts whose careers had developed along similar trajectories.

As 1993 progressed, the collaborations with eminent members of their new peer group continued. In March, a fleeting alt-rock supergroup was formed of Mike Mills on bass, Greg Dulli of The Afghan Whigs and Dave Pirner of Soul Asylum on vocals, Thurston Moore of Sonic Youth and Don Fleming of Gumball on guitar and Dave Grohl on drums. They went by the name of The Backbeat Band, and the music they recorded was used in the film *Backbeat*, a chronicle of The Beatles' early Hamburg years. In emulation of the Fab Four's early work, they committed to recording no more than two takes of every track, mostly the 50s rock'n'roll covers that made up those Hamburg setlists, and new wave veteran Don Was was enlisted to produce. Needless to say, Mills was thrilled to get his chance to touch the hem of Paul McCartney's garment.

By the time of the MTV Video Music Awards in the fall, R.E.M. agreed to perform two tracks live - 'Everybody Hurts' and 'Drive' - a big deal for them at this stage. The nerves were evidently real, as they even booked out two days in their home studio to prepare and rehearse, time that they also put to good use by having a whirl on some new material, including an embryonic 'E-Bow the Letter'. The show went steadily, and spirits were high enough that Stipe and Berry decided to join Pearl Jam on stage at the official afterparty.

It was a very rare live appearance for Stipe at the time, though. Indeed, his reluctance to put himself above the parapet had only served to fuel the flames on the scurrilous, bad faith rumour that he had contracted

AIDS Attempts to trace the allegation back to a source proved difficult, but it certainly coincided with the aftermath of the passing of Freddie Mercury. The Queen frontman had spent years rebuffing rumours about his own HIV positive status, until the very eve of his death when he issued a statement confirming that it was true. Less than a year later, *Automatic for the People* was on the shelves and yet this new, emerging rock star was conspicuously absent. It happened to do him no favours that his demeanour was skinny, verging on gaunt, and that there continued to be nods and winks about his sexuality, but no matter the extent of the band's vehement denials, the headlines continued.

The British press played more than their equal part in the shameful episode. Reference had been made to it in the *Melody Maker* review of the album, an irresponsible and shockingly unwise editorial decision that gave credence to something that was simply untrue. The British tabloids, already in a gutter-bound feeding frenzy at the time thanks to a circulation war, latched onto the rumours, sensing there was enough circumstantial evidence for mischievous editors to feign justification. Peter Buck, when asked, could not have stated the facts more plainly: "What can you say about it? We've all been tested. We have tons of insurance, millions of dollars' worth. Not that it's somebody's business, or that I care one way or the other what people think. But I know Michael passed the test just two months ago." Stipe, in his lone comment on the issue, was more succinct: "Bullshit".

It wasn't just Stipe that was in retreat from the public glare. Peter Buck had taken a literal escape from the hullabaloo by sojourning his way south of the border to Acapulco, Mexico, leaving behind the bit-projects that had kept him sane between stints with R.E.M., as well as the personal difficulties stemming from his broken-down marriage. The band were happy to let him have his space early in the new year, but by April 1993, it was decided that it would be best for the band to visit Buck down south for some clear-the-air conversations about where things currently stood.

Extravagant success was theirs, but without the regular churn of life on the road, they didn't really know how to be in a band. Very few people did – you can count on two hands the number of million-selling rock'n'roll groups that have been entirely tour-free for five years. In their early days, R.E.M. only bothered to record songs so that they could secure more live dates, but now the whole dynamic had been inverted.

Sure, the break had been necessary and the freedom was fun for a while, but were they now becoming directionless?

They had made two great records by slamming the door on outside influences, but the long-term repercussions of that strategy were now beginning to show. They seemed to be drifting apart, albeit with no great explosion, but rather just an imperceptible slide away from the tight unit that had survived those hard early years. Over four bumpy days, the four men spoke openly and practically about how they were going to move out of this fog, with Bill Berry being particularly eager to tour again. He argued that for a tour to work though, they would first need to create a harder-edged rock record, in order to bring the shows to life. The drummer even went as far as to offer an ultimatum that if they were not going to agree to get back on the road, then there may be no band left. Left to his own devices, Michael Stipe could happily have avoided dealing with the press and the public for another decade, but not at the risk of endangering the band's status, and by the end of the crisis talks a plan had been drafted for the next two years of R.E.M.

With all parties satisfied with the agreement, they went their separate ways again for the summer, now realising that it offered their last chance to enjoy their personal space for a while. Buck, along with his new partner Stephanie Dorgan, went on a six-week African safari, while Berry purchased a farm in rural Georgia, where he started to familiarise himself with a very different pace of life on a tractor.

The first pre-production sessions for *Monster*, the album Berry had envisaged as a steroid injection to their live setlists, took place in October in New Orleans. It was a time of invention and studio adventurism, with Mills embracing fuzzed-out bass tones and Peter Buck falling in love with the cock-rock overtones that wah-wah pedals and tremolo effects brought to his electric guitar. The ten session days were overseen by engineer Mark Howard,who then passed on the best bits to Litt, whom he had worked alongside on *Automatic,* ahead of the first set of formal recording sessions to come.

Those sessions would not arrive for some four months. River Phoenix, with whom Stipe had struck up a rare intimate friendship, passed away on 31 October as the result of an overdose after taking a speedball (a combination of heroin and cocaine) at Johnny Depp's Viper Room club in Hollywood. Stipe and Phoenix had been launched into the spotlight at roughly the same time, the latter through his role in *Stand by Me* in 1986, and they immediately recognised each other as kindred spirits. Phoenix might have been a decade younger than Stipe, but there were too many similarities for them not to connect: for one, Phoenix fronted his own band, the acclaimed Aleka's Attic, alongside his sister Rain, and even his most famous role came in a film named after a B-52's song, *My Own Private Idaho*. What's more, they were arguing for the same causes in public – environmental dangers, veganism, AIDS support – so their stars were destined to cross. Stipe found himself bereft at the loss, which he described as "the most shattering experience of my life". He was essentially unable to work for the rest of the year, and when they finally were able to reconvene in February, it was decided that *Monster* would be dedicated to Phoenix.

A ten-day period of tuning up the new material in Athens prepared them for the first serious attempt at recording the album in Atlanta in March 1994. Scott Litt joined midway through the stint, as did engineer Pat McCarthy, a Dubliner that Litt knew from his involvement with the band Counting Crows. By this point, the band were comfortable enough with the technical processes of a recording studio that they could operate without an outside producer, but Litt was always more than welcome when he could make it. He understood them as well as they understood themselves by now, after all. The band were very much back in their original formation for these songs, with the auxiliary instruments now almost entirely streamlined out of the process. Litt thought it would be wise to record the songs as live – standing on a makeshift stage, with a fully-operating PA system, as if playing before an audience. Buck had taken his tremolo obsession to the next level, drilling holes in gallon water bottles and putting microphones inside them, hoping to create the same kind of reverb that The Kinks' Dave Davies had done with his slashed amplifiers thirty years earlier.

Once again, recording was interrupted on several occasions. Mike Mills fell ill on two separate days, the second with appendicitis during the recording of 'What's the Frequency, Kenneth?', while Stipe had to leave when an abscessed tooth rendered him completely unable to sing. The singer also took a break to be with his sister Lynda, who had just given birth; likewise, Peter Buck became a father to twin girls Zoe and Zelda in April, so he took off to Seattle to be there too.

The most tragic of the interruptions, however, arrived on 5 April. With the pain of River Phoenix's death still raw, news of Kurt Cobain's passing came as another profound setback. Over the last three years, Cobain and Courtney Love had regularly spent late nights with either Stipe or Buck or both, shooting the breeze and sharing music. The Nirvana frontman, whose own reaction to sudden megastardom had been the album *In Utero*, a coarse, abrasive, jagged record designed to scare away half of his audience, was lost in admiration for R.E.M.'s coping mechanism. In reality, the two responses were similar, but in equal and opposite directions: R.E.M. had gone delicate and introspective to try to make sense of their new fame, lashing inwards where Nirvana had lashed out. Cobain had expressed his desire to take the acoustic route with future Nirvana records, inspired in no small part by the friendship between the two bands. But his heroin addiction was swamping his life, in such a way that even his wife and daughter could no longer pull him to the surface. Stipe recognised how severe Cobain's problems had become, and bought him a plane ticket to Atlanta so that he could join R.E.M. after Nirvana's return from a European tour, a trip that had included Cobain's first suicide attempt.

"I wanted to get him out of Seattle," Stipe later said. "That was my attempt to get him enough out of the head that he was in, that he wouldn't kill himself or hurt himself." As it was, Cobain never used the ticket. He checked himself out of rehab in Seattle and went missing; Love even telephoned Stephanie Dorgan, Buck's partner and Cobain and Love's next-door neighbour, asking her to check their house, but it was too late. *Automatic for the People* was the album found sitting in Cobain's CD player, the last record he ever heard. Over the following days, R.E.M. wrote the song 'Let Me In' in tribute to their fallen friend.

By the time R.E.M. arrived at Ocean Way Recording in Hollywood for the final leg of the *Monster* recording process in June, they were behind schedule for the first time in their careers. In addition to the interventions from real life, both welcome and unwelcome, the decision to record as though playing live had been one of the greatest factors in the slowing down of the process, with the 8-tracks they had used in Atlanta making life difficult at the mixing desk. Grieving and under time pressures, the band once again were starting to fracture. They could barely agree which songs deserved to make the cut and they were beginning to feel the heat from the record company.

The four members were all staying in separate parts of Los Angeles, rarely spending time together even in the studio, let alone away from it. A crisis meeting was called at Scott Litt's home studio, Louie's Clubhouse, in the San Fernando Valley. "We broke up," said Stipe about what went on that day. "We reached the point where none of us could speak to each other, and we were in a small room, and we just said, 'Fuck off', and that was it."

As dramatic as Stipe makes it sound, it was in hindsight nothing more than a necessary release of pressure. Mike Mills took it upon himself to act as peacemaker, the most eager of the quartet to patch things up and forge a new way forward. "We have to begin working as a unit again, which we haven't been doing very well lately," he argued. Broadly speaking, his intervention worked and the band agreed to a stricter schedule and to work rigidly and briskly to get the job over the line in time. The final mastered album was handed to Warners at the end of July, in time for the slated release date of 27 September.

Unlike *Out of Time* and *Automatic for the People*, the band's choice of lead single for *Monster* was the obvious contender, 'What's the Frequency, Kenneth?'. A punchy, impactful slice of muscular pop-rock, it is led by Buck's strange backwards guitar riff and Stipe's mysterious musings. His words are once again hard to decipher, but not in the mumbly way of the early records – it is like he has found a second, entirely separate mode of singing that also manages to completely obscure the lyrics. The vocals are not as high in the mix as on the previous two albums either, something Litt regretted almost as soon as the album was finished. He told the band for years after that he wished he had pushed the vocals higher and pulled the reins a little on the wild guitars, something he would eventually get his way with on the 25th anniversary re-release in 2019, which offered new mixes of all twelve tracks. In truth, though, it is the original album's strange balance that gives it its character and makes it a true outlier in the R.E.M. discography.

The phrase 'what's the frequency, Kenneth' had entered the peripheries of the zeitgeist in the late 1980s as a means of encapsulating a spirit of complete chaos and misunderstanding. It derived from a bizarre incident in 1986 when American news anchor Dan Rather was attacked while walking down Park Avenue in Manhattan by an assailant who kept shouting the phrase in question. The man was later confirmed to be William Tager, who believed that the television networks were beaming signals into his brain. He had mistaken Rather for Kenneth Burrows, the man Tager believed to be the primary instigator of the signals he was receiving. "It was the premier unsolved American surrealist act of the twentieth century," Stipe said about the story, although the song's lyrics make little direct reference to its details. Rather, Stipe has described the song as being "about an older guy who's trying to embrace and understand and latch onto a younger generation's energy and is completely horribly failing at it."

As a leadoff for the album, 'Kenneth' is an attention-catcher, not so much a return to driving rock music as a new diversion into virgin territory. Even at their most muscular, R.E.M.'s earlier records had never been so bare and direct in their raw, blood-dripping guitariness as this, and for *Monster* to follow it up directly with 'Crush with Eyeliner' only confirmed that this was an R.E.M. album like never before. 'Eyeliner' is a track teeming with the sleaze and swagger of 1970s glam rock, drawing from artists that R.E.M. had always loved but that had been more or less absent from the band's own DNA: New York Dolls, David Bowie, Iggy Pop, The Velvet Underground. Crunchy guitar chords, now entirely free from Buck's former arpeggio trademark, combine with a newly confrontational, brash demeanour from Stipe, pairing the band more closely with some of the emerging British acts of the day – Suede, Elastica, Pulp – than the vogue American bands that were still in thrall to grunge. There was a self-awareness to the original glam godfathers that chimed well with Stipe's instincts, and he now began to adopt characters that were deliberately and transparently at a distance from his authentic voice. As if to prove a point, 'Eyeliner' features backing vocal contributions from Sonic Youth's Thurston Moore; close your eyes and it could be Lou Reed himself.

'Star 69' is a shining example of the *Monster* aesthetic, its very title a play on the fiasco that surrounded 'Star Me Kitten', although directly referencing the number you dial in the US to trace the identity of your last caller. Mills describes the track as being driven by a "happy agitation", channelling some of the more glam-inspired punk bands like Buzzcocks and the Ramones. 'Bang and Blame' might be the summit of the form, with Buck's tremolo guitar now at a full-blown rage and Mills' fuzzed out bass never having sounded more suggestive. Stipe's effeminate, posturing vocals are joined by his sister Lynda's, as well as those of Rain Phoenix, to complete the album's most addictive and surly track.

'Strange Currencies', often compared to 'Everybody Hurts', largely thanks to its use of 6/4 time, slows the bluster, its guitars still screeching, but this time more for texture than propulsion. Stipe lifted elements of Michael Hutchence's style for his delivery on the verses, a singer Bono had introduced him to earlier in the decade and one that Stipe held in high regard. "He, more than any singer of our generation, could pick up a room in one hand and drop them on their head without thinking about it," Stipe said about the INXS frontman. 'Tongue', meanwhile, sees Stipe's voice hitting strained falsetto notes, more in homage to the likes of Smokey Robinson, while Mills taps into some Booker T. Jones energy on the organ.

The album's most intriguing, if not most successful, experiment is 'King of Comedy'. Written in the legendarily debauched Room 69 at Hollywood's Chateau Marmont during a blight of writer's block, Stipe started to reckon with the effects of fame and fortune. Given the adverse headlines he'd been faced with over the last two years, he opted to come out swinging, so to speak: "Make your money with a pretty face/Make it easy with product placement/Make it charged with controversy/I'm straight, I'm queer, I'm bi," he sings. Like the Martin Scorsese film of the same name, the song examines the corrosive effect of celebrity and the misguided ambitions of people that crave its status. It is perhaps appropriate, then, that Stipe's vocals are buried especially deep into the song's mix, while instrumental parts are warped and shimmered in a fashion similar to the sonic tampering that dominated U2's *Achtung Baby*, and in keeping with the rise of industrial music, another trend of the time. "We were all trying for something that we hadn't really done before: we were trying to make that song really mechanical and electronic and not human. We were trying to take the human element out of that song, and we might have succeeded a little too well," conceded Mills.

The other notable departure on *Monster* is 'Let Me In', the song written following Cobain's death. The mood turns inward, the ironic bravado dissolves away and while the muscle remains strong, the impetus runs dry. The song does not tackle grief in a literal sense, but its writing certainly helped to break grief's spell over the band, serving as a way for them to expunge their sorrow by writing a plea to their friend Kurt, albeit too late. "He gathered up his loved ones and he brought them all around to say goodbye, nice try," sings Stipe. The band knew they had done everything in their power to help Cobain, but it did nothing to ease the pain.

133

Monster returned R.E.M. to the top of the US album charts, and it was their first record to reach the top spot on both sides of the Atlantic. Early sales figures matched those of its two predecessors, even if its numbers did not continue to skyrocket over the years in quite the same way, but most of all it served its stated purpose of providing the band with ammunition for the mammoth tour that loomed ahead.

The first trial run for the new songs came a little sooner than that, though. Having gone down well the first time, it was no surprise that the band were invited back to play *Saturday Night Live* in late 1994, a show that would mark their first performance in public since their ascension to global domination. They played 'Kenneth', 'Bang and Blame' and 'I Don't Sleep, I Dream', the raunchier, slicker, more powerful version of R.E.M. now on full display, ready for its first close-up. It was certainly still them, but they had undeniably repositioned themselves musically in order to fit in with their new platform; 'Gardening at Night' this wasn't. In the five years since they last toured, an entire regeneration had taken place, a metamorphosis that had demanded that they leave behind their beautifully designed chrysalis and bloom into the fully mature, stadium-ready monster that their fanbase now required of them. They felt they were ready for it, but there was just no way to be sure.

'New Adventures in Hi-Fi'

R.E.M.'s first engagement of 1995 was not their return to the stage, but the wedding of Peter Buck and Stephanie Dorgan. Realising that the *Monster* tour was set to consume the next eleven months, the couple decided that their baby twins were ready for their own first world tour, and knowing that the opening fortnight of shows were scheduled for Australia and New Zealand at the height of the Southern Hemisphere summer, they took advantage of the timing and planned their nuptials as a way to launch a massive year in epic style. The band and extended crew – all 47 of them – were on hand at Cottesloe Beach near Perth on the Australian West coast for the affair, with tour support act Grant Lee Buffalo serving as the wedding band.

Spirits were still flying high when the opening show went down just 48 hours later at the Perth Entertainment Centre on 13 January. The band had felt the need to recruit two additional musicians in order to cover the increased musical range of the new material, as well as to provide enough horsepower to fill the arenas and stadiums that lay ahead of them. Buck had struck up a bond with Scott McCaughey back in Seattle, the two guitarists sharing a rare musical fanaticism. McCaughey was the frontman of The Young Fresh Fellows, a Seattle alt-rock group that pre-dated the city's recent meteoric rise, and his ability to flit between guitar, bass and keys made him an ideal fit to fill the auxiliary role that Peter Holsapple had vacated. McCaughey had also been the one to set Peter up with Stephanie, so he had that green tick by his name, too. The band earmarked Ken Stringfellow from The Posies as a possibility for the second opening, but his band were still active and he could not spare the time, so instead they opted for Nathan December, a fixture of the Los Angeles scene. As with Holsapple before them, it was set out contractually from the start that McCaughey and December were not members of R.E.M., nor would they have any claim to songwriting credit or any part to play in media interviews.

As the weeks and months rolled by, it became clear that R.E.M. were going to play fast and loose with their setlists, just as they always had done. Tracks from *Monster* dominated, with most shows including at least ten of the twelve songs, but that did not worry them. "We had enough hits that we could keep the more casual fans ameliorated or interested enough to stay for two hours," Stipe later reflected, "and then I think the real fans were excited to hear the new material." This was nothing new for R.E.M., and was one aspect of their 1980s incarnation that had not changed. The hits - 'Everybody Hurts', 'Losing My Religion', 'Man on the Moon', 'End of the World' - were also nearly ever-present, but the rest of the catalogue had to fight it out for inclusion. 'Fall on Me', 'So. Central Rain', 'Begin the Begin' and 'Finest Worksong' were examples of earlier songs that were played regularly, along with as many of the album tracks from *Out of Time* and *Automatic for the People*. Really, the task was trimming the sets down to *only* two hours, with essentially three entire new records' worth of material to play with. On top of that, the band still enjoyed throwing covers into every set, with Tori Amos' 'Winter', Jimmy Webb's 'Wichita Lineman' and Chris Isaak's 'Wicked Game' among the favourites this time around.

'Let Me In' turned out to provide one of the emotional highs most nights, a song that Stipe occasionally found hard to sing, heavy with the knowledge that the crossover between fans of R.E.M. and Nirvana was likely to be substantial. Peter Buck played a guitar on that song that Courtney Love had donated to the band after Kurt's death to add further gravity to the situation. At the other end of the scale, one of the unexpected hits of the shows was 'I Don't Sleep, I Dream', one of the first times that Stipe had been seen to play a guitar on stage. Admittedly, he was sticking to two chords and he tended to keep his amplifier turned down, but he was besotted with the image of the Presley uber-macho stance with a guitar strapped around his neck and he couldn't resist the chance to project some of that same alpha male sexuality, even if just for one song per night.

Stipe had now shaved his head and he regularly took to the stage with face paint, displaying a new brashness in an effort to fill the huge spaces that he as frontman was now expected to fill. This was the most confident Michael Stipe to date, and it was no coincidence that it came at the same time that he had taken steps to publicly embrace his true self for the first time. Having not done media for a few years, the *Monster* publicity tour had seen him address rumours about his sexuality for the first time. He gave interviews where he said that "labels are for canned food" and "I think a lot of people just assume that I'm queer and that's fine. I've never been ashamed of anything and I've never denied anything." He stopped short of a declarative statement, but he was no longer avoiding the subject, and even in the mid-1990s, that was a mildly radical act for somebody so public.

One of the benefits of success was that R.E.M. were able to amass a list of support acts that must rank as among the most impressive of any tour in history: Radiohead, Sonic Youth, PJ Harvey, Blur, Oasis, Crowded House, The Cranberries and Faith No More are just some of the acts that opened for them at various points during 1995, most of them joining for entire legs of the journey. They were also able to finally make a connection with Patti Smith, who joined R.E.M. on stage at three different shows during the summer, adding vocals to their version of her song 'Dancing Barefoot' and lending her weight to renditions of 'Let Me In'. Stipe, over the moon to be connected to the woman that had shifted his worldview in 1975, would gladly return the favour the following summer, joining Patti on stage at four of her own shows in Europe, singing 'Horses' and 'Because the Night' with her, no less.

Early reviews for the tour were broadly positive, if not exactly effusive with praise. In several cases, they were written from the perspective of long-term fans that could not help but view this dramatic sizing up of the R.E.M. machine as slightly unnatural and not in keeping with their vaunted authenticity. The band had inevitably changed since 1989, it was true, and the scale of production had certainly rocketed, but after having taken liberties by not touring at all for six years, these were the unavoidable consequences. Stipe admitted in the *Rough Cut* tour film that was released the following year that they knew this was almost certainly going to be the peak of their commercial success and if they weren't prepared to make the moves now to translate that success into something tangible, then it may well never happen. Besides, this was the reality of how many people wanted to see an R.E.M. show now. Their success had far outstripped their ability to continue playing the sorts of sweaty, small shows that the reviewers reminisced over. Life was so different now that Peter Buck took the drastic decision not to drink for the duration of the tour, a wise, if difficult, choice, given that his new family were on the ride with him.

They might have been getting smarter with their lifestyle choices, but the tour was to be defined by a series of health-related crises that were out of their control. On 1 March in Lausanne, Switzerland, the band were in the groove, dozens of shows deep and fully comfortable with their playing, when Peter Buck and Mike Mills noticed that their performance of 'Tongue' was falling behind time. They each looked over to the drumkit to find Bill Berry wincing in obvious pain. 'Tongue' had tended to be a set highlight, with a giant disco ball lowering over the crowd to fit the song's mood, but there was nothing to celebrate about what was happening onstage. Berry stood and staggered over to Buck, complaining of a serious headache, and then withdrew, collapsing backstage. The group, slightly in shock, convened and decided to continue the show, with Joey Peters from Grant Lee Buffalo filling in on drums, while Berry was treated by the medical staff on hand. Berry had been plagued by migraines in the past and assumed it was nothing more than a severe case, but when he got to his bed, he was unable to sleep and concern turned to panic.

He was taken to hospital in the dark of night, where a scan found two aneurysms on his brain, one of them already ruptured. If the rupture had led to internal bleeding, Berry's survival chances would have been bleak, but they were able to catch the emergency in time and, by stroke of luck, Lausanne was at the forefront of medical development. He was immediately taken into surgery. "If it had been in any number of cities we'd just been in, Bill would have died," Peter Buck later said. As it was, he was left unable to move for a day or two after surgery, but after three weeks he was fit enough to be discharged and shortly thereafter, the band flew back to the United States.

A total of 44 gigs had to be cancelled as a result. The band were severely shaken, a terrifying brush with death from within their ranks at a time that had been intended to be a creative and physical high. By the middle of May, they were able to get back together to rehearse for the first show back in Mountain View, California, the tour now re-dubbed the Aneurysm 95 Tour. Just six weeks later, they found themselves back in Switzerland and the doctors who saved Berry's life were invited backstage, where Stipe gave a speech thanking them.

Three days later, however, they were cancelling shows again. This time, Mike Mills was the patient, requiring abdominal surgery to remove an intestinal adhesion that had been bothering him for weeks but which had gone undiagnosed. It turned out to be due to a buildup of scar tissue from the appendectomy that he had had during the *Monster* sessions, and while the pain escalated to the point that emergency surgery was once again required, it only saw the band out of action for ten days. In August, during a scheduled off-period, Stipe also took ill, requiring a hernia operation on his diaphragm. This is the only one of the three surgeries that it can be argued stemmed from the stresses and strains of life on the road, seeing as a hernia in one's diaphragm could well be related to singing at the top of one's vocal range for two hours every night. Otherwise, the circumstances of these medical emergencies were nothing but a distressing freak of timing.

One reason that the unplanned pauses were frustrating was that they interrupted one of the most important parts of their plan for the year. As Buck said in *Rough Cut*, "We're going to tour and ideally record a live record of all new songs. I would love it if next September, we're touring America and we have ten new songs in the set that no-one's heard." The intention was that during the down periods between shows, they would be writing and developing new material that they could in turn rehearse during soundchecks and then slowly incorporate into the shows. If it was going well, the soundchecks could then be recorded and used as demos for the new album, or, in the best-case scenario, the soundcheck performances could be used as the actual master recordings for the album. Despite the interruptions, this was in fact happening: by August, there were new songs popping up in sets by the names of 'Undertow', 'Bittersweet Me', 'Binky the Doormat' and 'The Wake-Up Bomb', the last of which they chose to play to the world at the MTV Video Music Awards in September.

They ended the year with more than enough new songs to fill album number ten, most of them already set to tape from various arena stages around the country. They came off the end of the tour energised and felt it best to head straight into the studio while the material was still fresh. After a few weeks at John Keane's in Athens, they set up at Bad Animals Studios in Seattle for the spring with Scott Litt. What they found when they listened back to the tapes was almost exactly what they had hoped it would be.

The songs sounded like they had been written on the road. There was a sprawling, electric, adrenaline-fuelled energy to many of them, the sound of a band that was in that frazzled state somewhere between mania and exhaustion. The material had emerged from a natural habitat of constant travelling and the adulation of screaming crowds, so fast and so numb indeed. In many ways, these were the songs that *Monster* begat: where that album had been made in prolonged solitude, imagining the conditions of a major tour, these songs were the actual real-life results of that imagination. The band cited Neil Young's *Time Fades Away* as an example of the concept they were aiming for, and as the studio sessions continued, they knew they were getting to where they wanted to go.

Many of the songs only needed a few touches and overdubs in Seattle, while some were augmented with extra instrumentation. The studio time went smoothly and easily, although for the first time there was an air of unease between the band and Scott Litt. Although both parties have been tight-lipped about the exact details, it has been said that the band felt that Litt's concentration was no longer fixed on helping the band artistically, but rather on his own burgeoning career as a label owner with his new company Outpost. Buck in particular recalls a meeting that he flew in from Hawaii for, only for Litt to turn up late and to have forgotten to bring the tapes that the band were meeting to work on. It would be the last time R.E.M. and Scott Litt worked together.

The album, *New Adventures in Hi-Fi*, is their longest and baggiest record, clocking in at 65 minutes and featuring 14 tracks. It is also one of their easiest albums to like and has been named by both Michael Stipe and Mike Mills as in their top two or three favourites.

Opener 'How the West Was Won and Where It Got Us', the only track that was entirely conceived and recorded in the Seattle studio, is a strange, innovative track that once again finds R.E.M. intentionally shocking listeners who first turn on their new album. The song takes its sweet time, with Bill Berry playing what the liner notes credit as an 'Ennio whistle', a nod to the Morricone-penned spaghetti Western sounds that they were aiming for. The track sets up the imagery of the album – that itinerant, freewheeling, open-road wanderer, that romanticism of the Old West, that life lived off-script. A crazed, out-of-control piano break crackles at the centre of the song, giving a sense of a band that has slightly lost their grasp of their sanity - and likes it.

From there, we launch into 'The Wake-Up Bomb', a total about turn. The lyrics make literal the exuberant glam rock influences from *Monster* as Stipe sings, "Get drunk and sing along to Queen/Practice my T. Rex moves and make the scene". It is at least the match of 'Crush with Eyeliner' or 'Bang and Blame', a rousing, balls-out, not-to-be-over-analysed slice of fun that clearly demonstrates R.E.M. were having a blast throughout much of the *Monster* tour.

Just as listeners are thinking that they've identified the two poles that *New Adventures* exists between, though, the band throw out a third entirely distinct flavour. 'New Test Leper' returns them to the *Out of Time* mood with an acoustically strummed, contemplative track inspired by a chat show that Stipe had recently watched. Exactly who Stipe had observed being treated with dismissive judgement by the show's audience and perhaps even the host is unclear, but it left its mark on him. "Judge not lest ye be judged/What a beautiful refrain/The studio audience disagrees/Have his lambs all gone astray," he sings, before concluding, "What a sad parade". The song is about the treatment of marginalised groups in society, invoking the story of *The Elephant Man* as well as the teachings of Jesus to depict how far we are falling short in our collective tolerance. One can perhaps assume that the full title would read 'New Testament Leper'.

Religion is invoked on 'Undertow' too, but in much more suspicious, rebellious tones, amid a swampy aesthetic of thick walls of noise and Jonny Greenwood-like stabs of raw, serrated electric guitar. Stipe sings that he's drowning and it sure does sound like it. 'Departure' captures the on-the-road spirit of the album, a hot rush of a track whose very lyrics are about the breakneck, disorienting speed of their constant travel, with different vistas and tableaus flying past their bus windows every day, and with landscapes, languages and cultures changing too fast for the band to keep track of.

'Leave' opens gently, if ominously, with Berry's acoustic guitar and McCaughey's synthesiser, but those soon give way to a siren-like, incessant synth line that refuses to recede. The track is alarming in more than just that sense, too, with Stipe singing about being spiritually lost and seemingly without much sense of how to resolve it. Like 'How the West Was Won', 'Leave' offers something brand new from R.E.M., a song that suggests a future that they never quite reached, one where they expanded the form further outwards. They may still be largely tied to familiar song structures, but they're showing new ways of arranging the furniture and one of the greatest joys of listening to *New Adventures in Hi-Fi* is hearing the literal spirit of its title play out.

The album's two most enduring tracks are 'E-Bow the Letter' and 'Electrolite'. The former continues in the R.E.M. tradition of obtuse lead single choices (it scraped inside the top 50 in the US, but became their biggest UK hit to date, beating 'Shiny Happy People' by two places), with the first part of its title referring to the field-generating device that Peter Buck used on his guitar strings to elicit tones similar to those of a bow on violin strings, and the second part of the title referring to the source of the lyrics. The words are lifted, supposedly almost verbatim, from an unsent letter Stipe had written to River Phoenix before his death, imploring him to find a way out of his rapidly spiralling cycle of drug dependency. The letter/song speaks of the blurring of the lines between fame and success and the challenges and potential pitfalls faced by a young star with a fawning fanbase. It is one of the most mysterious and haunting tracks the band ever recorded, richly enhanced by the deep, spectral guest vocals of Patti Smith, who Stipe was finally able to coax into a recording studio after years of trying.

'Electrolite', on the other hand, is one of the lightest, breeziest songs ever included on an R.E.M. album. Stipe was inspired to write it after a 1994 earthquake that rocked the San Fernando Valley and damaged his home there, and it is his straight-ahead love letter to Hollywood and the wonder of standing at the top of the valley on Mulholland Drive, looking down on the City of Angels and imagining yourself as the next in the line of Martin Sheen, Steve McQueen and Jimmy Dean. There are striking similarities here to the piano part in 'Nightswimming', but as a way to round out the album, it is a pure charmer. Thom Yorke, a new friend of R.E.M. after sharing a leg of the *Monster* tour with them, has named it as his favourite R.E.M. song and Radiohead have even been known to include it as an extended intro to some performances of their song 'Everything in Its Right Place'.

With the album complete, the band were forced to finally focus on something that had been looming in the bigger picture for a while. *New Adventures* was to be the fifth album of the five-album deal that R.E.M. had signed with Warner Bros in 1988; after its release, they would be free agents once again. In the years since the contract had been signed, Warners had endured an incredibly turbulent time. Their parent company Warner Communications had been bought out by the media empire Time, Inc. in 1990, creating the even more powerful conglomerate Time Warner in the process. The old guard of top-ranking music executives – Ahmet Ertegun, the former Led Zeppelin mentor and chief executive of Atlantic Records, and Mo Ostin, the Warners CEO with whom R.E.M. had a great relationship – were being forced out. The deep ties that these labels had with the creative histories of their past were being slashed and many artists in their employ were furious about it, R.E.M. chief among them. Just as they had been in 1988, the band suddenly found themselves in an incredibly powerful negotiating position. And yet, before they could get there, there was an even more pressing legal concern demanding their attention.

The R.E.M. unit had remained remarkably stable from the moment that it was first formed. The four band members, plus manager Jefferson Holt and legal counsel Bertis Downs, had always appeared to move in total lockstep, but in May 1996, that suddenly stopped. The band made an announcement that they had terminated their deal with Holt and that they would no longer be working with him. For those following the band closely, it was a major surprise. Holt had risen to such a privileged and visible position as the band's manager, present at nearly every show and recording session for years and credited publicly by the band whenever possible. His working reputation within the industry was considered to be among the best of any artist manager. The mystery of the separation was clarified somewhat by an article in the *Los Angeles Times* on 21 June 1996 by Chuck Philips, which detailed allegations made by a member of staff from the band's home office in Athens who accused Holt of sexual harassment. The band, once they had received the news of these allegations earlier in the year, had their team conduct an investigation into the matter and although both R.E.M. and Holt agreed that the terms of their termination would remain confidential, the fact that such drastic action was taken so swiftly and unceremoniously tells its own story. Bertis Downs assumed management of the band from that point forward and R.E.M. never spoke about Jefferson Holt again.

With one seismic career decision made, R.E.M. were immediately facing another. Mo Ostin and his partner Lenny Waronker, having been forced out of Time Warner, were swiftly hired by DreamWorks SKG – a seemingly artist-friendly new initiative launched by Steven Spielberg, film producer Jeffrey Katzenberg and music impresario David Geffen – to lead their music department. If trust in executive level decisions had been the key factor in R.E.M.'s choice, DreamWorks would have been difficult to turn down.

But there was no getting away from the fact that the infrastructure at Warners had become so familiar to the R.E.M. machine and the working relationships that had been established at every level were so beneficial to all parties that the allure of staying with the same company was strong. What's more, Warners had delivered in spades on the international success that they had originally promised, with the band now pound-for-pound more successful in the UK than they were in the US and with stadium shows easily selling out in four different continents. They had proven to be trustworthy in their commitment to allowing the band all of the artistic freedom that they craved too, accepting their oddball choices for lead singles without question and never offering any more pushback on their idiosyncrasies than I.R.S. had done.

Warners were desperate to re-sign them. All of the major corporate upheaval had produced some substantial negative press and they needed to show the world that they were able to hold on to one of their most prized assets. They made a bold offer, with a key clause that was similar to the one that Jay Boberg and Miles Copeland had hoped would keep the band at I.R.S. in 1988 – an increase on royalties on the back catalogue. R.E.M. may have quietly suspected that *New Adventures* was not about to be as much of a megahit as the last three albums (admittedly, they thought this every time), and they had seriously good reason to believe that their commercial success had already reached a peak that was never to be replicated, so this was now an incredibly enticing offer. If they were to receive higher profits on future sales and royalties relating to the music on *Out of Time* and *Automatic for the People* than they were already getting, that was big.

The announcement was made in August 1996 that Time Warner had indeed secured R.E.M. for another five albums. The deal was widely reported to be worth $80 million, which is believed to have been the most expensive recording contract in history at that point. Naturally, the band were coy about the financial details, but Peter Buck did once concede that he did believe it to have been the biggest contract ever signed by a recording act. Warners would have calculated that $80 million was a number they could afford: as Tony Fletcher reported in *Perfect Circle*, the first four R.E.M. albums on Warners had brought in sales income of approximately $300 million against only $10 million in combined advances, so the band were making the company serious money. It is rumoured that $20 million of the new deal related to the back catalogue royalties, so in essence Warners were handing R.E.M. $20 million as a back-dated royalty cheque. Plus, they would be receiving $10 million advances for each of their next five albums, on top of the money they were making from the fact that they still owned their own publishing.

It was an eye-watering deal. As a consequence, the band found themselves at the centre of a storm of negative publicity for the first time. R.E.M., the outsiders that had held themselves and others to the highest of moral and ethical standards, were now being attacked for their greed and corporate calculation. The biggest payday ever received by a recording artist? How could that possibly align with their philanthropic, left-wing, anti-imperialist mindset? What artistic purity is it possible to claim when you are taking that much money from one of the largest and most powerful media companies on the planet?

It must be said that the band were in such a strong position in 1996 partly through a fortunate set of circumstances that were well beyond their control. Just as they had done in 1988, the cards had fallen their way and the timing was such that they were able to cash out at the top end of what would have been considered feasible. On the other hand, they had earned this money by proving to the company that they were capable of selling an average of ten million records every two years, a fact that earned Time Warner a lot more than they were paying R.E.M. Were Warners taking a gamble on how the next five albums were going to perform? Absolutely. And with public perception now altered, were R.E.M. now under immense pressure to produce something to justify their new richest-band-in-the-world status? You bet they were.

'Up'

For the first time in four years, R.E.M. were back at the drawing board. The start of 1997 marked the beginning of a new album cycle, but they had no material. They convened at Peter Buck's latest new property, this time in Hawaii, where he showed the rest of the band the fruits of his labour from the few months since they had last been together.

Buck and Scott McCaughey had been tinkering with an assortment of drum machines and analogue synthesisers in their home studio, creating rudimentary backing tracks, over which they would later improvise melodies and guitar parts. He sheepishly played a few examples of the half-finished demos to his bandmates, figuring the new approach could open some new pathways for the band's creativity, and even a possible reinvention of the R.E.M. sound. Even he wasn't sure the ideas were worth the time of day – was this even R.E.M. if he'd been working on the tracks by himself for so long? Well, it was, because when the other three quarters of the band heard them, they were excited.

Michael Stipe's imagination was particularly sparked, recognising that the sparseness of the arrangements could create the space for him to delve a little deeper into his subconscious hinterland. He felt that his best writing, whether it was 'E-Bow the Letter', 'Undertow' or 'Country Feedback', had come when he was able to tap into liminal, non-literal language, so he felt a shift away from the familiar, finite world of organic instrumentation might lead to more such inspiration. Mike Mills was always interested in the challenge of new musical frontiers, so he was quick to sign up too. Bill Berry, the rest of the band noticed, was a little more apathetic.

They spent a pleasant few days exploring the possibilities a little further, before going their separate ways again for the spring. Buck was still spending most of his time in Seattle, where he would play gigs here and there, either as part of The Minus 5, with McCaughey, or in Tuatara, an instrumental group that featured, among others, the drummer Barrett Martin from Screaming Trees and bassist Justin Harwood from The Chills. The two bands greatly overlapped and a rolling revue by the name of The Magnificent Seven vs. The United States that included the extended gang as well as American Music Club singer Mark Eitzel would end up touring the country over a four-month period leading into the summer.

Over the same period, Stipe began to try his hand at film production. He had been taken by a script by Todd Haynes, the director of *Safe* and *Superstar: The Karen Carpenter Story*, and decided that he and his company Single Cell Pictures would try to get it into the production stage. The film was called *Velvet Goldmine*, named after an obscure Bowie song, and it was a glorification of the same wild, androgynous extravagance of 1970s glam culture that R.E.M. had recently been exploring themselves. Stipe took the executive producer role seriously, for once revelling in responsibilities that were much closer to business than to creativity; he would deal with financiers and studios directly, driven by his passion for the subject matter and the satisfaction of getting something of value through a system that only cared about the bottom line.

Stipe tasked himself with sourcing the right musicians to fill both the on- and off-screen roles, scouting the band Placebo in London and identifying them as the closest incarnation of the Iggy Pop/Lou Reed/ New York Dolls aesthetic as he was going to find. Jonathan Rhys Meyers would play the role that was styled after Bowie, while Ewan McGregor took on the Iggy-inspired part. Stipe assembled two bands to come up with the music: The Venus in Furs, comprised of Radiohead's Thom Yorke and Jonny Greenwood, Roxy Music's Andy McKay and Suede's Bernard Butler, dealt with the British material, while the Wylde Ratttz, made up of Sonic Youth's Thurston Moore, Minutemen's Mike Watt and The Stooges' Ron Asheton, produced the New York-inspired music. The film is as mystifying and nonsensical as it is dazzling and ambitious and it would go on to be nominated for the Palme d'Or at the 1998 Cannes Film Festival.

After the extended break, it was time to knuckle down and get to work on the new record and a month of sessions were booked out at West Clayton Street Studios in Athens. The night before the first day, Mike Mills' home phone rang at an unusually late hour; he answered, to be met with the voice of his old Macon friend, Bill Berry. The news he heard floored him.

Mills, Berry and Stipe had all noticed a difference in Berry since the aneurysm. During the *New Adventures in Hi-Fi* sessions, he had seemed distant, dispassionate, anhedonic. They knew that his marriage with Mari was on the rocks, although they may not have realised that divorce proceedings were already progressing. There was a sense too that he had taken the departure of Jefferson Holt far worse than the rest of the band had done. When they were in Hawaii, Berry would take himself off and spend long stretches of time alone. He was clearly wrestling with major, personal emotional conflict. On that first band meeting on the morning of 9 October 1997, Berry took his three bandmates into a quiet room and told them that he had decided to leave the band.

It was a calm, level-headed Berry that spoke with them. He explained with care that if a consequence of his decision would be that the band would come to an end, then he would not do it, but that he had come to a settled conclusion that this was his preference. His farm in Watkinsville had become something he was increasingly passionate about, his health scare on the last tour had forced him to make some major adjustments to the way that he viewed his life, his bank account was in a healthier condition than he'd ever imagined it would be and the breakdown in his marriage had caused him to seek a new start in the professional part of his life.

Needless to say, the band were shocked. Even Mills, who had had half a day to wrap his head around the news, was struggling to process it. They tried everything they could to make him reconsider, offering to let him record his percussion parts at home and to let him sit out the world tours, but they didn't even get close. To get to seventeen years without a change in a band's lineup is virtually unheard of and now, very suddenly, they were learning why.

The sessions were cancelled. The band had repeatedly stated in the press, as recently as 1995, that they could never carry on if one member left, but now here they were, loving being in R.E.M., proud of their recent work, motivated by the new material - and about to lose one of their founding members. They were trapped inside a torture device. The one thing they knew was that they wanted to control the narrative of how this news would reach the outside world, so a press release was drafted and a series of magazine, newspaper and television interviews were arranged for a date that all four would attend at the end of the month.

Above all, they wanted to display that this was not a sham statement where they were pretending to separate with mutual consent. They wanted to prove that what were telling their fans was the full story: one member of the band had taken an honest decision that he wanted to leave and the other three had the grace to sign off on it. As Berry himself said that day, "I'm just not as enthusiastic as I have been in the past about doing this anymore. I have the best job in the world, but I'm kind of ready to sit back and reflect and maybe not be a pop star anymore." He would also concede to a local Athens newspaper that, "I'd be lying if I said my brain surgery two or three years ago didn't have a little to do with it."

Over three months passed before the remaining R.E.M. trio could get to the stage where they were comfortable with moving on. "For me, Mike and Peter," said Stipe, "as R.E.M., are we still R.E.M.? I guess a three-legged dog is still a dog. It just has to learn to run differently." And with that mindset, a two-month spell was booked at San Francisco's Toast Studio, where they set about recording the album that became *Up*. Pat McCarthy stepped into Scott Litt's shoes, with Radiohead producer Nigel Godrich hired as assistant producer. Barrett Martin, with whom Buck had spent a third of 1997 on the road, was brought in as the drummer for the sessions.

In some senses, the timing of losing their drummer had not been as damaging for them as it could have been. After all, they had already familiarised themselves with the idea of electronic and synthetic percussion, so pushing themselves a little further down that path wasn't too great a risk. More pressing to them was how their creative stimulus had changed. Buck had turned 40 since their last album and Mills and Stipe were not far behind. The whole world knew about their financial situation too, so they couldn't pretend to share the everyday material struggles of their average listener anymore either. And they had still never really had the chance before now to reckon with the terrifying levels of success that were now theirs. They knew they didn't want to write for any particular audience other than themselves, but they were nevertheless aware that they were now being judged by their success at least as much as by their art.

There were now essentially two brands of R.E.M. fans: on the one hand, you had the survivors from the early years, and their younger equivalents, who were the die-hards that appreciated them for who they were and would be ready for whatever artistic about turns they might choose to make, and on the other, there were the more casual fans that they had amassed in the early 1990s, and it was this latter group that they were now very much in danger of losing. It's hard enough to keep most people interested in rock music past a certain point in their lives – usually when the sudden reality of mortgages and marriages rear their head – and while R.E.M. were hardly shining examples of this themselves, they were well aware that they were outliers. Most people past that point tend to turn to music, if they still do at all, as a comfort blanket or a hit of nostalgia, a reminder of younger, more carefree times. Getting them to invest in the continued development of their favourite bands is a challenge; sure, they might still catch them when they pass through town, if the babysitter is free, but that's often about it.

It's why you can barely find a band that stays close to the commercial centre of new music for more than a decade or so. Rare individual popstars are able to evolve and reinvent themselves, but they do it by appealing to new generations as they show up, which is far more difficult for guitar bands. For the few successful bands that don't split up, the options are to resort to the legends circuit and cash out in that stale and ever-decreasing cycle or to retreat into your own nature and find a creative niche that will appeal to a core fanbase. But for an $80 million band, neither of these options seemed to cut it. The Rolling Stones and The Who, dinosaurs before R.E.M. even formed, had essentially stopped being a creative force at around the age that R.E.M. now were, choosing to tour their first two decades of material until they were no longer capable of doing so. There ended the list of bands R.E.M. could look to for examples of where to go next. U2 and Metallica were contemporaries in similar positions. The long-term plight of the stadium-filling band that were expected to stay creative and relevant was a story that R.E.M. themselves were now writing.

Feeling the burden of these pressures, the recording of *Up* was a long, drawn-out affair. They went back to John Keane's studio in Athens with the songs far from complete. Stipe was struggling with his worst case of writer's block to date and all that did was leave Buck, Mills and McCarthy with enough time to mess around with the recordings so much that they started to dislike them. The remixes of the remixes were starting to make the songs sound artificial to their ears. The impact of Berry's departure was now being felt in earnest, a slow-releasing toxin that was spreading to every part of the R.E.M. organism. Being so close to home was only compounding the problem. Stipe said that the "darker times were darker than ever" during those months and that he felt at times they were making "R.E.M.'s last will and testament".

A crisis meeting was called in Idaho, attended by the trio and Bertis Downs, with Pat McCarthy joining them on the last day. Mills described the mood: "The essential thing is that you've got to realise that the band is more important than your hurt feelings. And if it comes to the point where the band is not more important than those particular personal feelings, then maybe it is time to move on." As it would transpire, these clear-the-air talks were ultimately the booster they needed, a more personally confessional coming together than any of the previous ones that had happened during other periods of internal crisis. They emerged from them stronger and were thus able to power through the final stages of getting the album finished.

Up is an oddly misshapen album, a product of its turbulent provenance. Its strongest calling card is Michael Stipe's evolution into an elite, poetic people-watcher, with a series of beautifully observed character studies, such as the middle-aged teacher with a drinking habit and a backlog of regret in 'Sad Professor' or the signee to a twelve-step program that has seen the process ultimately backfire, only to create a character incapable of remorse in 'The Apologist'. We are now a long way from there being any questions of autobiography in Stipe's creation of these protagonists: these are American archetypes that he has hewn from his experiences on this Earth and they are a joy to behold.

'Airportman' is another, creating a meditative portrait of a jetsetting businessman, but it is also the latest deliberate curveball to open an R.E.M. album. Immediately, its intro beckons us into a synthetic world, its electronic drumbeat and thinner range of frequencies mingling with textured sheens of guitar tones, while Stipe's voice is almost unrecongisable in its hushed restraint. The much-discussed use of electronica on *Up* is actually largely deployed to add atmospheric depth, although in the rare moments that it takes a tighter grip, as on 'Hope', it does seem that the supposed limitlessness of the possibilities that the technology allows for has been lost on the band. That track's blindingly obvious similarity to Leonard Cohen's 'Suzanne' led to Cohen being given an official songwriting credit, although it is said that the band only noticed this after they had recorded it, which seems hard to believe.

'Lotus' is the one hangover from the mood of the last two albums, a guitar pop song that plods along and is a little on the predictable side. It marks Stipe's second reference to the lotus-eaters in as many albums (after 'Be Mine'), the people of Greek myth who become hooked on the plant's narcotic powers and choose to live a simple existence away from the real-life stresses of the rest of the world. It may reflect a longing inside Stipe for the life that he might have led had R.E.M. not grown so out of control. Along with tracks like 'Walk Unafraid' and 'You're in the Air', it is an example of the band's transition into a musical middle class, where they no longer really ruffle feathers or challenge the status quo, but at their best can still express beautiful and profound observations with a poetic sweep that distinguished them from the mediocrity that surrounded them in the pop charts and radio playlists.

The only two tracks on *Up* that clock in at under four minutes are the only two to have a legacy beyond the album's existence, which may be no coincidence. 'At My Most Beautiful' has been described as Stipe's most direct love song, a safe bet seeing as it is impossible to imagine there ever having been a more unswerving, unabashed love song written in all human history. There is a clear Beach Boys influence on the harmonies, the melodic nakedness of the song's composition and its sincerity - it's a true heart-warmer. 'Daysleeper', meanwhile, is one of the band's strongest singles, a song that will pang with anyone who has ever been stuck in a going-nowhere, thankless and spiritually unfulfilling job. Here, we get the finest character study of all, a worker stuck in the receiving department of some corporate office every 3am, his nights coloured headache grey and his circadian rhythms a distant memory. It deserved better than to stall at #57 on the Billboard Hot 100 as the album's lead single; in the UK, it fared much better, reaching #6, further underscoring how much more the band's commercial success had endured there than at home.

Up's own chart trajectory marked a dramatic dropoff. It debuted at a respectable #3 in the US, but it was out of the top ten as soon as week two; even by the following summer, it hadn't reached one million domestic sales. The band's constant predictions that their success was about to plummet had finally borne fruit. Not to say that it was a calamity – most bands can only dream of releasing one album as lucrative as *Up* – but this was the game R.E.M. were being forced to play now. Warners may not have said anything to them, but the label certainly now had material evidence to support their concerns that their gamble had been overly ambitious.

The band first emerged back into the public eye in the summer of 1998 so that they could continue to support the cause of Tibetan freedom, a subject that had gained huge traction within the music community over the previous decade. An all-star cast massed at the Robert F. Kennedy Memorial Stadium in Washington, D.C. that June in order to play before a crowd of over 65,000. R.E.M. took their place amid a lineup that also included Red Hot Chili Peppers, Beck, Radiohead, Tracy Chapman, Dave Matthews Band, Pearl Jam and Beastie Boys, although like most on the bill, they had to wait an extra 24 hours to take the stage as a major lightning strike derailed the original day's action, injuring eleven people. Their eventual set – eight tracks including 'Be Mine' and 'E-Bow the Letter' with vocals from Thom Yorke – was their first ever public performance without Bill Berry, with both Barrett Martin and Joey Waronker drafted in to help replace him. Waronker, as the son of former Warners president Lenny, was already acquainted with R.E.M. and was part of Beck's touring band, so his credentials were impeccable. The overall performance that day, however, was not as strong as the band had hoped, and would have done little to settle their existential fears about the long-term health of R.E.M.

To further compound things, once *Up* was released, they were signed up for by far their most extensive media tour. They appeared on every major television outlet that would have them, from David Letterman, Jay Leno and Jon Stewart to a feature length MTV special and an episode of *VH1 Storytellers*. It extended to Europe too, where they did their first ever session for John Peel, made appearances on *Top of the Pops* and *TFI Friday* and had the rare distinction of having a full episode of *Later...with Jools Holland* devoted to them (even more rarely, they played a live version of 'Perfect Circle'). As if to prove how far their fame had reached, they concluded with a special guest appearance on *Sesame Street*, where they played a reworked version of 'Shiny Happy People' named 'Furry Happy Monsters', with the band bobbing along with some of their most brightly-coloured, enthusiastic fans to date.

They were playing these shows as a six-piece, with McCaughey, Waronker and Ken Stringfellow completing the line-up, and by the time they were through, they felt confident enough to go back on their decision not to play live until after the next album, and a whirlwind 50-show tour was set up for North America and Europe. They seemed at ease, delving into parts of the back catalogue that hadn't been aired for some time; suddenly, it was not unusual to hear 'Driver 8', 'Gardening at Night' or 'Pretty Persuasion' at an R.E.M. show again. The European leg included some of the continent's elite festivals, including Roskilde, Rock Werchter and a show headlining Glastonbury's Pyramid Stage in front of nearly 100,000 people, easily their biggest crowd ever. Stipe paused the show to introduce a rendition of 'Sweetness Follows' that he dedicated to Jean Eavis, the wife of festival founder Michael who had died in the weeks before the show.

The success of the shows in the summer of 1999 were a massive reassurance to the band. They felt loved again and remembered the joys of the road. It felt like they had re-connected to the outside world too, so much so that when they got a business call from Danny DeVito in the same year, it didn't even seem that weird. DeVito told them he was producing a film about the life of Andy Kaufman and they not only wanted to call it *Man on the Moon*, but they wanted R.E.M. to write and record the film's soundtrack. The band were thrilled. Stipe had been enthused by his experience with *Velvet Goldmine*, which had ended up with Academy Award nominations, and his production company was now working on *Being John Malkovich*, which would turn out to be a modern-day masterpiece. They read the Scott Alexander/Larry Karaszewski script for *Man on the Moon*, loved it, and booked some time at John Keane's to get to work. Director Milos Forman asked them to write a "sisterpiece" to the song 'Man on the Moon', not a small request, and their response to the challenge was 'The Great Beyond', a song that became R.E.M.'s biggest ever hit in the UK.

The rest of the soundtrack consisted of little more than instrumental snippets, excerpts of dialogue from the film, alternate versions of 'Man on the Moon' and a whimsical duet between Stipe and the film's star Jim Carrey on an old obscurity titled 'This Friendly World', a favourite of Kaufman's. The film, released just before Christmas 1999, would turn out to be a relative flop, despite Carrey being one of the era's most bankable leading names. It was in large part down to the fact that the Generation X crowd were far less familiar with the legend of Kaufman than R.E.M.'s punk generation had been, although the film endures decades later thanks to the behind-the-scenes documentary *Jim and Andy: The Great Beyond*, which became a major Netflix hit in 2017.

'The Great Beyond' mirrors 'Man on the Moon' in several ways. "There is nothing up my sleeve," Stipe sings this time around, in retort to the famous line from the earlier song's chorus, before going on to argue that while it may be true that we are all older now, there is still beauty in believing in something that the world is telling you cannot be true. As the 21st century arrived, R.E.M. had been through their darkest hour and despite the signs from the ether seeming bleak, they had come out the other side with renewed energy. Maybe it was time to truly believe again.

'Reveal' and 'Around the Sun'

The millennium was barely a month old when R.E.M. decided to convert this positive energy into new music. Pre-recording sessions were held throughout February at West Clayton Street Studio, with Stipe, Buck, Mills, McCaughey, Waronker and Stringfellow all in action. There was a shared desire to make the conditions for the next album as different as possible from the *Up* fiasco, and that meant no artificial time pressures, as much close collaboration as possible between band members, a return to the familiar band structure and a toning down of the electronic ingredients.

There was a feeling of gratitude toward Pat McCarthy for having been the outside voice of calm during the most alarming moments of panic too, so he was quickly invited back to produce, this time with assistant Jamie Candiloro. As the days and weeks passed, it became apparent that there was another big shift occurring too: the songs were trending towards a return to the bittersweet melancholy that had been at the heart of their early 1990s material.

The bulk of the song building and recording happened at the Warehouse Studio in Vancouver, just a short hop from Buck's base in Seattle, although the lyrics came together somewhere else entirely. Michael Stipe had felt that the primary cause of his crippling writer's block during *Up* stemmed from being too close to home, so he booked a place as far away as he could think of, holing himself away in an old country home outside Dublin. He would be alone with the recordings and his concentration. If he hit roadblocks, he would simply pop over to some other European city for a long weekend to let his hair down and blow the cobwebs away, before returning to his base and getting back down to work. It was the grandest rockstar indulgence of his career, but it kept him in a positive mindset and even if the process took some four months, it resulted in a set of lyrics that he was proud of.

It took the best part of a year, but by the end of 2000, they had completed the album. Mike Mills found himself part of the most surreal band lineup of his life that December, sharing a stage in Austin, Texas with tennis aces John McEnroe and Jim Courier on guitar and bass respectively, Metallica's Lars Ulrich on drums and himself on keys. It was the end of a long day that had seen them play a series of charity tennis matches (Mills and Courier would lose out to Ulrich and McEnroe in the final), but one imagines that as thrilling as it might have been for Mills to play with such legends of the sport, it was nothing to the rush that McEnroe and Courier got by jamming with some of the planet's biggest rockstars. They motored through exactly the staples that one would expect: 'Sweet Home Alabama', 'Johnny B. Goode', 'Purple Haze', et al.

It was hardly an appropriate warm-up for what was about to happen on the other side of the New Year. R.E.M. had never played in South America, but when the third edition of the Rock in Rio Festival decided it was going to try to break some all-time attendance records, they were bound to be on the invitation list. On 13 January 2001, R.E.M. played in front of 190,000 people, dwarfing their Glastonbury crowd. Four days later, they played another mammoth show in Buenos Aires. These were massive successes, further bolstering the mood of the band. They were now comfortable in their own stadium skins and they felt good at what they did.

And then, a setback. The band were due to play another marquee show, this time in London's Trafalgar Square, and Peter Buck was to join the rest of the band there a few days ahead of time. Seattle to London is a ten-hour flight, and even in British Airways first class, that is a gruelling experience. For Buck, though, this would become a defining night in his life. A friend had given him some Ambien sleeping pills to get him through it as smoothly as possible, but Buck, perhaps not realising that they are not to be mixed with alcohol, proceeded to knock back a number of the complementary wines. He has always maintained that he remembers nothing of what happened after that, but it has been described by all who saw it as nothing short of a drunken rampage. It was serious enough that Flight Captain Tom Payne held a crisis meeting with his staff and considered making an emergency landing at the first available airport, but ultimately decided he could make it to Heathrow and then have Buck arrested on landing. The guitarist was charged with two counts of common assault, one of criminal damage, one of disobeying an aircraft commander, one of threatening behaviour and one of being drunk on an aircraft. He appeared at court two days later and was released on £30,000 bail. Bertis Downs was with him and read an official statement, in which Buck said he was, "very sorry for the incident and, of course, very embarrassed about the whole thing."

Buck was pleading not guilty to all charges, in a contrast to the sentiments expressed in the statement, and if found guilty would be facing up to four years in prison. A trial date was set for 12 November, where the prosecutor laid out the precise charges: that he had consumed fifteen glasses of red wine in three hours, was belligerent and disrespectful to other passengers, that he tore up the Captain's yellow card warning, assaulted the cabin services director with a tub of yoghurt, flipped over the catering trolley and concealed a knife up his sleeve.

The trial was taking place some eight weeks after the attacks of 11 September and there was a sense both in the media and in the aviation industry that all in-flight misbehaviour should be dealt with extremely seriously. (Stipe, incidentally, had been in Greenwich Village in downtown Manhattan that day and was seen by many on the streets in the hours afterwards frozen in the same shock and disbelief as the rest of New York.) The challenge for the prosecution was that Buck was not the only one acting up on that flight – R.E.M. tour manager Bob Whittaker was with Buck and also took a dose of the Ambien and mixed it with wine. If he had been seen by witnesses as also having been guilty of misbehaviour (he was), then it was going to be markedly more difficult to ascertain the exact allegations against either man. The judge discharged the jury for this reason and set a retrial for 18 March 2002.

During the eventual proceedings, several members of the British Airways staff from the flight stood as prosecution witnesses and confirmed the reports. The British press had been transfixed by this story from day one and the hysteria peaked when Buck's defence witnesses were called: Bono took to the stand to defend Buck's character as a non-confrontational, responsible family-man. Michael Stipe and Mike Mills did the same, vouching for his reputation as a gentle, distinctly unaggressive man. The closing witness, his wife Stephanie Dorgan, was a former lawyer and her wording will have done her husband a major favour. The jury finally returned their verdict on 5 April, finding Buck not guilty on all charges. Anyone who followed the minutiae of the case is likely to find that all sides were making reasonable assertions: Buck had been unaware of the danger of mixing the pills with alcohol and his behaviour truly was out of character, but nevertheless his actions were terrifying for all involved. As luck would have it, the day of his acquittal coincided with the 22nd anniversary of the band's debut show, and, filled with the relief of not losing the services of their guitarist, they celebrated in their typically un-excessive and well-mannered way.

If anything, the scandal had only served to heighten the profile of the release of their new album, *Reveal*, in May 2001, just weeks after the original incident. In contrast to that hubbub, though, *Reveal* actually offered listeners their most tranquilised, easy-going R.E.M. listening experience to date. It was the sound of the band as they really were during the recording process: content, positive and unhassled. Lead single 'Imitation of Life' was typical, evoking the nostalgia of youth and of skipping through endless warm summer evenings, just as everyone seems to think that they actually did. However, in the same vein as the 1959 Douglas Sirk Hollywood melodrama from which it borrows its name, the song also seems to be concealing something far more sinister, akin to the festering ear beneath the surface of the picket-fence idyll at the start of David Lynch's *Blue Velvet*. This is just an imitation, after all.

The other standout pop nugget on *Reveal* is 'All the Way to Reno (You're Gonna Be a Star)', complete with a twanging country swing and a polished, clean finish. Guitar notes ring clear over hi-res percussion, while a series of earwormy hooks burrow into your subconscious. But like 'Imitation of Life', there is a cynical kernel at the heart of the song: Reno, after all, is the not-even-Las-Vegas of tacky showbiz, a Nevada city with a glamour so faded that no amount of neon saturation can make it sparkle. The would-be star that Stipe addresses in the song should have their heart on their sleeve, but as he sings, "You may as well have had 'kick me' fastened on your sleeve", such is the target that her naivete is going to make her. As absurdly enjoyable as it is as a slice of pop escapism, 'All the Way to Reno' is as darkly bitter as Elliott Smith's 'Angeles' on the subject of the showbusiness industry's ability to abuse the hopes and dreams of struggling artists.

'The Lifting' offers us a prequel to 'Daysleeper', where we catch our lead character earlier in their life, at a time when they were not so ground down by the monotony of working life and still holding onto their dreams. It is yet another example of a R.E.M. song set at least partly in an airport, which was a recurring motif at this point in their career - a reflection of the amount of time spent hanging around airports in their real lives. The track comes in on a bed of sampled electronic strings and synth squelches, but this amount of digital tampering is kept fairly minimal on *Reveal*. 'She Just Wants to Be', for example, is driven by plucked acoustic strings and bare vocals, as well as a chorus strong enough to match the album's singles.

'Disappear' sprouted from the private phone conversations that Stipe shared with Thom Yorke around this time. Like Cobain before him, Yorke looked to Stipe as one of the few fellow outsider, neurotic, anxious figures to have been flung into the global spotlight and he sought his advice wherever possible. Stipe told him to always remind himself, 'I'm not here, this isn't happening', which Yorke would use to devastating effect on Radiohead's stunning track 'How to Disappear Completely' on *Kid A*. As a riposte, 'Disappear' finds Stipe singing, "I looked for you and everywhere/Tell me why you're here/I came to disappear"; Stipe has said that he is not sure if it was hearing the Radiohead song that inspired these lyrics or if his words to Yorke were still rattling around his own head, but Yorke has said that Stipe deserves the credit for both songs either way.

Much of *Reveal* drifts by in a haze. 'Summer Turns to High' is typical, sounding a little like an offcut from The Beach Boys' *Surf's Up* played at half-speed. The track is the essence of the album, flush with the treats of summer: the sunshine and flowers, birds and butterflies, sweetness and love. *Reveal* as a whole was often compared with *Automatic for the People* at the time, and while they definitely share a heartworn wistfulness, this album does not touch the profound emotional depth of its older relative, and lacks its musical diversity too. Much of *Reveal* is genuinely beautiful, but it is one-paced and drifts too easily into daydream.

On release, it peaked at #6 in the US charts, their lowest since the 1980s. 'Imitation of Life' maxed out at a disappointing #83, although this was to be the highest home singles chart placing for the rest of their career. Internationally, though, their numbers went from strength to strength. *Reveal* returned them to #1 on the UK albums chart, their fifth time hitting the top in six efforts. It sold one million copies in Europe in its first month, more than double the number that it shifted over the same time period in the States. 'Imitation of Life' even became their first ever #1 single in Japan.

The accompanying press tour also focused on the European market, leading some to wonder if Warners were actually contributing to the underwhelming response back home. An extended run of television appearances in the UK included returns to *Top of the Pops* and *Jools Holland* and a debut on *CD:UK*, while back home they were at least granted another feature length *MTV Unplugged* episode. By far the most prestigious moment for the band came in July when they were invited onto the hallowed grounds of *The Simpsons* to record voice parts for the Season 13 episode 'Homer to the Moe', where they played self-deprecating versions of themselves as Homer's house band when he opens his own bar.

R.E.M. were back in the studio one final time in 2001 to record a new track for the soundtrack to the film *Vanilla Sky*. Director Cameron Crowe wanted something original and the band delved into their back catalogue, looking for one of the strongest of their songs that had never had a full release. They would scroll back as far as 1979 and the very earliest writing sessions between Stipe and Buck, before the line-up of the band had even been completed, to find 'All the Right Friends'. They had considered it to be a major breakthrough in their writing at the time and it came close to making the tracklisting for both *Chronic Town* and *Murmur*, falling just short both times and then disappearing from setlists after 1983. It speaks to the affection that they still had for it that they felt it worth revisiting nearly two decades later, and they turned it around in one day's studio work in Seattle.

Most of 2002 passed without activity, save for occasional benefit concerts, such as for the Gay Men's Health Crisis to commemorate the 20-year fight against AIDS, or the Bridge School Benefit, an ongoing series of annual charity gigs in Mountain View, California. Peter Buck, once his date with destiny with the British court system was behind him, was restless and set up a summer of touring with his band The Minus 5, with McCaughey and Barrett Martin and others. He was spending much more time with that crowd than with R.E.M. at this point, including an entire leg supporting Wilco around the US.

Warners felt that after seven albums with them, it was time to look at a compilation album for R.E.M. The only previous such releases for the band had been issued by I.R.S. and there would certainly be no possibility at this point for the two halves of the band's career to be included alongside one another on the same album, so plans were drawn up to assemble a greatest hits package drawn from the material from *Green* onwards. It was decided that there should be two new tracks included, so the band went back to the studio in Vancouver to work on 'Bad Day' and 'Animal'. The former dated back to the *Lifes Rich Pageant* days, and although it fell through the cracks then, it certainly set the template for 'It's the End of the World as We Know It' a year later. With only a few lyrical tweaks to update it, the band were happy to give it its moment in the sun now. 'Animal' was a new composition, one of their most interesting in years, with backwards-guitars that invoked Indian classical music in much the same way that The Chemical Brothers and The Beatles before them had explored.

These sessions, which were completed in the spring of 2003, were the first to feature Bill Rieflin on drums. He had been friends with McCaughey since the punk years of the late 70s in Seattle and had risen to acclaim in the late 80s with Chicago industrial rockers Ministry. The band immediately liked the muscularity of his work and he would stick with them for the remainder of their time together, with Joey Waronker leaving to pursue a career as one of the most sought-after session drummers in the world. In addition to the songs for the compilation, they were testing out dozens of new compositions, with an eye towards the next album. One of them, 'Final Straw', a rudimentary anti-Iraq War protest song, was even released via their own website, www.remhq.com. It was still considered highly unusual for bands to release their music directly to their fanbase in 2003 and the band were excited by the possibilities to make connections to their audience that the internet offered. A series of live sessions, essentially pre-tour rehearsals, were also made available 'as-live' on the site, and later in the year entire live shows from the tour were offered as downloads. R.E.M. had always enjoyed serving their hardcore fans with their annual Christmas fan singles dating back to the mid-80s, and this new medium just made that process all the more straight-forward.

It was during one of the final pre-tour rehearsals at West Clayton Street Studios that the band received a surprise visitor. Dressed head-to-toe in chef's whites, armed with sushi, poppadoms and chutney, Bill Berry poked his head round the door. He wanted the others to come and spend a day at his farm and the very next day, they obliged, delighted to have the chance for an extended catch-up.

The tour began in Europe and found the band plundering their early careers' work much more liberally than they had done over the last decade. Considering they were about to release a greatest hits album that featured nothing from before 1988, they started finding space for songs like 'Feeling Gravitys Pull', 'Maps and Legends' and 'Little America'. The North American leg began at the end of August, and on the penultimate night in Raleigh, North Carolina, Berry even joined them on stage to sing backing vocals on 'Radio Free Europe', and then to play drums on, poignantly, 'Permanent Vacation', a song from 1981/2 that they had recently re-discovered.

In Time: The Best of R.E.M. 1988-2003 dropped in October 2003, selling much more strongly in the US than the previous two albums had done, which could either be read as reassurance that people were still interested, or as confirmation that they only cared about the old material. As ever with greatest hits albums, special attention was paid to what was included and also what was not: here, the band carefully spread out the material so that *Reveal* was the only album to have more than one of its songs appear in the first eleven tracks on the record. Remarkably, *Out of Time* was only represented with one song, whereas *Up* had two, with no space for 'Near Wild Heaven', 'Radio Song' or 'Shiny Happy People', let alone any of the lesser lights that were firm band and fan favourites such as 'Country Feedback', 'World Leader Pretend' and 'Find the River'.

If they had delayed the greatest hits album for another year, it is hard to imagine that more than one song from the record they were about to record could possibly have made the cut. The sessions for *Around the Sun* began in Peter Buck's home studio in Seattle in December 2003 and went on continuously until July. They first moved back to Athens, and then onto the Compass Point Studios in Nassau, Bahamas, before finally ending up at the Hit Factory in Miami; if the process for *Reveal* had been gradual, then this was downright glacial. They were still happy with the results from the recording of the last album and hoped that the same attitude of operating as if the release date never needed to arrive, would work again. In fact, what they were doing was falling for the cliches of indulgence that come with bottomless reserves. This was a band that was once proud to say that they could produce an album every twelve months, each one different to the one before. Now it was taking them three times as long, without any substantial sonic development. On top of that, Pat McCarthy found it hard to assert his authority over the trio, such was their power by now, and the whole thing became stagnant.

Even at the time of its release, members of the band were speaking in code about how they felt that they had let the sessions get out of their control. A few years later, they were ready to tell the whole truth. "The album just wasn't really listenable," said Peter Buck. "Because it sounds like what it is: a bunch of people that are so bored with the material that they can't stand it anymore." The whole saga dragged on for so long that they were trapped listening to the same core recordings for a virtual eternity, tweaking them until all traces of life had been erased. "The songs on *Around the Sun* are great," Michael Stipe said, "but in the process of recording, we lost our focus as a band."

The album leads off with its one stab at immortality, 'Leaving New York'. Tapping back into the early R.E.M. hallmark of echoed, overlapping backing vocals, it boasts one of their all-time catchiest choruses, good enough to rival 'Fall on Me' and 'Man on the Moon'. It also smartly plays up the romantic allure of New York City, which had seen a resurgent spike following 9/11, and while there is nothing nakedly political about the track, just glorying in the city's afterglow was enough to position it as a statement of sorts in 2004. And yet, despite its formidable strengths, the song seems to come to a shuddering halt during the verses: too slow, too formulaic.

This problem plays out across all 55 of *Around the Sun*'s minutes. 'Electron Blue' and 'Wanderlust' bear traces of pop potential, but the life is smothered out of them by the weirdly slumpish pacing. It is made more frustrating by the fact that Stipe is clearly motivated here to use his writing in order to speak out in a way that he hadn't since *Green*. 'Final Straw', the song they rush-released online just five days after the US and their allies launched their 'shock and awe' bombing campaign to mark the start of the Iraq War, finds Stipe once again voicing his opposition to President Bush, albeit a new one. Stipe had described himself in the past as the world's angriest pacifist and those instincts are on full display on 'Final Straw': "If hatred makes a play on me tomorrow/And forgiveness takes a back seat to revenge/There's a hurt down deep that has not been corrected/There's a voice in me that says you will not win". Suffice to say, that voice in him would be proven right.

'Final Straw' plays out like an early 60s Greenwich Village protest folk song, driven by strummed acoustic guitar and half-spoken, pained vocals. It sits apart from the album around it, a quietly effective statement. Similar subject matter motivates 'The Outsiders', with Stipe more subtly throwing shade at the callow incompetence of the new Bush administration ("Drawing patterns with a cork on the tablecloth"), although once again the track itself is sluggish and spiritless. A guest verse from legendary rapper Q-Tip brings some much-needed variety, as well as the album's most pointedly provocative political statement: "I wanna float a quote from Martin Luther King/I am not afraid", he says, referencing Dr. King's 'Letter from Birmingham Jail', in which he called for direct action from the people in order to break morally unjust laws. This guest feature is a step up from the better-known KRS-One appearance on 'Radio Song', with Stipe letting Q-Tip carry the brunt of the song's message. With a better framework around it, 'The Outsiders' could have been an R.E.M. classic.

The album only reached #13 on the US charts, lower than their final I.R.S. album, *Document*. It still made #1 in the UK, though, and 'Leaving New York' became the hit there that it deserved to be, reaching the top five. For the first time, they were facing widespread negative reviews for an album and the momentum they had rescued from the *Up* sessions seemed to be slipping away. As the album was released in early October 2004, the band were in the middle of a whistlestop tour around the major US cities as part of the Vote for Change Tour, alongside Bruce Springsteen and Bright Eyes. It was election time again, and once again there was a Bush to whack. Springsteen would join the band for 'Man on the Moon', Stipe would sing 'Because the Night' with the Boss and Buck and Mills would get to join in on 'Born to Run'. They were most definitely having fun - until election day when George W. Bush saw off the lukewarm challenge of John Kerry with relative ease.

A week later, R.E.M. embarked on their third major world tour, after the ones following the releases of *Green* and *Monster*. It would see them take in the bowls, stadiums, amphitheatres and arenas of 114 cities in twenty countries and five continents. The shows were massively populated and well-received, but it was a bloated experience. On 2 July 2005, they appeared at the Live 8 event in Hyde Park, London, introduced by Ricky Gervais, playing in the afternoon so that they could fly to Switzerland that night to make their gig in St. Gallen. It had, perhaps, become too big. If they were going to wrestle back control, they were going to have to look inwards.

'Accelerate' and 'Collapse into Now'

Being a band in their mid-40s, R.E.M. could be forgiven for taking a long sabbatical after such an enormous global tour and for the next eighteen months, they were barely active.

Michael Stipe took to a recording studio as a solo artist for the first time in late 2005, making an EP under his own name as a benefit release for the victims of the destruction caused by Hurricane Katrina. Produced in Manhattan by Smashing Pumpkins guitarist James Iha, the release consisted of different versions of the song 'In the Sun', originally written and recorded by Akron, Ohio indie folkster Joseph Arthur in 2000. Among the alternate versions on the EP was a duet between Stipe and his latest superstar protégé, Coldplay's Chris Martin. Like Cobain and Yorke before him, Martin recognised Stipe's value as a godfather figure; unlike them, Martin brought no reflected credibility to the Stipe brand.

R.E.M.'s few engagements of 2006 were chiefly memorable for one reason: they nearly all featured Bill Berry back in the mix. At the Athens date of The Minus 5's tour in April, Berry, Mills and Stipe all clambered on stage between the end of the main set and the encore at the Georgia Theater, joining Buck, McCaughey and Rieflin. With Mike Mills on keys and Bill Berry on bass, they played a version of 'Country Feedback', and it gave them a buzz that they could not ignore. In September, they even found themselves back in the studio together, recording a version of John Lennon's '#9 Dream' for an Amnesty International album titled *Instant Karma*.

A few days later they were on stage again, this time back at their old haunt the 40 Watt Club. A group of the newest Athens bands (Tin Cup Prophette, Modern Skirts, The Observatory) had been assembled for a charity night called 'Finest Worksongs: Athens Bands Play the Music of R.E.M.', and the original quartet made a surprise appearance themselves, playing 'Begin the Begin' and 'So Central Rain' and then joining in with the ensemble encore of 'It's the End of the World as We Know It'. They were predictably treated like messiahs, but they played the spot because they were tuning up for something bigger.

Within the space of a few months, R.E.M. had been reminded of their senior status with invitations into two separate music halls of fame. First up was the Georgia Music Hall of Fame, where they were inducted alongside Gregg Allman, one of the forces against which R.E.M. had initially been compelled to form, and pop/R&B producers Dallas Austin and Jermaine Dupri. Introduced by former Georgia Senator Max Cleland, the band, including Berry, played 'Begin the Begin', 'Losing My Religion' and 'Man on the Moon'. It was a proud moment as the band had always gone out of their way to represent their home state whenever possible. What's more, a quick glance down the list of previous inductees highlights how against the grain R.E.M.'s musical style had been for Georgia at the time, with the bulk of artists coming either from the Southern rock, funk, blues or country spheres.

Far more people witnessed their induction into the Rock and Roll Hall of Fame the following March. Due to the Hall's arcane eligibility rules, an artist can only be inducted twenty-five years after the release of their first record, so with the silver anniversary of *Chronic Town* now upon them, R.E.M. were privileged to be inducted at the first opportunity. The other recipients that day at New York's Waldorf Astoria were The Ronettes, Van Halen, Grandmaster Flash & The Furious Five and, fittingly, Patti Smith, but R.E.M. were deemed to be that year's headline act, going on last. Eddie Vedder gave a charming and impressively funny induction speech, before Mike Mills said a few words, most notably to thank Ian Copeland, who had recently passed away, and then Michael Stipe gave a typically gracious and thoughtful acceptance speech, thanking all of the major players in the band's story, with the notable exception of Jefferson Holt. They played 'Begin the Begin', 'Gardening at Night', 'Man on the Moon' with Vedder, and 'I Wanna Be Your Dog' with Patti Smith and Lenny Kaye, perhaps in protest at The Stooges' ongoing absence from the Hall (they were finally admitted in 2010).

If Bill Berry enjoyed these one-off engagements, it was still not enough to completely lure him out of band retirement, and when work began on album number fourteen, Bill Rieflin resumed his place behind the kit. There was to be someone new at the production desk, though, with the band still reeling from how badly the *Around the Sun* sessions had spiralled out of control. U2's The Edge recommended Jacknife Lee, who had lent his hand to 2004's *How to Dismantle an Atomic Bomb*, and so a meeting was set up. Lee was another Dubliner, who by a preposterous coincidence had been in a teenage new wave cover band with Pat McCarthy in the 1980s. By 1994, he was a member of the moderately successful punk band Compulsion, before pursuing a solo career producing his own electronica under the Jacknife Lee name (the Jacknife part came from the opening line of Radiohead's 'Airbag'). His big break arrived in the early 2000s as a producer of huge hit albums for Snow Patrol, from which he was able to ingratiate himself into the British indie scene of the day – Editors, Bloc Party and Kasabian were all clients of his.

Jacknife had seen R.E.M. when they played in Dublin way back on the Green tour, but he needed to do some catching up with their recent work before his meeting with them. If he was nervous, then finding out that Thom Yorke was also going to be present at the meeting cannot have helped. Above all else, the band needed to hear that he had the same notions of how to put things right as they did. His use of the words "visceral and thrilling" when describing his vision for the album confirmed this and he was brought into the fold shortly thereafter.

The first decision that they needed to make was where to record. The band wanted to return to The Warehouse in Vancouver, but Jacknife was of the opinion that a return to a studio they already knew could lead to them falling back into the old bad habits, too familiar and complacent in their surroundings. They reached a happy compromise: they would base themselves in Vancouver, but at a different studio, The Armoury.

They were happy there and were able to lay down around twenty demos of new songs. After three weeks, Jacknife sensed that it was time for another move, though, and he recommended the remote Grouse Lodge Recording Studios in County Westmeath in his home country, somewhere he had worked with Snow Patrol and Editors in the past. He liked the venue's remoteness and the band didn't mind that either, familiar as they were with Bearsville Studios in Woodstock, New York. There were evening curfews of 7pm at the Grouse Lodge, which would put a cap on the endless tinkering that had plagued *Around the Sun*, and the band were happy to comply, with the on-site pub giving them enough extra-curricular activity to get them through the three weeks.

Bertis Downs made the trip to Ireland with them, and he came up with the most radical plan of the band's career so far in terms of preparing new material when he suggested that R.E.M. should play five shows trialling all of the new unreleased material at Dublin's Olympia Theatre in front of a full paying audience. Stipe called the idea an "experiment in terror", realising that it forced him to meet a concrete lyric-writing deadline; his delays had been another one of the major factors that had seen the last few recording processes grind to a halt. The band agreed to Downs' idea and the shows sold out instantly. The new material leapt out of the traps, and to round out the setlists, the band reached for some deep 1980s cuts like 'Second Guessing', 'Letter Never Sent' and 'Kohoutek'. The shows were a major success, according to the band, producer, manager, fans and critics alike.

The final leg of the sessions saw the band truly return to their roots, shacking up at the Seney-Stovall Chapel in Athens, where back in 1986 they had recorded that heart-melting version of 'All I Have to Do is Dream' for *Athens, Ga: Inside/Out*. Three weeks later, the *Accelerate* album was complete.

The record did exactly what the band needed it to do. Opener 'Living Well is the Best Revenge' is most definitely an acceleration, with supercharged guitars sounding clean and direct and ready for war. Stipe said that the lyric was about "that puff adder Bill O'Reilly, although his shrill offspring are even more venal and pathetic than he was." He separately explained that, "I tore into this vocal because someone who I really, really admired forever kind of bad-mouthed R.E.M. and I was like, 'fuck you! Sing like this, you talented fuck'." The two targets seem equally caught in the crosshairs in Stipe's chorus: "All your sad and lost apostles hum my name and flare their nostrils/Choking on the bones you toss to them." The vocals are frayed and imperfect, giving the impression that Stipe is mid-rage, postulating and barely able to control himself. This is what *Accelerate* was: un-manicured and not thwarted by misguided attempts to perfect its sheen.

'Man-Sized Wreath' was inspired by the day that the then-President George W. Bush visited the band's home state to honour Dr. Martin Luther King, Jr., an act of faux-sincerity that Stipe was not about to let pass. "Nature abhors a vacuum, but what's that between your ears?", he sings. Guitars are cranked up yet further to almost siren-like intensity and on the climactic end-chorus line, it sounds like a dozen Stipes screaming "Give me some". With the benefit of an extra few election cycles of hindsight, the performative fury of the liberal left during the late George W. Bush years can seem a little disproportionate, given how much further there was to sink, but Stipe, still one of the thought-leaders of his cohort, accurately captured the mood of the day.

'Supernatural Superserious' keeps the momentum going, with Stipe offering up reminders of teenage shame and of hiding one's true self; it might stop a little short of 'Drive' in terms of a pledge to offer reassurance to anyone going through the same, but the message is still there. There may be very little musical variety across these opening three tracks, but they are as good a rock version of R.E.M. as anything on *New Adventures in Hi-Fi*.

The mood varies on 'Hollow Man', with an unvarnished, cracked vocal from Stipe, and on 'Houston', a song about the people forced to flee their home cities because of Hurricane Katrina and the heartless comments from ex-First Lady and the then-president's mother Barbara Bush, who said that, "so many of the people were underprivileged anyway, so this is working well for them". The song attempts to reinstate the dignity of these Americans, with Mills' organ keys lending it a necessarily sombre tone.

'Mr. Richards' and 'Until the Day is Done' continue the album-wide theme of full-frontal despair at the Bush administration, with the former an attack on every faceless, bureaucratic, self-serving yes-man that works for these regimes and proudly signs their dirty deeds through, while the first verse of the latter is dominated by the Iraq War ("The battle's been lost, the war is not won"). Stipe goes on to cover plenty of other political ground on 'Until the Day is Done' – the broken US media cycle, the further foreign policy disasters, the triumph of the "business-first flat earthers" - but instead of bluster and rage, the track plays out as a lament, with prominent acoustic strings and Stipe sounding audibly wounded, a fitting sister song to *Around the Sun's* 'Final Straw'.

The lyrics of 'Sing for the Submarine' make reference to several songs from the band's back catalogue: 'World Leader Pretend', 'Feeling Gravitys Pull', 'Losing My Religion', 'It's the End of the World as We Know It', among others. "It's placed in that dream world, the older R.E.M. songs in there are like a legend on a map," Stipe told Pitchfork, with a sly meta-reference, "to all the other songs in our catalogue that also come from my dream world." Stipe's dream world appears to be starkly post-apocalyptic, but one where he himself seems immune from any imminent threat, perhaps casting some light on how he is able to summon such richly cinematic imagery.

Accelerate blazes out with 'Horse to Water' and 'I'm Gonna DJ', two tracks that barely cover four minutes between them. It is the album in miniature: sonic nuance is out and primal, visceral impulse is in. R.E.M. could pass as a sludgy, early-90s alt-rock band here, the sort of thing they were almost defined as being in opposition to at the time. Above all, they are convincing, meaning that the album clears its most important hurdle. Such was the aftershock of the bruising *Around the Sun* experience that they desperately wanted to prove that they could still seize an audience's attention and have something stirring to contribute. Even if it could be said that the album is somewhat frozen in fear, terrified of the consequences of leaving the fast lane, R.E.M. were back on top again, in control of their narrative and firmly back in the cultural conversation once more.

The album went as high as #2 on the US charts, up from *Around the Sun*'s #13 and their highest position since *New Adventures in Hi-Fi*. It provided them with yet another UK #1 album too, and it delivered their best reviews in over a decade. The ensuing media tour, never any band's favourite part of the job, was a significantly more pleasant experience now that they knew that the mood surrounding the album was positive.

Their latest world tour began outside Vancouver in May 2008, with indie heavyweights The National and Modest Mouse both supporting. At this time, Modest Mouse boasted Johnny Marr as a full-time member, and the chance to bring Marr and Peter Buck together at last was too much to resist. From their earliest days, the two guitarists' playing styles had been endlessly compared to one another, particularly in the UK press, with The Smiths' debut album arriving six weeks before the release of *Reckoning*. Marr joined R.E.M. on stage every night for 'Fall on Me', later expanding it to include 'Pretty Persuasion' and 'Man on the Moon' too.

At a gig in Raleigh, North Carolina in June, Mitch Easter and Don Dixon were on hand to guest on guitars for 'Sitting Still', a song from the album they had been so instrumental in steering a whole quarter of a century earlier. This was also the first R.E.M. tour to feature an extensive South American leg, including a night in Santiago on 4 November when, during the encore, Bertis Downs ran onstage with his laptop, breathlessly announcing that Barack Obama looked very likely to have won the election. Stipe put on an Obama Hope t-shirt and four audience members wearing the same were invited on stage to sing and dance along to 'Radio Free Europe'. When the tour concluded in Mexico City later that month, nobody in attendance realised that they were watching the last ever major R.E.M. concert.

One final public performance remained, at no less an institution than New York City's Carnegie Hall. A charity tribute show was thrown for the band, with an all-star array of friends and acquaintances, including The dB's, Throwing Muses, Vic Chesnutt, Apples in Stereo, Bob Mould, The Feelies and, inevitably, Patti Smith, queuing up to perform their favourites of the band's songs. The band took to the stage with Smith to perform 'E-Bow the Letter' that night, their final public performance for a paying audience, at one of the world's most prestigious and coveted live music spaces. And still nobody realised it.

The band ploughed on regardless, reconvening in May 2009 at Jackpot! Studios in Portland, once again with Jacknife Lee producing. Michael Stipe, as so often before, did not attend these demo recording sessions, but Buck, Mills, Rieflin and McCaughey came up with fourteen instrumentals that they were happy with. Portland was now McCaughey's home, and it was soon to be Buck's too, with the guitarist having fallen in love with a woman there, following the beginning of his divorce proceedings with Dorgan.

The band moved to The Music Shed in New Orleans to begin the recording sessions proper, first in November 2009 and then again the following May. A three-week spell at Berlin's legendary Hansa Studios, the site of Bowie, Iggy and Brian Eno's legendary days, saw album number fifteen blossom into full life. They were a confident and creative band again, and felt able to start letting a little freelance experimentation seep back into the process. One final flurry of activity in Nashville remained before they had their next album finished and ready to put on display to the world.

Where *Accelerate* had been scared to risk variety, here they were willing to shake it up again, feeling newly re-secure about their talents. From the very outset of 'Discoverer', the guitars dominate, but not in that sledgehammer attack way of *Accelerate*'s loudest moments. There is a tactility this time, and space for Mike Mills' basslines to re-emerge.

The track is also notable for discarding the political subject matter, leaning instead into more personal, introspective material.

They chose as the lead single 'Mine Smell Like Honey', the album's busiest song, complete with frantic drums, scuzzy guitars, an animated vocal take and towering harmony vocals. The whole vehicle charges through at juggernaut pace, and while it is not on the shortlist of R.E.M.'s greatest singles, it at least allowed the college radio stations – or their 2011 equivalents – an excuse to give the band one last shot at hanging with the Vampire Weekends and Kurt Viles on the new music playlists.

The other standout rock song on the album is 'Alligator_Aviator_ Autopilot_Antimatter', a title that cannot help but bring to mind David Bowie's famous refrain of "he's chameleon, comedian, Corinthian and caricature" from 'The Bewlay Brothers'. The track features guest vocals from dance-punk agent provocateur Peaches, described by Stipe as "the inner voice of teenage testosterone". They had met at a bar during their Berlin stay and such was the band's admiration for her that they allowed her to take a whole bridge as sole lead vocalist; only Q-Tip had been given such a prominent guest role before. Lenny Kaye's screeching, retro guitar solo, dripping in the sweat and grime of the original CBGB's, is the perfect final ingredient. This is a legitimately exciting, convulsing slice of smart, subversive rock music from a band in their fourth decade together, no mean feat.

'Überlin' seems to be about the experience of being an outsider in an unfamiliar city, looking for a spontaneous, life-changing experience. It is prettily arranged, with the echoey, multi-tracked "I know" refrain finding our character walking out alone onto the wire, desperately trying to reassure himself that he really might know. The surge as the chorus arrives, "I am flying on a star into a meteor tonight" as our character reaches whatever spiritual high he was looking for from this voyage, is galvanising. It is one of the most beautiful tracks of the last leg of the band's career, one that never had its fair chance in the spotlight.

More moving still is 'Oh My Heart', the sole R.E.M. song on which Scott McCaughey receives a writing credit. The song is a sequel to *Accelerate*'s 'Houston', as we hear about that song's central character returning from Texas to his New Orleans home and finding it ruined ("I came home to a city half erased"). A brief snatch of mournful horns introduce the song, a nod to the traditional jazz funerals associated with the city, before giving way to McCaughey's accordion and Peter

Buck's mandolin, the band reaching back into their own past to bring the maximum empathetic response to this unfolding tragedy. On 'Houston', Stipe sang, "If the storm doesn't kill me, the government will"; here, he replies, "The storm didn't kill me, the government changed". It is probably the most deeply felt vocal of Stipe's career, a staggeringly effective three-word chorus.

A song like 'Walk It Back' further demonstrates the maturity in Stipe's voice, his deep-chested register over Mike Mills' stately piano piece almost reminiscent of Bill Callahan. And then, on album closer 'Blue', we hear a very different Stipe. The song had emerged towards the end of the Berlin sessions, but as little more than a few chords and a beat. Unconvinced, the band gave it a final chance to materialise into something greater in Nashville, at which point Stipe decided to try speaking a beat poem over the top of it. He had written the piece back in Germany but he couldn't find a home for it. The band were immediately intrigued by the combination and when Patti Smith showed up in the studio a few days later, they finally knew how to get the track over the line. It is hard not to see the song as an accompaniment to 'E-Bow the Letter', with a similar gradual pacing, the mention in both lyrics of the time 4 a.m. and Stipe and Smith seemingly singing two different songs over the same chorus, but in fact 'Blue' is probably a closer relative to *Out of Time*'s 'Belong', Stipe's low, almost-whispered delivery spilling out at double pace.

While she was there, Patti Smith also came up with the album's eventual title. The band needed something and asked her to flick through the lyric sheets for the album, upon which she suggested *Collapse into Now* from Stipe's 'Blue' poem. The band loved it. They also knew by then that 'Blue' had to close the album, such was its departure from the rest of the material, but they had something even more special in mind. As the track fades out, we hear a full-throated reprise of 'Discoverer', the album's opening track. It is a reflective and out-of-character choice for R.E.M. to have made; it is almost as if they were deliberately trying to put a full stop at the end of something.

The Split

"I think I'll sing and rhyme/I'll give it one more time/I'll show the kids how to do it fine"

"You tell me which part of my story, baby, stuck"

"It's just like me to overstay my welcome, man"

"I just had to get that off my chest/Now it's time to get on with the rest/All the best"

Which lyric of *Collapse into Now*'s second track 'All the Best' do you think makes it the most obvious that R.E.M. were trying to say goodbye? Michael Stipe thought he was making it as obvious as he possibly could, but upon the album's release every one of his messages flew cleanly under everybody's radar.

"That whole record was a whole big goodbye," he told *The Quietus* a year later. "I'm shocked no-one noticed." Hell, even the cover of *Collapse into Now* shows Stipe with his hand in the air, waving goodbye.

The band had been contemplating the matter for some time. They all knew that *Collapse into Now* was going to be the album that fulfilled their contractual obligations with Warners, and even before they got down to work on it, there was a sense of finality in the air.

"I think we all came to the similar realisation during the '08 tour," Mike Mills said in 2017. "I remember the last show was in Mexico City, and I remember going out on stage by myself after it was over thinking, 'I'll probably never do this again'."

Peter Buck also remembers that night in Mexico City as having a poignant weight to it, remembering an exchange he had with Stipe that involved them agreeing that it was likely to be the last time that they would play these songs together.

If the band members had come to that conclusion, they certainly kept the secret well. Jacknife Lee was not told, for example, even if he was able to pick up on the signals during the weeks they spent together recording the final album. "We never really spoke about it," he told Tony Fletcher. "Though there were a few moments individually where we touched on it." Scott McCaughey and Bill Rieflin also did not realise they were contributing to the band's final work.

Whatever way they looked at it, the band were going to have to make a big decision once album number fifteen was finished. If they were to continue, they would either have to sign a new contract with Warners or one of the other major labels, or they would have to burrow their way back into the independent market. These would both have been enormous commitments to make. They had completed the three contracts they had signed, itself a remarkable achievement for a rock band, and in order to complete a fourth, they would have to be betting that the next decade or so of their lives would continue to be as fruitful and artistically satisfying as the last couple of years had been, and not a return to the stifling anguish of the early-2000s. They would doubtless have had to commit to yet more extensive touring, gambling on that not being a drain on their physical and mental health. What's more, they would have found themselves being increasingly expected to lean on the old hits with every passing year, their days of relevance seeming to recede indefinitely into the rear-view mirror. It all sounded like a little too great of a risk.

By choosing to call it a day, they would be offering themselves the chance to go out on a relative high. The *Accelerate/Collapse into Now* double header had returned them to a status that they were proud of and the 2008 tour captured them in excellent live form. It would also be the ultimate act of self-control and independence, both qualities that they had always held dear.

And besides, whatever new deal they were offered would necessarily have been very different to what they had been enjoying up until now. They were still a highly valuable asset for any media company, but not in the way that they had been in 1996, or even 1988, and not just because of any decline in their popularity. The music business had changed beyond recognition in the first decade of the 21st century, with record sales having fallen through the floor thanks to illegal downloading, leaving space for the imminent arrival of streaming services that could get away with passing miniscule profits onto artists. Bands like Radiohead had taken to self-releasing their music, but the long-term effects of that kind of strategy remained unclear at the time. For R.E.M., how much more industry upheaval were they willing to endure in their fourth decade together as a band? What more unforeseeable problems would arise and what were the chances that they would only make their life more complicated?

The business side of the band was already draining their energy. Peter Buck told *Rolling Stone* in 2016 that while the band were making their decision, he compiled a five-page list of the things that he could no longer bear about being in R.E.M.. It contained, he said, "everything except writing songs, playing songs and recording them." The politics of being in one of the world's biggest bands was something that none of R.E.M. had anticipated, with endless, aimless corporate meetings bloating their schedules and eating into their love of the job.

To make matters worse, there was yet more turmoil at Warners in the year leading up to the release of *Collapse into Now*, which was another contributing factor in their ultimate decision. Chairman Tom Whalley, who had always been a devout supporter of R.E.M. from within the upper echelons of the organisation, was let go in 2010, as was Ethan Kaplan, the Senior Vice President of Emerging Technology and owner of the online R.E.M. fan community *Murmurs* on the side. When *Rolling Stone* interviewed Kaplan about why he thought the band made their decision, he spoke with a degree of inside knowledge. "I can understand that after how hard they worked for how long," he said, "the thought of going back to 'paying dues' with new label staff, in a very weird industry, was too much."

The final decision was made early on in the recording sessions for *Collapse into Now*. Stipe confided in Buck and Mills that after the record was finished, he was going to need to take a break away from the band. As Buck explained to *Rolling Stone,* he replied, "How about forever?", and the three men exchanged glances, before Mills said, "Sounds right to me." At that moment, the band's ending was confirmed.

The recording process continued, the album was released and received well by audiences and critics, but no accompanying tour was announced and the band kept promotion to interviews only, with no television or radio performances. Still, nobody in the outside world considered anything about it to be suspicious, and when an announcement popped up on the band's official website on 21 September 2011, it took everybody by surprise.

"To our Fans and Friends: As R.E.M., and as lifelong friends and co-conspirators, we have decided to call it a day as a band. We walk away with a great sense of gratitude, of finality, and of astonishment at all we have accomplished. To anyone who ever felt touched by our music, our deepest thanks for listening."

A few hours later, the band's individual members added personal comments to the statement. Mike Mills was the first to attempt to clarify the situation: "We feel kind of like pioneers in this. There's no disharmony here, no falling-outs, no lawyers squaring off. We've made this decision together, amicably and with each other's best interests at heart. The time just feels right."

Michael Stipe struck the right tone, too. "I hope our fans realise this wasn't an easy decision; but all things must end, and we wanted to do it right, to do it our way," he said. "A wise man once said, 'The skill in attending a party is knowing when it's time to leave'. We built something extraordinary together. We did this thing. And now we're going to walk away from it."

It cannot be overstated how highly unusual it is for a band of R.E.M.'s enormous global stature to bring their career to a close this elegantly. The bands that have reached similar or even greater levels of success have tended to either stick together doggedly, in the face of all challenges (Queen, The Rolling Stones, AC/DC, U2), find themselves struck by tragedy (Led Zeppelin, The Doors, Nirvana), or descend into bitter, resentful acrimony (The Beatles, Pink Floyd, Fleetwood Mac, Eagles). With this move, R.E.M. were acting in a typically thoughtful, sensitive manner, not prepossessed with ego or vanity. They ended the band in the spirit with which they started it, and with which they had maintained it for their entire adult lives.

Understandably, their fans wanted to know a lot more and so the three remaining members agreed to tour the television studios and magazine columns to help explain what had come across as a shockingly sudden decision. Speaking to *The Guardian*, Stipe refused to discuss which of the three of them had made the final decision, in an effort to preserve the sense of unity that they felt it was important to convey. It is no surprise, though, that people were suspicious, expecting that before long the secrets would spill out. But there were no secrets – they really were voluntarily ending their band during good times. It was only hard to believe because there was virtually no precedent for it.

It took until 2016 for any of them to open up a bit more on the subject. *Rolling Stone* teased out of Peter Buck that managing the R.E.M. estate continued to take up a sizeable chunk of their lives, partly due to the fact that Bertis Downs had once convinced them that they should own their own masters. There were staff to employ, buildings to run, a publishing company to oversee, but just no shows to play or records to make. He also warned fans not to expect a slew of posthumous R.E.M. albums featuring unreleased tracks, in the manner of Prince or Amy Winehouse. Part of what pleased him about R.E.M.'s legacy was that they had a tight discography with minimal overflow; besides, for every album, they included virtually all of the tracks that they felt were worth releasing anyway. "I'm really proud of the body of work," he said. "There are a couple of records that aren't great. But there are a couple of Bob Dylan records that aren't great."

To accompany the announcement of the split, they also revealed that they would release a definitive compilation album. In other circumstances, news of yet another greatest hits album might have set a few eyes rolling, but it now seemed like a beautifully fitting way to send the band off. Titled *Part Lies, Part Heart, Part Truth, Part Garbage 1982-2011* after an offhand line that Peter Buck made about the band in a 1988 interview, the album was all the more poignant as it marked the first time ever that elements from the entirety of the band's catalogue would be included on the same record. Unlike 2003's *In Time*, or the various efforts at repackaging the I.R.S. years, this was to be a true all-in-one career retrospective, covering the first release until the last.

Even at forty tracks, this proved difficult. Once again, 'Near Wild Heaven' missed out, as did 'Drive', 'Find the River' and, perhaps most surprisingly, 'E-Bow the Letter'. Stipe took the lead on assembling the tracklisting, making room for a few choice album track favourites like 'Begin the Begin', 'Country Feedback' and 'New Test Leper'; tacked onto the end were three new songs, the final R.E.M. songs to be released. 'A Month of Saturdays' and 'Hallelujah' were holdovers from the *Collapse into Now* sessions; in fairness, it is possible to see why they were deemed unready for that album. The best of the three is 'We All Go Back to Where We Belong', an ornate, teary-eyed little number that recalls the dreamy sunny afternoon dynamics of *Reveal*. It came together during a few days of sessions in Athens in July that the band took on independently, working in a studio without a record deal for the first time ever. They had already resolved that the band was ending, but they took the time for one final stint, although Peter Buck was forced to miss out, due to suffering from a debilitating back injury that kept him at home in Portland. His guitar parts were taken from an earlier demo, while Stipe, Mills and Jacknife Lee assembled the track together. It was the fruit of their final labour, and while it was not an all-time spectacle to bring the curtain down, the song serves as a charming footnote for the band to bow out on nonetheless.

As if to prove a point, they even went out as a non-band to promote the album in November. It was the first taste of what would go on to be the abiding spirit of the post-R.E.M. years: it was not at all unusual to see any combination of members appearing together, giving interviews about the band's history or about the events of the day. Even once they had moved past the deliberately visual togetherness that they presented in the immediate aftermath of the split, it would become clear over the years that they had indeed remained close friends and were more than happy to work together in non-music-making ways.

Peter Buck was not a part of the promotional tour for *Part Lies*, because he was off playing with The Minus 5 in San Francisco. This was one part of the guitarist's life that was not about to change. In 2012, he toured as part of the Baseball Project and as a member of Robyn Hitchcock's backing band The Venus 3 (the other two of the three being McCaughey and Rieflin). That same year, Buck released a self-titled solo album on Mississippi Records, which included some of his first ever recorded vocals as well as contributions from Mike Mills on bass, Lenny Kaye on guitar and Corin Tucker from Sleater-Kinney on guest vocals. Per Buck's request, the album was a vinyl-only release, as was its follow up, 2014's *I Am Back to Blow Your Mind Once Again*.

Buck married for the third time in 2013, having settled in Portland with Chloe Johnson. His musical activities only expanded after that, including guest spots on records by First Aid Kit, The Jayhawks and, amazingly, The Monkees, as well as forming two noteworthy new groups: Arthur Buck, a collaboration with Joseph Arthur that produced one self-titled album in 2018, and, most successfully of all, Filthy Friends, which sprung from a series of low-key shows that Buck and Corin Tucker played together in the Pacific Northwest in late 2012. The duo found that they enjoyed working together too much to let it go and formed the band not long after, before securing a deal with the prominent Portland indie label Kill Rock Stars. Their first two albums, 2017's *Invitation* and 2019's *Emerald Valley*, with McCaughey and Rieflin contributing alongside others, capture both the brash, forthright character of Tucker's Sleater-Kinney and the bold, muscular and melodic punch of late-period R.E.M., both very strong records.

Tragically, this project would mark the end of Bill Rieflin's playing career. The drummer had been diagnosed with cancer as early as 2012, and his battle against it ended on 24 March 2020, as announced by his friend and recent bandmate in King Crimson, Robert Fripp. He was just 59. Scott McCaughey also had a serious health scare just three years earlier, suffering a stroke in November 2017. His friends rallied around him and organised two benefit shows to aid with his medical bills, which included performances by Berry, Buck, Mills, Tucker, The Decemberists and James Mercer from The Shins. Fortunately, McCaughey made a strong recovery and was playing publicly again less than a year later.

Mike Mills also remained busy in music after the split. He has been a prominent figure in the project Big Star's Third, a group of musicians that have toured sporadically since 2010 in order to play the entirety of the 1975 album *Third* by the sublime Memphis power pop group Big Star. The idea began in the 2000s when old R.E.M. friend Chris Stamey from The dB's tried to get the original Big Star to reform for a summer of shows, only for frontman Alex Chilton to pass away before arrangements could be finalised. Instead, Stamey, Mills, *Murmur* producer Mitch Easter and an assembly of their friends put together a touring show that has also variously included Sharon Van Etten, Kurt Vile, Cat Power and Aimee Mann, as well as Big Star's original drummer Jody Stephens, with Mills taking the tracks 'September Gurls' and 'Jesus Christ' for himself (R.E.M. had recorded a cover of the latter for their 2002 fan club single).

Mills has also appeared regularly with the Baseball Project, a band formed in 2007 by McCaughey and Steve Wynn, the former frontman of The Dream Syndicate, while backstage at R.E.M.'s Rock and Roll Hall of Fame induction. The group wrote and performed songs about various oddball and eccentric characters from baseball history, releasing three niche albums between 2008 and 2014, all featuring Mills and Buck playing together once again.

The former R.E.M. bassist also took the opportunity in 2016 to exercise his classical training by composing 'Concerto for Violin, Rock

Band and String Orchestra' with his childhood friend, the violinist Robert McDuffie, later touring the piece in 2019 as part of an ensemble group of home-state musicians under the banner 'A Night of Georgia Music'. Mills also guested on the single 'After It's Gone' by Drive-By Truckers frontman Patterson Hood in 2012, which was recorded for the Protect Downtown Athens organisation, protesting against the building of a massive Walmart store on a beloved historical site in the city. It is so on brand for an R.E.M. member that it could be a pastiche, but the sentiments were real, proving that the band's loyalties to their hometown never wavered.

Maintaining the same workmanlike musical profile was never going to be quite so easy for Michael Stipe. His every move continued to make headline news on online music platforms after the split, possibly even more so, with fans desperate to gain an inkling into what the singer's next chapter might look like. His first major appearance was to sing an acoustic version of 'Losing My Religion' alongside Chris Martin at Madison Square Garden for '12-12-12: The Concert for Sandy Relief'; aside from that, he seemed to be doing a good job of staying in the corner and out of the spotlight.

He took the chance to pour more of his time into his other great love, visual art, resulting in three photograph albums, all on the Damiani label: *Volume 1* in 2018, *Our Interference Times: A Visual Record* in 2019 and *Portraits: Still Life* in 2021. In 2014, he also accepted the request of the Rock and Roll Hall of Fame to give the induction speech for his friends in Nirvana, speaking in lyrical prose about the importance of musicians to the lives of their fans. And slowly, as the years passed, he began making surprise live appearances on music stages again, whether it was as the unannounced opener for Patti Smith at New York's Webster Hall, playing covers of Perfume Genius songs, or singing 'Ashes to Ashes' at a David Bowie tribute concert at Carnegie Hall.

He could also be found drumming up support at political rallies for the socialist presidential candidate Bernie Sanders in 2016. Suffice to say, that campaign did not end the way that Stipe, or anyone on the left, or indeed many people in the centre, had hoped. The band had their own run ins with Donald Trump that year when his team chose to use 'It's the End of the World as We Know It' at one of their rallies. It could only have been seen as the actions of a troll, and it did not take long for R.E.M.'s legal team to respond. Beyond the obvious call to cease and desist from using the song, the message stated that America should "not allow grandstanding politicians to distract us from the pressing issues of the day", arguing that "there are things of greater importance at stake here". If it was a response marked with dignity, then Stipe's own personal reaction, shared via Mike Mills' Twitter account, cut a little sharper: "Go fuck yourselves, the lot of you – you sad, attention grabbing, power-hungry little men. Do not use our music or my voice for your moronic charade of a campaign."

Shortly after Trump's victory, Stipe appeared on Alec Baldwin's podcast and came close to a direct confrontation with the host, who had impersonated Trump in a series of extremely high-profile skits on *Saturday Night Live* in the run-up to the vote. "What does it feel like from the inside?" asked Stipe. "Warhol said there's no such thing as bad publicity. How have we created this monster?" It was an accusatory audio finger jab, a snapshot of the head-spinning despair that was everywhere at the time. The interview uncovered several other fascinating scraps of information, including a revelation that Prince held a personal grudge against the band after he found out that they owned their own masters and he didn't, and the intriguing nugget that Stipe had been offered the Kevin Spacey role in David Fincher's *Se7en*, but had to turn it down because it conflicted with the Monster tour.

It took several years, but eventually Stipe started making music again too. In 2018, he took on the biggest producing role of his career when he helped to oversee the New York electroclash outfit Fischerspooner's fourth and final album, *Sir*. Stipe was an old friend and brief romantic partner of the group's Casey Spooner and revelled in the chance to explore the music's intersection between new technologies and the human experience. Once the collaborations had started, they kept coming: he contributed vocals to Rain Phoenix's beautiful acoustic indie track 'Time is the Killer' in 2019; a year later, he sang on the lockdown ballad 'No Time for Love Like Now' by Big Red Machine, a project led by Aaron Dessner of The National and Justin Vernon of Bon Iver; in 2022, his husky, reflective vocals featured on 'Family Ties', a smart, infectious, slow-burning electro-R&B track by Mykki Blanco.

Most intriguing of all though are the rare solo tracks that have emerged. A forty-second teaser track 'Future, if Future' was the first out of the traps, with Stipe releasing this snippet on Instagram in 2018 in conjunction with a March for Our Lives rally in support of gun control legislation. It was only a taste, but its twitching, glitchy electronic production called to mind similar work by St. Vincent and it excited fans that there might be a broader project on its way. 'Your Capricious Soul', his first full, original solo song, co-written with Athens producer Andy Lemaster, followed in 2019. The track builds on the same digital foundations of 'Future, if Future', while expanding the palette to let in a swelling horn section, crackling tambourine flourishes and a touch of vocoder, potentially inspired by his admiration for Perfume Genius. Lyrically, Stipe is back in a familiar zone, offering support to an adolescent generation in danger of being led astray by the modern world, recalling the sentiments of 'Drive' and 'Supernatural Superserious'. It was around the release of the next song, 2020's 'Drive to the Ocean', the best of the tracks so far, that Stipe confirmed that he was indeed working on a full solo album. The song continues Stipe's lifelong obsession with the poetic role of the radio in his consciousness, as well as featuring his most daring and idiosyncratic use of synthesisers to date. Stipe indicated his intention to compose the album's tracks alone, and if 'Drive to the Ocean' is any indication, it suggests that an entirely new musical path may just be opening up to him as he enters his sixties.

Their occasional appearances and the attention that they received reaffirmed what should already have been clear: R.E.M. had become a permanent part of our shared cultural consciousness, and even in their supposed absence, they continued to be on hand to offer a steadying, reassuring hand on the shoulder when the world became difficult. When Hurricane Dorian ravaged the Bahamas in 2014, R.E.M. released the song 'Fascinating' via Bandcamp to help with the relief fund. The song had been discarded at the last minute during the *Reveal* sessions and then re-recorded in the Bahamian capital Nassau during their spell at Compass Point Studios making *Around the Sun*. It was another reminder that the band were still on call to help. When American late night talk shows were plumbing the depths of despair after the Trump election, Stipe was there alongside Stephen Colbert with a re-tooled version of 'End of the World' to offer a glimpse of light at the end of a horrific year. When Covid-19 struck and 'End of the World' was climbing up the US charts again as some kind of harbinger of global panic, Stipe issued a calm, sensible, handheld video of advice on how to care for your fellow citizen, long before governments were organised enough to do the same.

The band were also out on promotional tours semi-regularly as part of the ongoing 25th anniversary re-releases of their albums, including well-timed celebrations of *Out of Time* and *Automatic for the People*, their most beloved works. One thing that the re-issue series forced the band to do was to reckon more seriously with their history, and even with the benefit of hindsight, it was a lot to take in. The dust had been settling for a few years, and for the first time they were able to look back with clear eyes at what they had achieved.

This was a band that had to coax a reluctant frontman out of his crippling shyness before he ever climbed onto a stage. A band that developed inside their own bubble, evolving unnaturally and arriving at a curious, impenetrable playing style that nobody had been prepared for, but that within a few years had caused them to become the leaders of an underground movement. A band that, when they had reached the logical end point of how far the movement could take them, developed a second curious playing style, based on complex and therapeutic emotional expression, and conquered the world with it. They redefined what it was considered possible for a merry band of outsiders to achieve in the full, unbridled glare of the global public eye, and they held firm. They never wavered in their value system along the journey, nor compromised on their artistic principles. Other bands had done some of these things before, but nobody had done them all, and certainly not this weirdly or this successfully.

For as long as there are ways for music to be heard, R.E.M. will be there, a guiding light for the people of Earth that rejoice in the collision between pop and experimentation in music and that take refuge in the celebration of caring, progressive values. There was a time when R.E.M. worried whether they could find enough such people to fill a bar in their art school hometown, but just as the Sex Pistols had shown Peter Buck in 1978, you never know how many there are in your tribe until somebody gives you the reason to get together. Thanks to R.E.M.'s thirty-one years of giving us that reason, we now know that there were millions of us all along.

Lists

The Roots of R.E.M. Playlist
The Byrds – So You Want to Be a Rock 'n' Roll Star
The Supremes – I Hear a Symphony
The Troggs – I Can't Control Myself
The Monkees - (I'm Not Your) Steppin' Stone
The Lovin' Spoonful – Do You Believe in Magic?
Glen Campbell – Wichita Lineman
Neil Young & Crazy Horse – Cinnamon Girl
The Velvet Underground – What Goes On
Harry Nilsson – Don't Forget Me
The Beach Boys – Feel Flows
Big Star – Give Me Another Chance
R. Stevie Moore – Goodbye Piano
New York Dolls – Personality Crisis
Roxy Music – Editions of You
Patti Smith – Redondo Beach
David Bowie – Cracked Actor
Brian Eno – St. Elmo's Fire
The Modern Lovers – Pablo Picasso
Television - Venus
Wire - Mannequin
The Pop Group – We Are Time
The Raincoats – Only Loved at Night
LiLiPUT – Die Matrosen
Au Pairs – It's Obvious
Devo – Whip It

The Friends of R.E.M. Playlist
The B-52's – Rock Lobster
Gang of Four – At Home He's a Tourist

186

The dB's   Black and White
The Feelies – The Boy with the Perpetual Nervousness
Pylon – Cool
Tanzplagen – Treason
The Method Actors – Can't Act
Love Tractor – Pretty
Let's Active – Every Word Means No
Oh-OK – Lilting
Minutemen – Bob Dylan Wrote Propaganda Songs
Hüsker Dü – Don't Want to Know If You Are Lonely
The Replacements – Swingin' Party
The Dream Syndicate – Tell Me When It's Over
10,000 Maniacs – Candy Everybody Wants
Robyn Hitchcock & The Egyptians – Airscape
Sonic Youth – Silver Rocket
Nirvana – Come as You Are
Pearl Jam – Black
U2 – The Fly
Radiohead – Talk Show Host
PJ Harvey – To Bring You My Love
Billy Bragg & Wilco – Way Over Yonder in the Minor Key
Modest Mouse – Dashboard
Vic Chesnutt – Guilty by Association

Best R.E.M. Opening Lines

1. "Empty prayer, empty mouths/Combien reaction?" ('Talk About the Passion')
2. "Birdie in the hand for life's rich demand/The insurgency began and you missed it" ('Begin the Begin')
3. "That's great, it starts with an earthquake/Birds and snakes, an aeroplane/ Lenny Bruce is not afraid" ('It's the End of the World as We Know It')
4. "With the restraint of New Order covers, Young Marble Giants, I sat quietly, waiting" ('That Someone is You')
5. "This could be the saddest dusk I've ever seen/I turn to a miracle, high-alive" ('Half a World Away')
6. "Could it be that one small voice doesn't count in the room" ('Shaking Through')
7. "These bastards stole their power from the victims of the us v. them years" ('Ignoreland')

8. "I can't see myself at thirty/I don't buy a lacquered thirty" ('Little America')

9. "She didn't want to get pinned down by her prior town/Get me to the train on time" ('Auctioneer (Another Engine)')

10. "Hello, I saw you, I know you, I knew you/I think I can remember your name" ('Pop Song 89')

Best R.E.M. Covers
1. 'All I Have to Do is Dream' (The Everly Brothers)
2. 'Crazy' (Pylon)
3. 'Dark Globe' (Syd Barrett)
4. 'Pale Blue Eyes' (The Velvet Underground)
5. 'Tighten Up' (Archie Bell & The Drells)
6. 'Superman' (The Clique)
7. 'Wall of Death' (Richard Thompson)
8. 'King of the Road' (Roger Miller)
9. '#9 Dream' (John Lennon)
10. 'Strange' (Wire)

Best Covers of R.E.M. Songs
1. Pavement – 'Camera'
2. !!! – 'Man on the Moon'
3. First Aid Kit – 'Walk Unafraid'
4. Jawbreaker – 'Pretty Persuasion'
5. Hem – 'South Central Rain'
6. Old 97's – 'Driver 8'
7. Patti Smith – 'Everybody Hurts'
8. 10,000 Maniacs – '(Don't Go Back to) Rockville'
9. Dolapdere Big Gang – 'Losing My Religion'
10. Fischerspooner – 'Fascinating'

Best R.E.M. Rarities
1. 'Star Me Kitten', featuring vocals from 82-year-old William S. Burroughs, released on the album *Songs in the Key of X: Music From and Inspired by The X Files* in 1996.
2. 'Voice of Harold'. Michael Stipe reads the liner notes to an old gospel record over the backing to '7 Chinese Bros.', released as a b-side on the 'So. Central Rain' 12" single.

3. 'Radio Free Europe (Radio Dub Version)'. Mitch Easter's 'dub' remix of his version of R.E.M.'s debut single, available online.
4. 'Fall on Me', from R.E.M.'s *MTV Unplugged* appearance in 1991.
5. 'Ages of You', released as a b-side on the 'Wendell Gee' single. It had been close to inclusion for *Chronic Town*, missing out at the last minute.
6. 'Fretless', from the soundtrack to Wim Wenders' *Until the End of the World*, released in 1991.
7. 'Perfect Circle', from R.E.M.'s *Later...with Jools Holland* appearance in 1998.
8. 'White Tornado', released as a b-side on the 'Superman' single in 1986. It had been recorded on the same day as the 'Radio Free Europe' single in 1981.
9. 'Leave (Alternate Version)', a stripped-down version of the *New Adventures in Hi-Fi* track, included on the soundtrack to Danny Boyle's *A Life Less Ordinary* in 1997.
10. 'Happy Furry Monsters', from R.E.M.'s *Sesame Street* appearance in 1999.

Best R.E.M. *Billboard Hot 100* Hits

1. 'So. Central Rain (I'm Sorry)' (#85, 1984)
2. 'Fall on Me' (#94, 1986)
3. 'E-Bow the Letter' (#49, 1996)
4. 'Losing My Religion' (#4, 1991)
5. 'It's the End of the World as We Know It (And I Feel Fine)' (#69, 1987)
6. 'Radio Free Europe' (#78, 1983)
7. 'Drive' (#28, 1992)
8. 'Daysleeper' (#57, 1998)
9. 'Electrolite' (#96, 1996)
10. 'The Great Beyond' (#57, 2000)
11. 'Shiny Happy People' (#10, 1991)
12. 'Everybody Hurts' (#29, 1993)
13. 'Bang and Blame' (#19, 1994)
14. 'Imitation of Life' (#83, 2001)
15. 'The One I Love' (#9, 1987)
16. 'Pop Song 89' (#86, 1989)
17. 'Man on the Moon' (#30, 1992)
18. 'What's the Frequency, Kenneth?' (#21, 1994)
19. 'Strange Currencies' (#47, 1995)
20. 'Supernatural Superserious' (#85, 2008)

Best R.E.M. *Billboard Hot 100* Hits That Never Were
1. '(Don't Go Back to) Rockville'
2. 'You Are the Everything'
3. 'Near Wild Heaven'
4. 'Nightswimming'
5. 'Driver 8'
6. 'Leaving New York'
7. 'Perfect Circle'
8. 'All the Way to Reno (You're Gonna Be a Star)'
9. 'Talk About the Passion'
10. 'Finest Worksong'
11. 'The Sidewinder Sleeps Tonite'
12. 'We Walk'
13. 'Gardening at Night'
14. 'Orange Crush'
15. 'Pretty Persuasion'
16. 'Crush with Eyeliner'
17. 'Bad Day'
18. 'Cant Get There from Here'
19. 'Überlin'
20. 'At My Most Beautiful'

R.E.M. Albums Ranked
1. *Automatic for the People* (1992)
2. *Reckoning* (1984)
3. *Out of Time* (1991)
4. *Murmur* (1983)
5. *Fables of the Reconstruction* (1985)
6. *Green* (1988)
7. *New Adventures in Hi-Fi* (1996)
8. *Document* (1987)
9. *Monster* (1994)
10. *Lifes Rich Pageant* (1986)
11. *Accelerate* (2008)
12. *Collapse into Now* (2011)
13. *Up* (1998)
14. *Reveal* (2001)
15. *Around the Sun* (2004)

Acknowledgements

Writing a book is as hard as all previous book writers have led you to believe. I spent most of the process alternating between serious doubt at my ability to complete the task and outright denial of the book's very existence. If it was not for a group of special people, I would have been right.

Thanks to Marc Burrows for bringing the prospect of this into my life for the first time, and for invaluable advice along the way. Your writing and insight have been a guiding light.

Thanks to Jonathan Wright, Charlotte Mitchell, Laura Hirst and everybody else at Pen & Sword for your unwavering patience, support and confidence in this first-time book writer.

Thanks to Hank Grebe, Dean Brush and gert74 for your generosity in our use of your excellent photography.

Thanks to Mélanie Dangereuse de Clegane for your outstandingly meticulous, collaborative and judge-free editing, detangling my worst impulses. The book became far better for your input.

Thanks to James Glossop for proofreading.

Thanks to Claire, Luke, Phoebe and Lois for putting in the hard yards, lifting my confidence when my motivation was flagging, providing a place of warmth and zen, and maintaining belief in me when you saw mine dwindling. Your love is in these pages.

Thanks to Loz and Alex for your unconditional friendship and steadfast capacity for putting up with my need to release the pressure, you can't know how grateful I am.

Thanks to Dad for ingraining in me a love for music, the stranger the better. You made me curious enough about the world to make this even a slim possibility.

Thanks to Mum for being the one true constant. Your desire to explore and to understand the world is inspiring and your love for words and music is fundamental to who I am. I hope I can reciprocate your love, you have made me very lucky.

Thanks to Michael, Peter, Mike and Bill. I hope I didn't ruin it.